The Changing Lives of
American Women

The Changing Lives of
American
Women

Steven D. McLaughlin

Barbara D. Melber

John O. G. Billy

Denise M. Zimmerle

Linda D. Winges

Terry R. Johnson

The University of North Carolina Press
Chapel Hill & London

The paper in this book meets the
guidelines for permanence and durability
of the Committee on Production
Guidelines for Book Longevity of the
Council on Library Resources.

92 91 90 89 88   5 4 3 2 1

Library of Congress Cataloging-in-Publication Data
The Changing lives of American women /
by Steven D. McLaughlin . . . [et al.].
p. cm.
Bibliography: p.
Includes index.
ISBN 0-8078-1813-5 (alk. paper)
1. Women—United States—Social conditions. 2. Women—United
States—Attitudes. 3. Attitude change. 4. Life cycle, Human.
I. McLaughlin, Steven D.
HQ1421.C47   1988   88-9699
305.4'2'0973—dc19   CIP

Contents

PART FOUR

Summary and Outlook

Tables

Figures

Foreword

By Glen H. Elder, Jr.

Howard W. Odum Distinguished Professor of Sociology
The University of North Carolina at Chapel Hill

Dramatic social changes over the past half century are finally beginning to receive the attention they deserve, an observation that applies to women's lives in general and to the current volume in particular. The authors skillfully identify basic features of women's changing lives, from greater personal control over life outcomes to their greater independence relative to family claims, and sum up the general picture with a concept of the new woman as a primary individual.

The story focuses on the women who married and gave birth to children in the baby boom of postwar America, the women of the baby-boom generation itself, and their daughters, who are encountering a period of higher levels of women's paid employment, marital instability, and economic pressure. Across the generations we see the rise of the primary individual among women who feel more personal efficacy and less constraint from family, and who are timing family events later in their lives in response to career needs and personal desires. Within a broader time span, this "new" life course can actually be seen to have more in common with the lives of women around 1900 than with the lives of mothers of the baby boom. The latter now appear among all generations of the twentieth century to be the unique group, given their pattern of early marriage and parenthood.

The remarkable array of social changes in women's lives calls for an approach that relates lives to a changing society, a task well suited to the life-course perspective, as this book demonstrates. Indeed, the life-course perspective emerged in response to the issues, sensitivities, and dislocations of the 1960s. Social discontinuities at the time prompted new questions linking life-course development, genera-

xiii

tional change, and history. Out of this intellectual context and a deeper appreciation of the historical and social meanings of age came a view of the life course shaped by social institutions and historical forces. Longitudinal and retrospective life history data were mobilized in response to the new questions and approaches of this emerging field of study. Also, techniques of analysis were developed for modeling the ever-changing dynamics of an evolving life course.

Age patterns in the life course are expressed in the timing of an event or transition (such as marriage, first birth, etc.), in the sequence of events or transitions (e.g., marriage before or after the first birth), and in time spent in a situation or social role, the duration. By analyzing life-course change in terms of these components, McLaughlin et al. show that variation in the timing of events represents a major aspect of observed change. Delayed marriage and parenthood, as well as divorce, are far more common among the baby-boom women than their mothers. In addition, the sequence in which marriage is followed by births is less common today than in past generations. Marriage and parenthood have become more differentiated and independent spheres. Perhaps the most telling story of all involves the time women devote to family and work domains. Across the generations, family time has decreased, while work time and independent living have increased. Together, these trends document a rise in the primary woman that is paralleled by a decline in the primacy of marriage and the family.

This diverse portrait of change in women's lives brings to mind the limitations of a still popular model of family development—the normative family cycle, which depicts a process of family expansion and contraction, formation and dissolution. The cycle begins with marriage and continues with the stages of childbearing and child-rearing, followed by the departure of children, the empty nest, and widowhood in old age. This family cycle applies to a single marriage that survives into middle or old age, an accomplishment made less common by high mortality in the nineteenth century and by divorce and separation today.

The family cycle also provides an account of only one area of change, phases of parenthood. Not too many years ago social scientists did not view these stages in relation to marital interaction over time or to worklife and earnings, as if careers could be understood by viewing them in isolation. The concept of interdependent lives is now commonplace in studies of families, which focus on the interdependence of work, marriage, and parenthood, as well as the ties between individuals and the lives of non-kin. Recently, life-course studies have brought greater sensitivity to problems of interdependence in women's lives. Indeed, some fruits of this effort are apparent in this volume. The fate of marriage depends on worklife and earnings, and parenthood varies according to the quality of marriage.

Using the empirical literature and some data analyses, McLaughlin et al. achieve a valuable beginning in charting the life patterns of American women across historical time and, to a lesser extent, across the lifetime of individual women and cohorts. Left untouched is the task of linking actual social changes (recessions, war mobilization, etc.) to women's lives and then tracing these influences over the life course. In this study we learn about the life patterns of women born at different times, but not about historical factors that might explain the variations. Though some factors are mentioned, they are not empirically studied. Explicit linkages between historical change and women's lives and families deserve priority in future research. Interrelated lives represent one medium for tracing historical effects. War, for example, may be experienced both directly and indirectly through the lives of family and friends.

A second task involves analyzing connections across a woman's life. Young daughters may learn maternal behavior from their mothers, but the consequences of this learning hinge on whether this behavior will persist over time. The perpetuation of marital instability across the generations often reflects a dynamic in which unstable parents produce unstable family relationships, which in turn increase the risk of unstable work and family behavior in the next generation. However, very little is known about this transmission process. Lastly, more research in women's lives is needed on the relation between early and later events in the life course. What are the consequences of teenage pregnancy, early marriage, and early parenthood? Does the formation of the adult life course have consequences for the latter years of life?

Central themes from this study serve as guidelines for efforts to assess the changing lives of women and their families. For example, the rise of women as primary individuals refers to a process by which they have assumed an increasingly larger amount of control over their life situation and outcomes. How will subsequent technological and social trends influence this trend, such as the improvement of tests to determine fetal normality and its influence on women's decisions to have children later in life? The spread of day care is another important factor in future equations.

Whatever the nature of social change, this volume underscores the importance of a broad historical timeline in studies of successive generations or cohorts. By comparing the baby-boom mothers with their daughters, we see an emerging new pattern of delayed family formation. But this apparent newness quickly fades when we consider all generations in this century. The baby-boom daughters established a life course that closely resembles the life course of their great-grandmothers, a similarity that highlights notable areas of change. Early death was more a source of family breakup than divorce for the great-grandmother generation, whereas the opposite pattern applies to the younger generation of women today. History reveals both continuity and change across generations of women's lives in this century.

Prefatory Note

By D. Claeys Bahrenburg

Executive Vice-President, Hearst Magazines

In 1984, as publisher of *Cosmopolitan* magazine, I commissioned the renowned Human Affairs Research Centers of the Battelle Memorial Institute to conduct a wide-ranging study of American women. Under the editorship of Helen Gurley Brown, *Cosmopolitan* began to respond to changes in the lives of young women that became apparent in the mid-1960s. Partly through the success of the magazine, everyone became aware of these changes, but it seemed that their causes and implications were little understood. We saw an opportunity to make a contribution to all marketers to women by summing up what was known about all American women from the vantage points of several disciplines and in historical perspective. At the time, we scarcely realized that the report would make a significant contribution to social science as well.

Battelle's research, under the direction of Dr. Steven D. McLaughlin, broke new ground in a number of ways. In 1986, the year the first part of our study was released, the *New York Times* reported our finding that "it is the mothers of the baby boom, rather than their daughters, who departed from many historic demographic trends." As a result of this "discovery" (which is now universally accepted), marketers no longer benchmark their projections of women's consumer behavior on the "aberrant" generation that gave birth to the baby boom.

In the second part of our study, released in the fall of 1986, Battelle demonstrated that changes in women's demographic behavior (increased labor force participation by women with preschool-age children, women's commitment to lifelong labor force participation, etc.) were followed by a rapid attitudinal shift in the late 1960s and early 1970s that favored such behavior. The authors concluded that women's return to long-term demographic trends is complete, and that the attitudes now firmly in place insure stability of the life course for the foreseeable future.

A major problem for our times was crystallized by the study: While women's attitudes have converged with men's regarding lifelong labor force participation, their commitment to "traditional" family values has not appreciably lessened. The result is structural tension in the home and workplace. In the past, this was viewed primarily as a problem for individual working mothers and career women who plan to have children, rather than as a social and economic problem we all must face together.

But the tide has turned. Basing his remarks on Battelle's findings, Congressman Bill Green, of Manhattan, read into the *Congressional Record* of 5 February 1987, the following:

> Polling of teenage women shows that the vast majority expect to have careers throughout their adulthood—while also choosing to be married and have children. There clearly is no reason to expect a reversal in the future and so society and government need to accept this new/old role of women—and to plan accordingly.
>
> . . . Government's decisions on issues such as the marriage tax, day care, education, volunteerism, employment, and retirement will have to be based on the fact that what is called the primary woman—one with her own plans and activities—is back to stay.

Not only are enlightened legislators mandating maternity leave, leaders in the business community also are adopting policies that acknowledge the widespread reality of women as "primary individuals."

We are delighted that the University of North Carolina Press has now published our earlier findings in this revised, compact, and highly readable edition. These findings not only provide an interesting history lesson and meticulously researched casebook study; what is more important, they are actively changing perceptions about American women, in both the private and public sectors. Itself a catalyst for change, *Cosmopolitan* is pleased to have sponsored this remarkable and thought-provoking research.

Acknowledgments

During the early stages of the project culminating in this book, Battelle formed an advisory panel to provide guidance on technical aspects of the report and style of presentation. The members of this panel are gratefully acknowledged: Barbara Creaturo, senior editor, *Cosmopolitan* magazine; Dr. Glen H. Elder, Howard W. Odum Distinguished Professor of Sociology, University of North Carolina at Chapel Hill; Dr. Robert T. Michael, director of the National Opinion Research Center, Chicago; Dr. Jeylan T. Mortimer, professor of sociology, University of Minnesota; Karen Ritchie, senior vice-president, Lintas: Campbell-Ewald Company; Dr. Linda Waite, senior social scientist, The Rand Corporation.

In large part, this book is the direct result of intensive collaboration between the authors and members of *Cosmopolitan*'s staff who were responsible for overseeing the research project. During the early phases of the work *Cosmopolitan*'s marketing director, Norma Saulino, made a number of important contributions to the project's direction and scope. Daniel D'Arezzo, who succeeded Ms. Saulino as marketing director, played a central role in the project from its inception and contributed to all phases of the effort.

Thanks are also due Battelle staff members for their contributions to the reports issued by *Cosmopolitan*: David Sommers for data analysis and graphics, Cheryl Geisendorfer for graphics, and Anita Stocker for graphics and manuscript preparation. At different stages of the project, Wendell Ricketts, Rosalie West, and Ron Leamon copyedited and proofread the manuscript with unstinting attention to detail. In addition, Paul Betz of the University of North Carolina Press went far beyond the normal obligations of an editor in creating a single book from pieces of three separate research reports.

Special thanks are due Charles Rodin, who fostered the idea of a major piece of research on women and brought *Cosmopolitan* and Battelle together to produce it.

Part One
Perspective and Approach

1

Introduction

Recent decades have witnessed enormous and far-reaching demographic changes in the lives of American women. These changes touch almost every aspect of life—education, marriage, divorce, employment, sexual behavior, childbearing, and living arrangements. In fact, it is difficult to avoid the media's persistent messages regarding the new American woman. We know that women are entering higher levels of education in unprecedented numbers, going into professions traditionally reserved for men, delaying marriage and remaining employed after they are married as well as after their first child is born, divorcing at higher rates, and heading a greater number of households. It is not surprising to find these changes the subject of intensive study by social scientists, policymakers, market researchers, as well as the media.

A great deal of knowledge has been accumulated from these studies, but it remains scattered over a wide range of technical reports, articles, and books, making it largely inaccessible to the general public. The professional demographic literature tends to be highly specialized, giving in-depth attention to narrowly defined research issues. Thus, we have an extensive body of literature on the changes in women's education as well as separate bodies of literature on changes in marriage, employment, fertility, and living arrangements. However, social scientists seldom are able to step back from the details of this technical literature and consider what these changes mean in a broader context. Although we know that change in one area is related to change in another (e.g., changes in fertility are related to changes in women's labor force participation), we know

3

little about the simultaneous impact of these many changes on the day-to-day life of American women. The purpose of this book is to synthesize what is currently known about the basic demographic changes affecting women's lives and to do so in a manner that puts the vast array of demographic changes in a single theoretical perspective.

AN OVERVIEW OF THE BOOK

In the process of bringing together demographic information about the changes affecting women's lives, we have identified two major underlying themes. The first suggests that recent demographic changes are related in their origins, and the second places these changes in a new, broader historical perspective.

The most important general conclusion is that the significance of the family within the lives of American women has declined in recent years. Whether by choice or necessity, women today spend more of their lives as single, independent adults with an interest in controlling and organizing their lives to meet personal and career objectives. This rise in the independence of women serves to explain and integrate seemingly disparate changes in education, employment, marriage, and childbearing. It also serves as a focus for speculations about the future implications of these life-course changes.

Facing a world of increasingly attractive labor-market opportunities, women are acquiring more education—not to find a man but to get a job. The link between education and future employment can be seen in the increasing numbers of women enrolling in professional schools and in the continuation of schooling after marriage. The changing patterns with respect to marriage also indicate increased independence for women. As educational attainment among women rises, marriage is being postponed or, in some cases, avoided altogether, as can be seen in increases in nonmarital sexual activity and cohabitation. The divorce rate is higher and the average duration of marriage is becoming shorter, particularly among women with high earnings or the potential for high earnings. The emerging patterns of labor force participation (more continuous employment, entry into occupations dominated by males, and higher wages) have allowed women to consider a life of independence before, during, and after marriage or to remain single, and there has been an enormous increase in the number of women living alone, particularly younger women. The increased effectiveness of birth control methods has added to the ability of women to control their fertility to fit their lifestyle objectives.

All of these changes point to a rise in the primacy of the individual woman that is paralleled by a decline in marriage and the family.[1] In general, these demographic changes have been driven by economic, technological, and cultural developments that have permitted women greater control over their lives. This new control is reflected in complex life-course changes that can be roughly summarized as a movement away from the orderly progression of the 1950s (student, then jobholder, then wife, then mother) to participation in several roles simultaneously.

The composite portrait of American women today clearly indicates that they are spending less of their lives in traditional family living arrangements—less time married, less time with dependent children, more time in independent living situations, and more time employed. We expect this pattern to continue. Women's day-to-day lives will be less dependent on their family affiliations; their economic, social, and emotional needs will be increasingly met by combinations of individuals outside the household and outside the family unit. Family-based networks will continue to decline in importance as more women remain single, migrate to find or keep a career, have fewer children, get divorced, and (perhaps) remarry. This is not to say that the family is no longer an important social institution.

1. Our theme of the "rise of women as primary individuals" is in part adapted from F. E. Kobrin, who has done important research on changes in living arrangements and family structure in the United States (see Kobrin 1973, 1976a, 1976b). As the basis of her analysis, Kobrin examined U.S. Census data relating to "primary individuals," a census category that was created in 1947: "Primary individuals are considered those who live as heads of separate households, as well as the small proportion (mainly young) who head households containing nonrelatives" (Kobrin 1976b, p. 233). We use the term "primary individual" in this technical sense, but also in the broader sense of an individual who has at least the potential for being economically self-sufficient and socially autonomous. The increasing number of women who share with their husbands the responsibility for the economic welfare of the home could thus be termed "primary individuals," even if the Census Bureau does not identify them as such.

Most women still value marriage and the family, and still spend a significant part of their lives as wives and mothers. Nevertheless, the family's influence over their lives is declining.

The second theme that is followed throughout the book is the importance of examining the more recent changes in the life course of American women within a broader historical perspective. The demographic behavior of today's young adult women (roughly defined as women between 18 and 44 years of age) is frequently compared to the behavior of their mothers' generation. The result is a picture of dramatic social change. Compared to their mothers, today's women have made enormous gains in educational attainment both in absolute terms and relative to men; significantly postponed marriage and childbearing; entered the labor force in unprecedented numbers and in new occupations, particularly as married women with children; increased the divorce rates considerably; had much smaller families; been much more likely to live alone as young women; and headed families more often.

All these changes have appropriately received a great deal of attention and are the subject of many debates among the general public, the mass media, the academic community, and policymakers. The positions taken in these debates range from concern for the stability of our basic social institutions to a welcoming of a new era of individual autonomy and freedom from the stereotyped and limiting roles of men and women that characterized previous generations.

When viewed in a longer historical perspective, however, a very different picture emerges. In particular, the mothers of the baby boom, the cohort against which contemporary women are most frequently compared, departed from several long-term demographic levels and trends to which their daughters are now returning.[2] In

2. For the benefit of the nonspecialist, we should explain that in our usage the term "cohort" signifies a group of individuals who have in common a meaningful demographic event. In many instances in this book, the term identifies a group of individuals born in a given year, and we refer to "birth cohorts" when there is a need to be technically explicit. In other instances, we use the term "cohort" in the sense often attached to the term "generation"—i.e., a group of people born within a span of years that are linked by a notable demographic pattern. For example, the cohort (or generation) of women born during the 1930s exhibited unusually high childbearing rates during the 1950s, which resulted, of course, in the baby-boom cohort (or generation).

many respects today's young women are more demographically similar to their grandmothers than to their mothers. However, this current demographic behavior is driven by an environment that differs greatly from that of the grandmothers. The longer-term historical perspective shows that in many areas women are not breaking new ground but are returning to old ground for new reasons. Support for this position comes from our findings in the following areas:

1. Education: Women are returning to a level of education similar to the level held by men. This is a position that was characteristic of the first half of the twentieth century and was lost by the cohort of women who reached adulthood during World War II.

2. Marriage: The proportion of women who eventually marry and the average age at marriage are currently similar to patterns in evidence during the first half of the twentieth century. The rise in the marriage rate and the decline in age at marriage experienced by the mothers of the baby boom were unique historical events.

3. Divorce and fertility: Throughout the twentieth century the divorce rate has increased, with one major fluctuation. The peak in divorce in the mid-1940s was followed by a sharp decline in the 1950s because of the unique marital behavior of the mothers of the baby-boom children. Since that time, the divorce rates have continued the previous pattern of steady increases. The same can be said of fertility behavior. The total fertility rate has been declining for two hundred years with only minor fluctuations except for the rise in fertility during the 1950s. More recent fertility rates represent a return to this long-term downward trend.

4. Labor force participation: The rapid increase of women in the labor force is unprecedented. However, when participation in the labor force is recognized as a form of participation in the production of goods and services, the recent entry of women takes on a different image. When the United States was primarily an agricultural society, the family served as the locus of both production and consumption. As such, it enabled women to be major participants in the productive process. With industrialization and urbanization, the production role shifted outside the family and was assumed by the male, while the family became the unit of consumption. The return of women to the labor force and the recent trend toward being employed over the life course represents women's regaining a central role in the productive process, which they lost during the Industrial Revolution.

The application of this longer historical perspective is also useful when considering the future life course of women, particularly when combined with the theme of the rise of the primary individual. Some demographers expect that the small birth cohort that is now following the baby boom into the labor market will return to the lower age at marriage and the higher fertility that characterized the mothers of the baby boom because of the relative economic prosperity expected for small birth cohorts. We do not expect this to happen for several reasons. First, the more permanent place of women in the labor market, their higher wages, and their entry into male-dominated occupations will increase the supply of labor, and the resulting wage competition will lessen the relative prosperity of the small cohort. Second, the basic relationship of women to the family and to the economy has changed such that even in the face of economic prosperity we do not expect women to return to a dependent, family-centered lifestyle.

THE LIFE-COURSE PERSPECTIVE

As we have noted, the sources of information concerning demographic behavior are varied and diffuse. In order to present a coherent picture of how the lives of American women have changed, we needed to find a way of integrating data on different types of behavior that might otherwise seem coincidental in their relationship. With this integration as an objective, we determined that we could most effectively use a theoretical approach from sociology known as the life-course perspective.

The power of the life-course perspective in the study of social change was first brought to the attention of sociologists and demographers by Glen Elder's now classic study *The Children of the Great Depression* (1974), and since the mid-1970s it has been refined and increasingly adopted by demographers, social psychologists, family scholars, and students of social change (e.g., Oppenheimer 1982; Kohn and Schooler 1983; Elder 1985).

The life-course perspective focuses attention on the changes individuals experience throughout their lives, with particular emphasis on the critical role of time—in its social, psychological, and biological aspects—in determining when these changes take place. From this perspective, a woman's life is profoundly affected not only by the social roles she occupies (e.g., wife, mother, jobholder) but by when she assumes those roles—at what age, in what sequence, and for what length of time. An individual woman's social role serves to define her relationship to an institution such as the educational system, the family, or the economy. All known societies regulate the manner in which individuals make transitions from one role to another as well as the timing and sequencing of these transitions. The life course of individuals is, therefore, determined in large part by the relationships of social institutions, such as the family and the economy, with each other. As technological and economic changes take place, the relationships between social institutions change, and these changes, in turn, have effects on the life-course experiences of individuals.

Each of the major changes to be considered in this book is a change in the life course of women. Changing trends in educational attainment, marriage rates, labor force participation, and fertility can be seen to have an impact on the life course of individuals if we recognize that they represent changes in when women assume various social roles. Women born in more recent decades spend more time in different combinations of roles. This is a profound change in the organization of the life course of individual women as well as a profound change for American society as a whole.

The life-course perspective is thus particularly valuable when applied to the study of social change. Considered in isolation, empirical findings such as increased educational attainment, decreased fertility, or the rise in age at first marriage are certainly important, but they do not describe how these changes are interrelated and how they influenced the way women lead their lives. When presented from the life-course perspective, however, demographic changes such as these can be interpreted as differences in the number of years women born in different decades spend in roles such as student, jobholder, wife, or various combinations of these three roles. The rise in educational attainment increases the proportion of life spent in the student role, the growing trend of returning to school after marriage and after having children increases the number of years spent in the combined roles of spouse and student, and the rise in labor force participation after marriage increases the number of years spent simultaneously in the roles of wife, mother, and jobholder.

Comparisons of the life-course patterns of groups of women born in different periods can unify seemingly unrelated demographic changes in the social organization of life.

Among the most widely studied transitions are those associated with the assumption of adulthood, including the completion of formal education, the first job, the formation of a separate household, marriage, and the birth of the first child. Other major transitions are divorce, the departure of the last child, retirement, and death of a spouse. The life-course perspective recognizes the importance of each of these role transitions but stresses the consequences of the age at which and the order in which they are assumed. Marriage, for example, is a critical role transition in its own right, but the life-course perspective focuses on the implications of when the transition was made (e.g., at age 17 versus 22 versus 34) and what other roles were occupied before, during, or after the marriage (e.g., student, jobholder, or mother).

The significant role transitions mentioned above are obviously important for individuals, but they are also important for society at large. The timing and sequencing of these transitions determine the size and fundamental character of a society's primary social institutions, such as the educational system, the economy, and the family, which are all grounded in the expectation that individuals will conform to the typical patterns of age and ordering that characterize entry into and exit from these institutions. To cite a couple of obvious examples: most occupations require some level of formal education prior to entry, and family law, as well as most of our family traditions, presupposes that marriage precedes the birth of the first child. Research has demonstrated that there are costs associated with deviations from this normative life script. For example, having a child "too early" is known to be associated with lower educational attainment, poverty, rapid subsequent fertility, divorce, lower IQ for the child, and welfare dependence.

Thus, there is a close interdependency between the welfare of the social system and the life course of its members. Changes in the life course have profound and far-reaching implications for the social system, and historical events that affect the social system (e.g., the Industrial Revolution, war, economic depressions) often influence the life course.

Perhaps the most dramatic social change to be considered in this book is the increased participation of women in the labor force, which has been labeled the "quiet revolution." In a subsequent chapter we will show that this revolution, like other presumably sudden changes, is more accurately described as a gradual increase beginning long before the revolution was presumed to begin. The truly revolutionary aspect of women's increased labor force participation is its place in the life course. That is, it is the new timing and sequencing patterns that are revolutionary, not the labor force participation itself. The single career woman, the married employed mother of preschool children, and the divorced employed female head of the household have had the greatest impact on the social system.

In the aggregate, these shifts have implications of such magnitude that no society leaves them unregulated. Though apparently the result of individual choices, they are far too important to society to be left to the individual. Consequently, every society has mechanisms of social control to ensure that the majority of its members move through the transition to adulthood as well as other transitions (e.g., going into retirement) in an orderly and predictable fashion. Changes in these transitions have enormous implications and are heralded as either dramatic social progress or serious deterioration of the social fabric.

In subsequent chapters, five separate bodies of literature dealing with demographic changes are summarized. Each of these demographic changes will be examined for its impact on when women assume important new roles, how many roles they maintain simultaneously, and how long they spend in various role combinations. Attention will be focused on the demographic behavior of women aged 15–44 because these years include the part of the life course during which most of the demographic behavior of interest takes place. The demographic changes examined are in the areas of educational attainment, marital and divorce patterns, premarital sexual activity, labor force participation, and childbearing.

TABLE 1.1
The Female Population of the United States, 1900–2010 (in Millions)

Age	1900	1910	1920	1930	1940	1950	1960	1970	1980	1984	1990	2000	2010
0–14	12.9	14.6	16.6	17.7	16.3	19.9	27.4	28.4	25.1	25.3	26.7	27.3	26.2
15–29	10.7	12.9	14.0	16.3	17.7	17.5	17.6	24.6	30.6	30.6	28.0	26.3	28.5
15–19	3.8	4.5	4.8	5.8	6.2	5.3	6.6	9.4	10.3	9.2	8.3	9.3	9.3
20–24	3.7	4.5	4.7	5.5	5.9	5.9	5.5	8.4	10.6	10.7	9.1	8.4	9.7
25–29	3.2	3.9	4.5	5.0	5.6	6.3	5.5	6.8	9.7	10.7	10.6	8.6	9.5
30–44	7.0	8.8	10.7	13.0	14.4	16.7	18.4	17.7	21.7	25.5	30.1	31.2	27.0
30–34	2.7	3.3	3.9	4.6	5.2	5.9	6.1	5.8	8.8	9.9	11.0	9.4	8.7
35–39	2.3	3.0	3.7	4.5	4.8	5.7	6.4	5.7	7.0	8.5	10.1	10.8	8.8
40–44	2.0	2.5	3.1	3.9	4.4	5.1	5.9	6.2	5.9	7.1	9.0	11.0	9.5
45–59	4.1	5.2	6.5	8.4	10.3	12.2	14.7	17.3	23.3	23.3	24.2	31.4	39.8
60–74	2.4*	3.1	3.9	5.1	6.9	9.5	12.8	15.3	8.8	9.4	10.1	9.9	11.2
75+									6.4	7.3	8.9	11.3	12.5
Total	37.1	44.6	51.7	60.5	65.6	75.8	90.9	104.3	115.9	121.4	128.0	137.4	145.2

Sources: For 1900–1970, U.S. Bureau of the Census 1975; for 1980, U.S. Bureau of the Census, *1980 Census of the Population: Characteristics of the Population* (Washington, D.C.: U.S. Government Printing Office, 1984); for 1984, U.S. Bureau of the Census, *Estimates of the Population of the United States by Age, Sex, and Race: 1980–1984* (Washington, D.C.: U.S. Government Printing Office, 1985), p. 25, #965; for 1990–2010, U.S. Bureau of the Census, *Projections of the Population of the United States by Age, Sex, and Race: 1983–2080* (Washington, D.C.: U.S. Government Printing Office, 1984), p. 25, #952.
Note: For 1900–1970, 60–74 includes 60 and all older ages.

THE CONTEMPORARY FEMALE POPULATION
IN THE UNITED STATES

To provide the demographic context for the specific behavioral changes to be discussed in this book, we need to discuss briefly the size and character of the basic population under consideration. Table 1.1 describes the size and age distribution of the female population between 1900 and 1980 as enumerated in the U.S. Census. In addition, the table provides relevant estimates of the female population as of March 1984, based on the 1984 annual demographic file of the Current Population Survey, the most recent population estimate available at the time this book was completed. Other data in Table 1.1 report the most commonly used projections of the female population by age for the years 1990, 2000, and 2010. (These are the Series B projections supplied by the U.S. Bureau of the Census.)

The impact of the baby boom on the size and age structure of the population can be readily seen in Table 1.1. Beginning in 1950 this large birth cohort can be followed as its members age into their late thirties and forties by 1990 and approach their sixties in the year 2010. In the fourteen years between 1970 and 1984 the number of women aged 30–44 increased by almost 8 million, an increase of 44 percent.

Table 1.1 also shows that after 1984 almost no growth is projected for the age group of 30-to-44-year-olds. This projection of a relatively flat population size disguises much change in distribution among life-course stages. In fact, women are entering stages of the life course at different ages and in different sequences, and are spending different proportions of their lives in these stages. These changes serve to redistribute the 56 million women aged 15–44 into categories of the life course with widely differing tastes, lifestyles, and types of economic behavior.

2

The Historical Context

Before considering the results of our analysis of recent changes in the life course of American women, we need to place these changes within a larger historical context. In this chapter we briefly describe the emergence of the modern form of the family and its relationship to the economic system. Most demographic changes affecting women stem from shifts in their relationship to both the family and the economy. Consequently, it is important to understand how these two institutions have changed, particularly in the ways they have defined new roles for women.

Most of the material presented in this chapter is based upon historical information, as opposed to social science data. Seldom does historical information provide an index of variability in trends or even a measure of the proportion of the population following a given pattern. Thus, it is the historian who must judge to what extent ideas and behavior became common among various segments of the population at any given time. In this respect, the following historical overview differs from the subsequent chapters, which are restricted to empirical research.

Contrary to much folk wisdom, the extended family, consisting of several generations living and working together on the family farm, was never a large part of American family life. The misconception that nonnuclear families were popular in the past arises because household size has drastically declined from 5.8 persons per household (16.6 persons per household, including slaves) in 1800 to 4.8 persons per household in 1900 and to 3.5 persons per household in 1950. The decline, however, is due to the disappearance of nonrelatives from the household (apprentices, servants, and boarders) as well as to the drop in the birthrate from 7.04 children per white woman at the beginning of the nineteenth century to 3.56 children per white woman by 1900 (Greven 1972; Pryor 1972; Laslett 1973; U.S. Bureau of the Census 1975).

Recent historical research (Greven 1966, 1970; Demos 1972; Pryor 1972; Goldin 1979) has confirmed that the "nuclear family," a married couple and their children, has always been the dominant household type in the United States. Even in colonial America, it was rare for three generations or two married couples to live in the same household. In the late seventeenth-century Plymouth Colony, for example, households typically consisted of a man, his wife, their children, and a servant. Occasionally a grandparent or, rarely, two grandparents lived with the family for a short time. Married siblings never occupied the same household (Demos 1972). "The classical family of Western nostalgia"—grandparents, parents, kids, and sometimes an aunt, uncle, and cousins—was the exception, not the rule (Goode 1963, p. 6).

For demographic reasons it was unlikely that three generations would live together because the relatively late age at marriage and short life expectancy meant that grandparents and grandchildren were rarely alive at the same time. Although life expectancy was greater and age at marriage younger in the colonies than in western Europe, families remained as nuclear in America as in Europe (Laslett 1973). Even in the twentieth century, when grandparents began living longer, the family remained nuclear (Kobrin 1978).

CHANGES IN THE ECONOMY

Although the nuclear family has always been the dominant household type in the United States, the economic roles of family members have undergone substantial change. The major force behind this change was the Industrial Revolution. During the tremendous economic expansion that accompanied it, the center of production moved from the home to the factory, and the population became increasingly concentrated in urban areas. Between 1820 and 1860, industrial production doubled every decade, and by 1860, 20 percent of the American population lived in cities compared to only 7 percent in 1820 (U.S. Bureau of the Census 1949). The combination of these shifts in economic production and population distribution contributed substantially to changes in the economic roles of family members.

In preindustrial America the home was typically the workplace—whether the work was farming (the occupation of the vast majority of American families), crafts, or trade. Although men, women, and children ordinarily performed different tasks, all of their work was integral to the successful production of household goods and the livelihood of the family. Even nonfarm families benefited economically from their children's labor. At 10 or 11 years of age many children were sent out to work as apprentices or servants in other households while their own families took in additional children as apprentices or servants. Women also contributed to the family's livelihood because, despite spending most of their married lives bearing children, they spent relatively little time caring for them. Older children or servants helped care for the very young ones, and once children were 6 or 7 they participated in many of the household chores. Moreover, childhood was not viewed as a distinct period of development that required special nurturance. By nineteenth- and twentieth-century standards, young children were relatively neglected and older children treated as adults (Ariès 1962; Shorter 1977).

Because children made an economic contribution early in life and were often the means of support for their parents later, they were not an economic drain and could, in fact, be an economic asset (Davis and Blake 1956). This economic relationship between parents and children remained unchanged even in the early stages of industrialization. Women and children were needed as cheap labor to mass-produce the household goods that once had been produced at home. Prior to the Industrial Revolution, spinning and weaving done at home were the most common occupations for women. The early mills simply transferred the place of employment. The shortage of male labor led to the proportionately large number of women employed in the mills. In addition, mill work was more attractive than domestic service because mill work paid better, even though women were paid one-third to one-half of the wages paid to men (Hymowitz and Weissman 1978).

As technology grew and the supply of immigrant labor to the United States increased, the labor of women and children was in less demand. In the 1820s New England mill owners recruited native-born women by proclaiming the benefits of hard work for everyone, but by the 1830s middle-class women were no longer employed in factories (Smelser and Halpern 1978). At the same time, children were spending more time at school; by 1870–90, schooling for children aged 6–12 was compulsory (Caldwell 1982).

Because of technology and new economies of scale, household goods could now be manufactured outside the home and sold at an affordable price. As a result, middle-class women and children shifted from being both economic producers and consumers to non-productive consumers. In their new role as consumers and with their time spent at school rather than at work, children became an expense rather than an economic asset (Caldwell 1982).

The popular idea that "a woman's place is in the home" developed only after industrialization had separated home from the place of work. The "cult of true womanhood" defined women of the middle and late nineteenth century as domestic, pious, pure, and submissive. Women were in charge of the home and children, while men earned a living away from home.

Prior to marriage and childbearing, middle-class American women spent several years of relative idleness in their parental home. During the late nineteenth century, about one-third of women aged 16–24 were neither in school nor at work. One of the few jobs considered respectable for these young women was schoolteaching, a job many of them held for an average of two years. As teachers, they earned half the salary of male schoolteachers and, since the position of school principal was reserved for males, had no upward mobility. Other positions that became available to women and were considered respectable for single middle-class women in the second half of the nineteenth century were librarian, retail sales clerk, and office clerk (Ryan 1983). For married middle-class women the only respectable means of earning money was taking in boarders. It is estimated that 20 to 30 percent of households in late-nineteenth-century cities contained boarders (Laslett 1973; Modell and Hareven 1973).

In the wake of the Industrial Revolution, when motherhood and domesticity became the career of middle-class women, lower-class families often lacked the economic means to keep their women home. In fact, the Industrial Revolution provided more opportunities for lower-class women to work outside the home and a greater economic need for them to do so. Lower-class women sought employment because their husbands' or fathers' factory jobs did not provide sufficient income for the family to survive. Between 1880 and 1910 the proportion of females in the labor force aged 14 and over rose from 14.7 to 24.8 percent (Ryan 1983). By 1900 there were almost 5 million female wage earners, comprising nearly one-fifth of the total labor force (U.S. Bureau of the Census 1949). Two million of these women were employed as domestics—maids, cooks, nurses, and laundresses—in private homes. In the South, these domestics were primarily black women; in the North, they were mostly recent immigrants. Three million women, mostly immigrants, worked in the northeastern garment, cigar-rolling, laundering, and food-processing industries (Hymowitz and Weissman 1981). But few of the women in the labor force made a living wage. For example, in Pittsburgh, 60 percent of female workers made less than the seven dollars per week that was considered essential for subsistence in 1906–1907. The average tenure was eleven years, and most women stopped working when they married (Ryan 1983).

Only about 2 percent of married women in 1890 were employed outside the home (U.S. Bureau of the Census 1949). Of those, many worked in the factories or as seasonal farmworkers only during periods of severe economic need. Other married women, as we saw earlier, took in boarders (Ryan 1983). Studies of Philadelphia in 1880 show that the way lower-class families reduced economic stress was to have children work rather than married women. Virtually all male heads of households in this study were employed (97 percent) while almost no married women were employed (4 percent). Although child-labor laws existed in a few states by the 1880s, they did not exist in Pennsylvania until 1901, when the state passed a compulsory-education act. The proportion of male children in Philadelphia who were less than 16 years old and who worked ranged from 45.6 percent for native-born white children to 68.8 percent for children born to German immigrants. Fewer girls than boys worked, although the proportion of girls who worked ranged from 38.9 percent for native-born white children to 57.7 percent for children of Irish immigrants. The greatest need for income came when the male head of the household was older and his earnings were declining relative to the number of family members to support. Thus, children were to a large extent the cause of, as well as the solution to, the economic problems of families in the late 1800s, not only in Philadelphia, but elsewhere in the United States as well (Goldin 1979; Haines 1981). An important effect of the Industrial Revolution on the family, then, was to pull lower-class women, primarily single women, out of the home, while isolating married and middle-class women within the home.

CHANGES IN THE FAMILY

As the family became more isolated from the economy and the schools, its functions became more specialized. No longer in charge of educating children or producing household goods, women became devoted to rearing children and promoting emotional relationships between family members (Parsons 1949). Moreover, the family became a refuge from and defense against the competitiveness and rapid change of the industrial world, "a haven in a heartless world" (Christopher Lasch in Degler 1980). Sennett (1970, p. 237), after studying a Chicago middle-class community of the late 1800s, concluded that family isolation was a "retreat from disorder" in an attempt to make the family a "bulwark against confusion" brought on by the Industrial Revolution.

The increase in the psychological function of the family is due in part to changes in the relationships between husbands and wives as well as between parents and children. With industrialization, young men were no longer reliant on the inheritance of farmland or a small business in order to marry. Marriage changed from an economic arrangement controlled by the older generation to an emotional bond between husbands and wives (Greven 1966), which raised social concern over the regulation of intimacy within marriage. Victorian morality can be seen thus as an attempt to control the sexual conduct and roles of men and women within their homes. As Smelser and Halpern (1978) contend, "In one respect, the Victorian family ideology—including its prudish components—was an exercise in 'overcontrol' of a new institution that was unfamiliar and appeared to be dangerously fragile" (p. S308). By making women exclusively responsible for the family at home, the "cult of true womanhood" was an effort to preserve the family in the wake of change.

Emotional ties between parents and children increased as well.

Children were regarded more sentimentally in the nineteenth century as mothers, freed from the role of economic producers, took on the exclusive care of young children. From about 1830 on, motherhood became a full-time job for middle-class women. Moreover, children lived at home longer. Instead of being sent out in their preteens to work for another family, children were staying home until their late teens or early twenties to continue schooling. Although a decline in infant mortality is often cited as a reason for the increased affectional ties between parents and children in the nineteenth century, it could not have been a factor because infant mortality did not drop significantly until the 1920s (Goldscheider 1971). Families had fewer children, an average of 3.56 by the end of the century, as compared to 7 or 8 at the beginning. The decline in fertility accompanied the change in attitudes toward children as children became increasingly expensive to raise (Caldwell 1982).

Although the emotional relationship between parents and children increased, parental control decreased. Children were no longer expected (and with child-labor laws, permitted) to work side by side with their parents. Moreover, children did not have to wait for an inheritance in order to marry. The loss of parental control reinforced the need for compulsory schooling, in order to keep young people out of trouble (Katz and Davey 1978).

Although the causal relationship between the rise of industrialism and the rise of the nuclear family is currently debated (Thadani 1978), both fueled a sense of individualism. Industrialism opened up new economic opportunities for individuals, so that they no longer needed to depend upon family-run farms or businesses for their livelihood. The nuclear family in turn further stressed individualism by its economic independence from extended family and its orientation toward nuclear-family members instead of the community or larger kin network. The decline in marital fertility represented an increased sense of individual freedom of choice, as well as a rational response to economic circumstances—to provide more for fewer children and for oneself (Lesthaeghe 1983).

THE TWENTIETH CENTURY:
FURTHER REDEFINITION OF WOMEN'S ROLES

After the turn of the century, married middle-class women's careers continued to be motherhood and domesticity. The decline in domestic workers after 1900, which was due to the expanding industrial economy and immigration restrictions, meant that middle-class women had to perform many household chores previously done by servants (Morison 1965). Housework became a "science" of killing germs and a study in efficiency. Colleges in the 1920s began adding domestic science courses to their curricula to satisfy their female students' interest in homemaking as a career. The increasing production of labor-saving devices, such as fast foods and appliances, supposedly took the drudgery out of housework as well as saved time. Yet standards of cleanliness demanded more cleaning ("spring cleaning" for colonial women was just that—a once-a-year ritual), and many of the appliances, such as the washing machine, added chores that for middle-class women had previously been done outside the home (Margolis 1984).

For single middle-class women, the dramatic increase in white-collar jobs open to women in the 1910s, prior to World War I, provided employment possibilities that were consistent with their social class. The proportion of women employed in white-collar jobs increased by 64 percent to become the major sector of female employment, even surpassing manufacturing. In 1910, 17 percent of female workers were in clerical or sales jobs; by 1920 the proportion had increased to 30 percent, where it remained for several decades (Chafe 1972). Whereas before 1900 over one-third of single middle-class women aged 16–24 were neither in school nor at work, by 1930 this fraction had dropped to only one-twentieth. For lower-class women clerical jobs were an attractive alternative to factory work. Wages for clerical jobs were typically two to three times what a female industrial worker could earn, and the working conditions and hours were better (Ryan 1983).

Despite the conclusion of a 1910 U.S. Bureau of Labor Statistics study that women worked outside the home because their husbands' or fathers' jobs were inadequate for family support, the "pin money" theory of women's employment continued to be used as justification for women's lower wages. It was believed that women worked for pocket money, which they spent for frivolous reasons rather than out of economic need. Yet until the 1920s the typical blue-collar worker's wages were insufficient to support a family (Dubnoff 1978). The middle-class ideal of the home as "a woman's place" did not fit the economic reality for most lower-class women. Yet the attitude that women's work outside the home was temporary, "a brief interlude in their lives before they could achieve their true calling as wives and mothers," lessened their commitment to employment and discouraged protest of their unequal pay and lower positions (Chafe 1972).

Most women, middle-class or lower-class, quit the labor force once they married. Some employers—most school boards, for example—prohibited the hiring of married women and fired female employees when they married. The public accepted the employment of single women, even single middle-class women, but rejected the idea of married women's taking a job. A Department of Labor report echoed public attitudes: "Practically every speaker . . . recognized that women's interest in industry was at best only temporary, a stop-gap between whatever girlhood lay behind her and marriage" (Rupp 1978, p. 61).

Despite the increase in well-educated middle-class women in the labor force, women did not make much progress in entering professional fields. As late as 1930, 57 percent of employed women were black or foreign-born, and they worked primarily as domestics or operatives in the apparel industry. Women were not allowed the roles of both employee and wife at the same time. Only 12 percent of women professionals in 1920 were married, and three-fourths of women who earned Ph.D.'s between 1877 and 1924 remained single (Chafe 1972). Thus few were willing to choose "celibate careerism" over marriage and motherhood. In some professional fields—medicine and dentistry, for example—the number of female practitioners actually declined from 1910 to 1920 despite a general population increase during this time and the addition of about 2 million women to the labor force. From 1920 to 1930 the proportion of employed women in professional occupations increased from 12 to 14 percent, although the professional fields they entered did not change. Three-quarters of professional women were in teaching, nursing, and other female-dominated fields. The percentage of female architects and lawyers remained constant from 1910 to 1930 (Chafe 1972).

The depression further restricted women's employment opportunities relative to men's. Employers denied women the right to work, and men were hired before women for jobs paying a living wage. The proportion of women in professional occupations fell from 14 percent in 1930 to 12 percent in 1940 (Chafe 1972).

Public sentiment was also against women's seeking employment, especially married women: a 1936 Gallup Poll showed that 82 percent of Americans thought that wives whose husbands were employed should not have a job. Gallup reported that he had "discovered an issue on which voters are about as solidly united as on any subject imaginable—including sin and hay fever" (Chafe 1972, p. 108). Nevertheless, the proportion of women in the labor force as a whole increased by 1 percent during the depression years, and the proportion of married women in the labor force increased by 4 percent (U.S. Bureau of the Census 1975). Forty percent of wives who entered the labor force during the depression were from the middle class. Their employment made it possible for their families to maintain a middle-class standard of living, despite their husbands' being out of work (Ryan 1983).

Unlike World War I, when only 5 percent of the women in the labor force were recent entrants, World War II had a tremendous impact on the employment of women. With 6.5 million more women employed as a result of the war, the proportion of the female population in the labor force jumped from 27.4 percent in 1940 to 35.0 percent in 1944 (U.S. Bureau of the Census 1975). Initially, single women filled the war-related jobs that were open, but eventually married women were called upon as more workers were needed. The war's impact on the employment of married women was augmented by the rise in the marriage rate between 1940 and 1944. Thus, there was both an increase in demand for female workers to fill war-related jobs and an increase in the proportion of women who were married. Seventy-five percent of the new workers in the early 1940s were housewives (Ryan 1983). The typical employed woman during the war was a middle-aged housewife—not a young single woman. In 1940 one-sixth of married women held jobs; by 1950 the proportion of married women who were employed had increased to over one-fourth (U.S. Bureau of the Census 1975). Furthermore, one-third of the new war workers had children under the age of 14 (Chafe 1972).

Public attitudes regarding suitable employment for women and married women who wished or needed to work outside the home changed dramatically in response to the crisis of war and the government's mass-media heroine, Rosie the Riveter. The U.S. Employment Service surveyed two hundred war jobs and concluded that women, with brief training, could fill 80 percent of the positions. In just five years public opinion of wives' working outside the home completely changed, from 80 percent disapproval in 1938 to over 60 percent approval in 1943 (Chafe 1972).

Contrary to what happened after World War I, the employment of women after World War II did not return to prewar levels, despite some public sentiment that it should. Many women were laid off when men returned from the war (women were laid off at a rate seventy-five times higher than men after the war) or voluntarily quit in the immediate postwar period (Chafe 1972). But by 1947, women reentering the job market began to make up for the immediate postwar losses, and by the mid-1950s the labor force participation rate of women was as high as it had been during the war. By 1952, 10.4 million wives had jobs, 2 million more than at the peak of World War II. In 1950, wives made up the majority, 52.1 percent, of women in the labor force, in contrast to 36.4 percent in 1940 (U.S. Bureau of the Census 1975). Almost one-fourth of wives working outside the home had children under 18 years of age (Chafe 1972).

After the war public attitudes toward women in the labor force, especially wives who continued working outside the home, was mixed. The Department of Labor issued a directive forbidding discrimination on the basis of race or sex, and the Secretary of Labor warned against restricting the hiring of married women. In 1944 Senator Harry Truman said: "Many women who have gone into factories and done such splendid work will want to continue working, and they are entitled to the chance to earn a good living at jobs they have shown they can do" (Chafe 1972, p. 176). Other Americans did not agree. Willard Waller, a Barnard sociologist, urged a return to what were perceived as traditional roles: "Women must bear and rear children; husbands must support them." Frederick Crawford, head of the National Association of Manufacturers, agreed: "From a humanitarian point of view, too many women should not stay in the labor force. The home is the basic American institution" (Chafe 1972, p. 176).

Many Americans believed that unless women returned home so

that the veterans could find work, the depression, with its relief rolls and breadlines, would return. Labor leaders also wanted women out of the way and used seniority lists and contract clauses to exclude them. But most women who worked outside the home wanted to continue in their jobs. A Women's Bureau survey of employed women in ten areas of the country showed that three-fourths of women who had taken jobs during the war wanted to continue working after the war. The greatest enthusiasm for employment came from women over 45 years old—80 percent of those women in the labor force wanted a permanent job (Chafe 1972). A factor contributing to the number of women continuing in the job market after the war was the inflationary economy of 1945–47. Thus, while many couples might, in principle, have believed that a woman's place was in the home, the wife had to have a job to help support their middle-class lifestyle. The emphasis was on being employed to provide a better home life, not on pursuing careers. The wife who sought employment to help the household did not challenge the traditional notion of her role; she simply modified it a bit. What is novel about the situation of women's holding jobs after the war is the change in definition of economic need. Before 1940, a wife entered the labor force if her husband's income was below poverty level; after 1950, a middle-class wife got a job so that she and her husband could enhance their material welfare (Chafe 1972).

The increase in the number of wives working outside the home was fueled mainly by entry into the labor force of women whose children were at least of school age. In 1950, just 12 percent of married women with children under 6 years old were employed (Waite 1981). In 1940, the average woman married at 21 years of age and had her first child at 23 years of age and her last child at 27 years of age. Thus, by the time she was 32 her youngest child was in grade school, and by the time she was 45 her youngest child was ready to leave home. Chafe (1972, p. 193) notes how the expansion of women's work roles in the 1940s did not constitute a challenge to the traditional definition of a woman's role: "The war had made employment for women over 35 an increasingly viable possibility, and it was not surprising that the bulk of new female workers during the 1940s came from the middle-aged segment of the population. From a social point of view, however, the most significant fact about such women was that they had already fulfilled their function as mothers. Their employment did not represent a 'feminist' threat." Further evidence that the public was not ready to accept employment of mothers with preschool-age children was the lack of support for child-care centers. Although "latchkey" children, delinquency, and runaways became subjects of national concern, the federal government avoided addressing the problem of child care. The public still preferred to think that mothers should stay home and that the government should not tamper with tradition (Chafe 1972).

Although the war changed the number, age, and marital status of women in the labor force, their position in the labor force was unchanged. During the war, wages for women increased as women shifted from low-paying jobs to aircraft-industry jobs or federal government jobs previously held by men. Black women especially benefited as the proportion employed as servants dropped from 72 to 48 percent in the war years. The unionization of women workers also increased by 400 percent during this period. But after the war, women in better-paying jobs were laid off, and when they returned to the labor force they were hired in traditionally female occupations. The result was that after the war, women were still paid less than men. Women in manufacturing earned 66 percent of what men in manufacturing earned. Whenever women constituted a majority in an industry, that industry paid below the national average wage. The proportion of women employed as professionals declined from 45 percent in 1940 to 38 percent in 1966, while the proportion of women employed as clerical workers increased from 53 percent in 1940 to 73 percent in 1968. Professional women were primarily in the traditional fields—nursing, teaching, librarianship, and social work. Increasingly, women were entering female-dominated fields in which the average pay was little more than half that of men's. A "pink-collar ghetto" was emerging (Ryan 1983, p. 281).

CONCLUSION

The separation of home and workplace, and of the roles of wife and husband, can be viewed as a functional separation of two institutions whose standards are at odds. The workplace is impersonal and objective; roles are defined by performance. In contrast, the home is personal and emotional; roles are defined by age and sex. With only one family member in the workplace, the nuclear family could avoid having its members compete with each other (Parsons 1949; Kanter 1978).

Far from remaining fixed, the institutions of the family, the economy, and the educational system have undergone tremendous change. Industrialism brought separation of the home and workplace, and women's roles became more narrowly defined as mother and home-maker. Yet the decline in fertility and the increase in life expectancy, as well as the economic vulnerability of such separate roles for men and women, have brought further change. In the following chapters we discuss the demographic changes that took place as women re-emerged from the home to the workplace.

Part Two
Behavioral Changes

3

Educational Attainment

We begin with education because completion of schooling is one of the primary points of transition to adulthood in American society. Changes in the timing and level of education are likely to affect the assumption of adult roles in society (Modell et al. 1976), and the amount of schooling men and women receive is closely linked to their potential employment opportunities, occupational status, and earnings (Duncan et al. 1972; Sewell and Hauser 1975). For women in particular, a higher level of education has meant a chance to achieve greater economic independence (Oppenheimer 1982). Furthermore, educational attainment is strongly associated with values, tastes, and attitudes (Davis 1982), and so it is to be expected that changes in women's aggregate level of education are related to shifts in their outlook on life and in their lifestyles.

Over the course of the twentieth century, both men and women have reached higher levels of education. Women, however, have made their greatest gains at different historical periods than men have, and women have also incorporated education into their life course in different ways. The last twenty years have witnessed the most significant increase in the level of women's education since 1900. College attendance among women has doubled—one out of five women obtained some college education in the mid-1960s compared to two out of five in the early 1980s. This steep rise has narrowed the gap in levels of education between men and women, in contrast to the period from 1940 to 1960 when the educational attainment of women declined relative to that of men.

As a result, women now participate more heavily in the labor force. Compared to twenty and even ten years ago, today's college-educated women are much more likely to have a job outside the home, and they are more strongly inclined to stay employed. The desire—or the need—to be in the labor force has become a major motivation for obtaining a higher level of education. Moreover, the number of women returning to school at later ages has greatly increased. Today, more than one-fourth of all women college students are over the age of 30.. A further consequence of the changes in educational attainment over the last two decades is that women have entered traditionally male-dominated fields in record numbers. Currently 20 to 30 percent of the new entrants into the professions of law, medicine, architecture, and business are women, compared to only about 5 percent in 1960.

Another important impact of the increase in the educational level of women has been the postponement of marriage and motherhood. In fact, women's attainment of a high level of education correlates with delayed marriage to a greater extent now than it did twenty years ago. As highly educated women remain single, prepare for long-term employment, and obtain job experience, their early adulthood is devoted to roles outside the family. This experience encourages a continuing participation in the labor force even after women have assumed family responsibilities as wives and mothers. The multiple roles that now characterize the lives of many women stem largely from the early commitments they make as single, independent individuals.

WOMEN'S EDUCATIONAL ATTAINMENT
RELATIVE TO MEN'S

Women have completed high school to the same or a slightly greater extent than men throughout this century; it is at the level of higher education that differences between men and women have emerged. Since 1900 the average level of education for both men and women in the United States has shown consistent increases. Women's educational attainment *relative* to men's, however, declined from the 1940s to the 1960s (Smith and Ward 1984; Hoffman 1975). The major explanation for this change in the pattern was the educational advantage afforded men through the GI Bill after World War II (Hoffman 1975).

FIGURE 3.1

Percentage of Men and Women Aged 24–29 Completing at Least One Year of College, 1900–1984

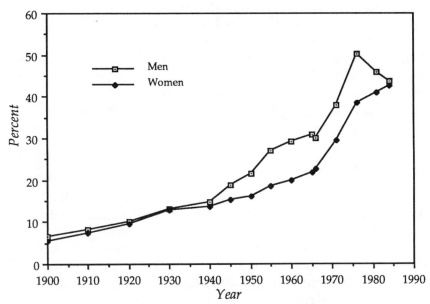

Sources: For 1900–1965 data on white males and white females aged 24–29, see Ridley 1969; for 1966–84 data on all males and females aged 25–29, see U.S. Bureau of the Census 1984c and U.S. Bureau of the Census, Personal Communication, September 1985.

While 6 percent of women and 7 percent of men aged 24–29 had completed at least one year of college in 1900, and this 1 percent difference continued through 1940 (when 14 percent of women and 15 percent of men had attained one year of college education), by 1965, 31 percent of men had completed one year of college compared with only 22 percent of women (Ridley 1969; see Figure 3.1). Men who reached adulthood in the 1960s attained an average of 2.8 more years of education than men who reached adulthood in the 1930s; between comparable groups of women the difference was 2.3 years (Smith and Ward 1984).

Only during the past twenty years have women been making gains at a faster pace than men, narrowing the gap in educational attainment (U.S. Bureau of the Census 1984a). This pattern has continued up to the present time. By 1981, 46 percent of men and 41 percent of women had completed at least one year of college. During the

1980s women's college attendance has continued to increase, while men's has declined slightly. In 1984, 44 percent of men aged 24–29 had finished at least one year of college compared to 43 percent of women in the same age group, returning women to the same position relative to men that they had maintained during the first half of this century (see Figure 3.1). The ratio of female to male college graduates (aged 24–29) also illustrates the recent convergence of female and male educational attainment. This ratio dropped from the 1950s level of .66 to .56 in 1960, then rose dramatically to .71 in 1970, to .85 in 1981 and to .89 by 1984 (U.S. Bureau of the Census 1976a, 1984a).

Gains in College-Level Education

Both the proportion of women aged 25–29 who attained at least one year of college education and the proportion who graduated from college almost doubled between 1966 and 1984, from 23 to 43 percent and from 11 to 21 percent, respectively (U.S. Bureau of the Census 1984a, Table B.1). As shown in Figure 3.2, in 1981 there were approximately 4 million women aged 25–34 who had some college education and another 4 million who were college graduates. Of the approximately 6.5-million increase in the population of women aged 25–34 from 1970 to 1981, close to 4 million attained some college education and approximately 2.5 million were graduated from high school, showing the dominance of growth at the college level of education during this period. The number of women aged 25–34 with less than a high school education has dropped steadily since 1940 in spite of growth in the population of women in this age group. In 1940, over half of these women had not been graduated from high school; by 1981 the proportion was less than 15 percent (see Figure 3.2).

The largest growth in women's college attendance in recent years has been at two-year colleges rather than at four-year institutions, so that a major part of the rapid expansion of women's college-level attainment has been achieved through enrollment in community colleges (U.S. Bureau of the Census 1984c). However, because women are more concentrated in two-year institutions than men, and these institutions are more limited in educational opportunities than four-year institutions, women continue to lag behind men in their educational achievement (Randour et al. 1982).

FIGURE 3.2

Educational Attainment of Women Aged 25–34, 1940–1981

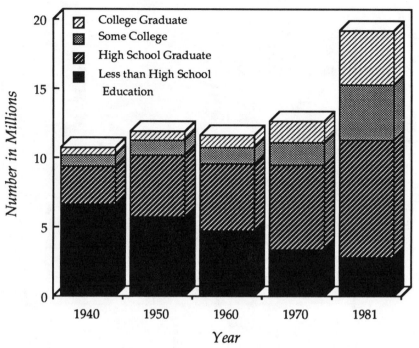

Source: U.S. Bureau of the Census 1984c.

With their rapid increase in college attendance, by 1983 women constituted over half of the student body at two-year colleges and close to half of the students attending four-year colleges. However, they had not yet achieved parity at the level of graduate education, where they comprised 44 percent of graduate students (see Figure 3.3).

Women's rising level of educational attainment also is evident in the proportion of degrees earned by women, which since 1950 has been steadily rising at all levels of higher education, but most notably at the bachelor's and master's levels (as shown in Figure 3.4). Women received only 24 to 30 percent of these two degrees in 1950, but 50 percent in 1982. While women also have made gains in doctoral degrees, they still receive less than one-third of such degrees. It is important to note, however, that the gains achieved from 1950

FIGURE 3.3

Women as a Percentage of the Student Body at Institutions of Higher Education, 1970–1983

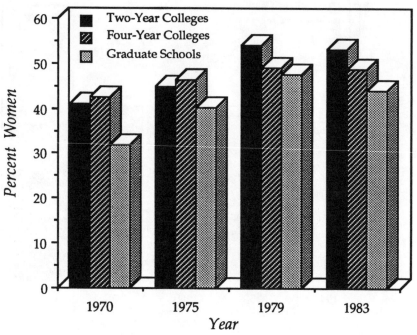

Source: U.S. Bureau of the Census 1984c.

through the early 1970s were in fact restoring an educational position that women had achieved earlier in the century. For example, in the 1971–72 academic year the proportion of bachelor's, master's, and doctoral degrees earned by women were 44 percent, 41 percent, and 16 percent, respectively. As shown in Figure 3.4, this is similar to the 40 percent of bachelor's and master's degrees and 15 percent of doctorates earned by women in 1930. It is only in the last decade that women have made gains beyond the levels established prior to the 1950s. Projections for women's participation in higher education indicate a leveling off by the end of this decade at the bachelor's and master's levels, as women are expected to continue to obtain approximately half of all these degrees in 1990. Continued growth in the proportion of female doctorates, however, is expected—a rise from less than one-third of doctorates earned by women in 1982 to 46

FIGURE 3.4

Percentage of B.A., M.A., and Ph.D. Degrees Earned by Women (Actual and Projected), 1930–1990

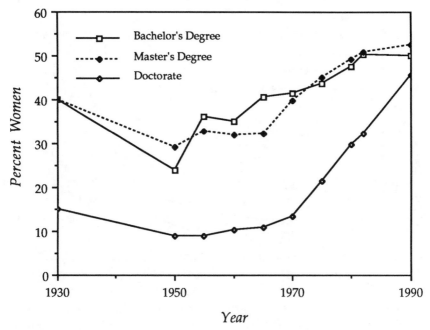

Sources: U.S. Bureau of the Census, Statistical Abstracts of the United States (1983, 1984, 1985); Westervelt 1975; National Center for Education Statistics, Digest of Education Statistics, 1983–1984.

percent by 1990 has been projected (National Center for Educational Statistics 1984).

The period from the 1960s to the 1980s has shown the greatest increase in the overall level of young women's education since 1900. Given the steep rise during this time, it is likely that while women's educational level will continue to increase over the next decade, the rate of change probably will slow as women's educational attainment converges with that of men.

The Reduction of Sex Segregation in Fields of Study

There have been significant changes in the fields of study women have entered in higher education since the 1960s. While women continue to dominate many traditionally female fields—e.g., education,

FIGURE 3.5

Percentage of Professional Degrees Earned by Women, 1955–1982

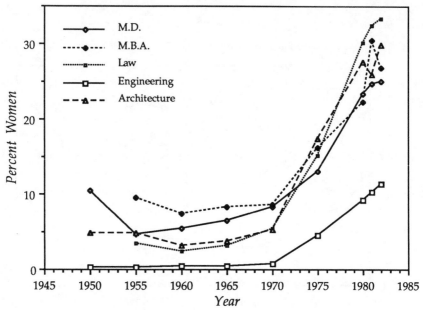

Sources: U.S. Bureau of the Census 1984i; National Center for Education Statistics, Digest of Education Statistics (1981).

foreign languages, health professions, home economics, and library science, where over three-quarters of degrees granted are obtained by women (Randour et al. 1982)—they have become a significant part of several male-dominated fields, particularly in the major professions (Melber 1981; Randour et al. 1982). The most dramatic changes have occurred in the professions of law and medicine (as shown in Figure 3.5). The number of women becoming lawyers increased from 230 in 1960 to approximately 12,000 in 1982, which represents a dramatic increase in law degrees earned by women, up from 3 to 33 percent. Similarly, the number of women who received medical degrees increased from 390 in 1960 to approximately 4,000 women in 1981, representing a jump from 6 to 25 percent of all medical degrees. Other male-dominated professional fields also have experienced high rates of change. In the rapidly growing area of business administration, over 10,000 women obtained master's degrees (M.B.A.'s) in 1982 compared to 160 in 1955, a rise from less than 4 percent to 27 percent of all M.B.A.'s awarded. Women now comprise more than 25 percent of all architecture graduates (2,500 female degree candidates in 1980) compared to 3 percent (fewer than 60 women) in 1960. Similarly, 170 women received engineering degrees in 1960 compared to over 9,000 women in 1982 (increasing from 1 to 11 percent of all engineering degrees).

There has been a parallel trend at the baccalaureate level in several other areas, although less dramatic than the rate of change in professional degrees. From 1965 to 1982, the proportion of bachelor's degrees earned by women in the field of business administration rose from 7 to 39 percent; in the biological sciences, from 28 to 45 percent, and in the physical sciences, from 13 to 26 percent (see Figure 3.6).

The result of these changes in areas of study is less overall sex segregation in higher education. However, the reduction in sex-specific areas of study has been almost exclusively the result of women's moving into traditionally male fields, while the traditionally female-dominated fields remain segregated.

The change in women's fields of specialization in recent years, and particularly the emphasis on professions, suggests that women now are selecting educational programs geared more toward future jobs than they have in earlier periods. The significant movement of women into law, medicine, architecture, and business, to the extent that they now comprise from one-fifth to over one-third of the new entrants into these professions, is evidence of a clear trend: women are participating in higher education to prepare for employment and, increasingly, for long-term careers. A greater orientation toward work appears to be an important factor in the dramatic changes in women's education over the past decade.

CHANGES IN THE TIMING AND DURATION OF EDUCATION

Women have expanded their participation in education to include a broader portion of their lives. This expansion involves both changes in the timing of education in terms of the ages at which women are enrolled in school and changes in the total number of years devoted to education.

There has been a consistent pattern of higher rates of school en-

FIGURE 3.6

Percentage of B.A. Degrees Earned by Women in Selected Fields,
1950–1982

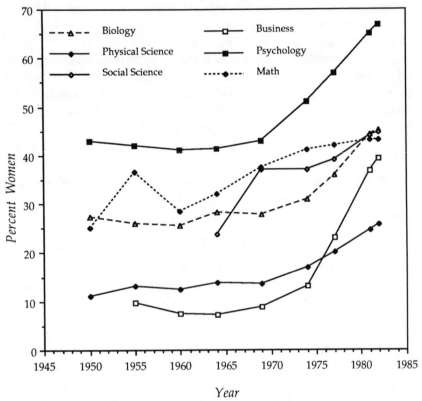

Year

Sources: U.S. Bureau of the Census, Statistical Abstracts of the United States (1967, 1971, 1979, 1984, 1985); National Center for Education Statistics, Digest of Education Statistics (1981).

rollment for women at all ages from the 1960s to the 1980s. For example, from 1965 to 1983 enrollment of women aged 18–19 increased from 38 to 50 percent; enrollment of women aged 25–29 increased from 3 to 9 percent; and for those aged 30–34, enrollment increased from 2 to 7 percent (U.S. Bureau of the Census 1984b, h; see Table 3.1). The increase in the age range for completing schooling also can be seen in the changes in the age distribution of women college students over the past twenty-five years. In 1960 women aged 25–29 made up approximately 8 percent of all female college students; by

TABLE 3.1

Male and Female College Enrollment by Age Group, 1965–1983

	Men		Women	
Year	25–29 (%)	30–34 (%)	25–29 (%)	30–34 (%)
1965	9.4	4.5	3.1	2.1
1970	11.0	5.3	4.3	3.1
1975	13.1	7.7	7.2	5.6
1980	9.8	5.9	8.8	7.0
1983	10.7	5.8	8.5	7.0

Source: U.S. Bureau of the Census 1984h, Table 3.

1983 they made up 14 percent. Similarly, the proportion of college women aged 30–34 increased from 5 to 11 percent from 1960 to 1983, and college women aged 35 and over increased from 11 percent in 1972 to 16 percent in 1983 (U.S. Bureau of the Census 1981, 1984h). Today, women aged 25 and over constitute over 40 percent of female college students.

This pattern of significant increases in school enrollment at older ages has not occurred among men. In contrast to the consistent upward trend documented for women, only minor changes in enrollment rates have occurred among adult men since 1965, increasing in some years and decreasing in others (U.S. Bureau of the Census 1981, 1984h; see Table 3.1).

In addition to there being a wider range in the ages of women attending school, the amount of time the average individual woman devotes to education has increased. This is due largely to the increased time necessary to complete higher levels of education, but also partially to a large increase in part-time schooling, particularly at older ages (Heyns and Bird 1982; U.S. Bureau of the Census 1981; see Table 3.2). Time spent in school for women aged 18–29 increased from an average of 1.4 years in 1960 to 1.9 years in 1970, and to 2.6 years in 1980 (Sweet and Teixeira 1984). Below, the implications of these changes in timing of enrollment for women's lives are addressed.

TABLE 3.2
College Enrollment by Age and Part-Time Attendance

Enrollment Status	Men		Women	
	25–34	35+	25–34	35+
Part-Time 1979	798,000	402,000	955,000	764,000
Percent Change 1974–1979	−1.4	+9.2	+66.4	+72.5
Full-Time 1979	558,000	81,000	364,000	147,000
Percent Change 1974–1979	−0.7	−22.9	+41.6	+42.7

Source: Magarell 1981.

THE IMPACT ON MARRIAGE, MOTHERHOOD, AND EMPLOYMENT

The increased age span over which women are obtaining education is associated with changes in the timing and sequencing of other life-course events, such as marriage, motherhood, and employment. Three major themes emerge when we consider the relationship of education to changes in women's life course: (1) the strong correlation between obtaining higher levels of education and remaining single and childless during young adulthood; (2) the increase in combining multiple roles over the life course, because as women attend school across a broader range of life-course stages, they are combining education with marriage, motherhood, and employment; and (3) the closer linkage of education to employment patterns over the life course.

Educational Attainment and the Timing
of Marriage and Motherhood

The general increase in the educational attainment of women over the past twenty years has significantly contributed to the rise in the ages at which women both marry and enter motherhood. While a positive relationship between level of education and later marriage has been observed throughout this century (Ryder and Westoff 1971a; U.S. Bureau of the Census 1969), this association appears to have strengthened over the past twenty years. As shown in Figure 3.7, the differences in age at first marriage among women with different educational levels have increased considerably. By 1980 women with some college education (more than 12 years of schooling) were getting married for the first time an average of 2.5 years later than female high school graduates (12 years of education) and an average of almost 4 years later than women with fewer than 12 years of schooling (Sweet and Teixeira 1984).

The apparent tendency of higher educational levels to effect later age at marriage and the significant increase in the average level of educational attainment for the total population of women have combined to increase the overall age at first marriage for American women. Average age at first marriage among women aged 18–29 increased by approximately two years, from 21 to 23, between 1960 and 1980 (Sweet and Teixeira 1984).

As described above, the average time spent on education by women aged 18–29 almost doubled between 1960 and 1980, increasing from 1.4 years to 2.6 years. There was only a minor change in the rate of school enrollment for single women between 1960 and 1980 (i.e., the proportion of single women in school increased slightly). The increase in average time spent on schooling can be explained in part by the increase in time women are remaining single, because single women are more often enrolled in school than married women.

The question arises as to the causal relationship between education and age at first marriage: Do women who marry early drop out of school or do women enrolled in school postpone marriage? Studies addressing this issue indicate that, while both processes occur, education has a stronger effect on delaying marriage than marriage has on leaving school. Marini (1978a) found that the effect of level of educational attainment on age at marriage was twice as strong as the

FIGURE 3.7

Time Spent Single from Ages 18 to 29, by Educational Level

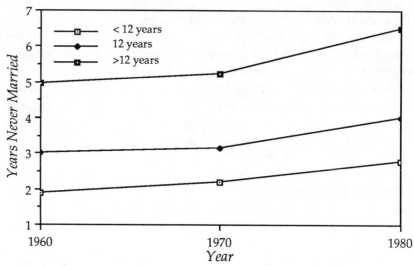

Source: Sweet and Teixeira 1984.

effect of age at marriage on educational attainment. Specifically, each additional year of education led to a delay in marriage of approximately eight months, while each additional year of being single resulted in less than four months of additional education. For men, a different pattern has been found. Although a higher educational level is related to a later age at marriage for men (but to a lesser extent than for women), the timing of marriage does not have a significant effect on men's educational attainment (Marini 1978a; Call and Otto 1979; Alexander and Reilly 1981).

The relationship of educational level and entry into motherhood follows a pattern similar to that of education and marriage—that is, a higher level of education is associated with a later age at the birth of the first child (Rindfuss et al. 1980; Rindfuss et al. 1983; Waite and Moore 1978; McLaughlin et al. 1985; Marini 1984a; Hofferth and Moore 1979). There also is evidence that the correlation between educational attainment and timing of motherhood has strengthened since the 1950s. College education was more highly associated with delayed fertility in the 1970s than in the 1950s, resembling the pattern found during the 1930s when late childbearing was closely linked to high levels of educational attainment (Rindfuss et al. 1984). The divergence of the pattern of the 1950s from other periods is evident here; women who had different levels of educational attainment followed a more homogeneous life course during that period than in either earlier or later decades (Uhlenberg 1974; Lopata and Norr 1980). During the 1950s, on the average, women of higher educational levels had their first child at an age similar to women with lower educational attainment. Today, education is a more critical factor in determining the timing of motherhood. Only among women who had their first child very early (at age 18 or younger) was there no effect of educational level on timing of entry into parenthood (Hofferth and Moore 1979). The effect of timing of motherhood on educational level has generally been found to be much weaker than the other way around (Marini 1984a; Rindfuss et al. 1980; Hofferth and Moore 1979), except for giving birth at age 18 or younger, which has been found to truncate educational attainment.

When the effects of education on the timing of marriage and the first child have been compared, educational level has been found to have a stronger impact on the timing of the first child than on the timing of marriage. As mentioned above, for each additional year of education attained by women, marriage is delayed by approximately eight months, whereas the first child is postponed by approximately a year (Marini 1984a). This is not surprising, since marriage places fewer constraints on activities outside the family than does the birth of a child.

The linkage between the level of educational attainment and the timing of entry into marriage and motherhood demonstrates the importance of recent changes in education for the life course of American women. As more women go on to college and delay marriage and motherhood, they spend a greater period of early adulthood independent of the traditional female roles of wife and mother. This longer period of single adulthood, particularly when many women have left their parents' homes and established separate households (as detailed in the following chapter), is a time when women's lives are organized around the demands of their own activities rather than around those of other family members. This experience of independent adulthood outside of marriage is likely to result in greater independence of women within marriage and parenthood as well.

The Trend toward Multiple Roles over the Life Course

The second distinct area of change, as mentioned above, is women's continued involvement in formal education across a broader range of life-course stages than in the past. According to Davis and Bumpass (1976), over 20 percent of married women have attended school at some time after marriage. The ages of these enrolled women suggest both an earlier return to school after marriage in recent years and the likelihood of a greater total participation in school over the life course for women married in the 1960s and 1970s relative to those married in the 1950s.

Returning to school after marriage generally occurs at two points in time: after a brief interruption, to complete a high school or college program; or after a period of approximately ten years, following the early child-rearing period (Davis and Bumpass 1976). The increase in women's enrollment after marriage has occurred both prior to and after their having children. From 1960 to 1980 school attendance of married women aged 18–29 without children increased from 14 to 22 percent. In the same period, school attendance of married women aged 18–29 with children increased from 4 percent to 13 percent (Sweet and Teixeira 1984).

While women's return to education after marriage and motherhood has not had a large impact on the overall level of educational attainment of the female population in the United States (i.e., the average number of years of schooling), it is significant for many women, both because the return is frequently for completion of a degree and because, for those who return after a long interruption, it often serves as a transition to labor force entry. Women who are separated or divorced are particularly likely to return to school (Davis and Bumpass 1976), suggesting a focus on education that is geared toward employment.

The prevalence of combining higher education with marriage and family contrasts with the life patterns of a significant portion of highly educated women in the early part of this century, when choosing education and employment more often meant forgoing marriage and family. Approximately 30 percent of graduates of a prestigious women's college from 1911–15 remained single throughout their lives (Giele 1984). Female college graduates of the 1960s, in contrast, have combined higher education and employment with family. Eighty-five percent of 1964 female college graduates with some work experience had married by 1982, and of these only 15 percent had not had children as of 1982 (Giele 1984). Furthermore, in recent years more highly educated women (those who have attended college and those who were graduated from college prior to marriage) are the ones who have returned to school after marriage at the highest rate: approximately 40 percent of these women surveyed in 1970 (Davis and Bumpass 1976).

The increase in combining schooling and labor force participation also demonstrates the significant trend toward multiple roles over the life course. Between 1960 and 1980 there was a large increase in the number of women who both worked and attended school. Working part time while attending high school has increased dramatically in recent decades. Since 1940 girls aged 16 have increased their labor force participation while in high school by a factor of 16 (Steinberg and Greenberger 1980). In 1980, approximately half of the time that women aged 18–29 spent in school, they were also employed, compared to about one-third of the time for women in the same age range in 1960 (Sweet and Teixeira 1984). The increasing pattern of women's working while going to school is further evidence of a trend toward greater independence of women as they take on more economic responsibility for the cost of their education.

Educational Attainment and Employment

Higher levels of educational attainment have always been associated with greater labor force participation of women. In recent years, however, this relationship has strengthened in the same way as has that between higher educational levels and greater delays in marriage and parenthood (Smith and Ward 1984; Michael 1985). As shown in Figures 3.8 and 3.9, labor force participation of college-educated women and high school graduates has increased substantially, with little change among those who do not complete high school.

Part of the rise in female labor force participation can be attributed to the overall increase in women's educational attainment. As more women attend college, more will enter the labor force because higher education correlates with employment. However, the greater effect

FIGURE 3.8

Labor Force Participation of Women Aged 25–34, by Educational Level, 1940–1983

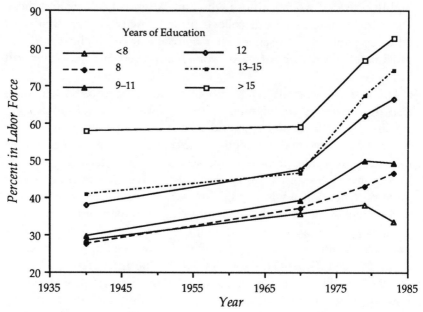

Source: Smith and Ward 1984.

of education on labor force participation is due to substantial increases today in employment of women who have attained higher educational levels as compared with women in earlier decades (Michael 1985; Smith and Ward 1984). Thus, it is not simply that there are more women college graduates today but, more important, women college graduates are more likely to be employed now than during the 1950s, 1960s, and 1970s. This substantial increase in the linkage of women's educational attainment to employment is consistent with women's changing to fields of study that are clearly directed toward careers.

The long-term association of a higher level of education with greater labor force participation of women has been explained as being driven by tastes and values acquired through higher education—e.g., an interest in meaningful work (Davis 1982)—and by the better employment opportunities available to those with more education.

FIGURE 3.9

Labor Force Participation of Women Aged 35–44, by Educational Level, 1940–1983

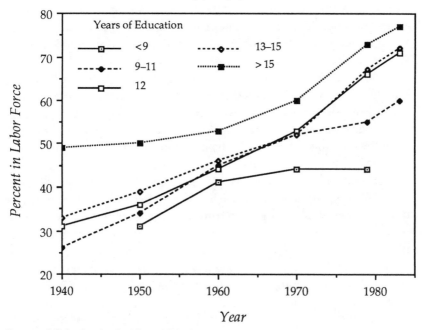

Sources: Michael 1985; Smith and Ward 1984.

The recent strengthening of this relationship suggests that now more women are participating in higher education in anticipation of employment than in the past.

EDUCATION AND THE LIFE COURSE OF WOMEN

Women's position in education has changed in many ways over the past thirty years. Their overall level of education has increased, and the gap between men and women in educational attainment has narrowed. However, it is important to emphasize that much of the gain achieved in the 1960s and 1970s merely restored the position in higher education that women held relative to men as early as the 1930s. The most significant changes have been: (1) the large increase in women's college attendance, doubling from the mid-1960s to the early 1980s; and (2) the substantial movement of women into major professional fields traditionally dominated by men.

Although level of education always has been associated with the extent of women's employment, historically the aggregate rise in women's labor force participation preceded the period of the most rapid increase in women's overall educational attainment (which did not occur until the 1960s and 1970s). As will be explained in Chapter 6, factors other than increased educational levels—primarily an expansion in female-dominated occupations—were largely responsible for the rise of women's employment in the 1950s. Educational gains have lagged behind women's gains in labor force participation. We hypothesize that the recent gains in women's educational attainment and, in particular, the current movement into a broader range of career fields are, to some extent, a response to the changes in labor force patterns of women in earlier years. Because of the increased demand for female workers during the 1950s, which brought older married women into the labor force, female employment came to be perceived less as a temporary experience before marriage and more as a long-term commitment extending over several stages in the life course. With this change, the nature of the job became a more important consideration for many individual women. The sharp increases in women's educational attainment began in the 1960s during the time that women were continuing to expand their labor force participation but were limited to female occupations. Educational gains then furthered women's employment opportunities. In recent years it appears that education has been a more significant force in the dramatic expansion of women's employment over the life course. There is evidence for this in the fact that women are increasingly entering career-oriented fields, which reflects a stronger relationship between educational level and labor force participation.

The change in the type of higher education women are obtaining has important implications for the occupational distribution of women. In spite of the dramatic increase in women's employment, there had been almost no change in occupational sex segregation until the 1980s, since women continued to move into a narrow band of female-dominated occupations. The recent entry of women into traditionally male fields is finally beginning to break this barrier. Over time this movement will lead to a reduction in the sex segregation of occupations, just as there has been some reduction in the sex segregation in educational fields in recent years.

Education has become a more critical factor in determining a woman's life course compared to thirty years ago. The long-term patterns of more highly educated women entering marriage and motherhood at later ages and spending more time employed have strengthened considerably in the past two decades. Women with different educational backgrounds follow more diverse paths now than in the past, both in terms of when they assume the traditional female roles of wife and mother and how long they spend in the role of jobholder over the life course. As we have seen above, the major change in women's educational attainment has been the increase in the proportion of women who obtain some college-level education, and the patterns of this growing group of highly educated women appear to be setting the new trends in women's life course.

As women who obtain a high level of education remain single longer, prepare for employment, and obtain some job experience, they are consolidating resources and leading their early adult lives as independent individuals rather than entering adulthood in the roles of dependent wife and mother. This period is one during which women are most similar to men in their role obligations and lifestyles. Early adulthood is a time of rapid attitude change and development, after which established orientations tend to show greater stability over time (Glenn 1980). The formative attitudes and values established during this period of independence are likely to have lasting consequences for women.

The longer period of schooling for women reflects women's changing allocation of time at different stages in the life course. In contrast to a sequential pattern more typical of the 1950s, women are increasingly combining a broad range of activities across stages, simultaneously working, going to school, and parenting. Furthermore, the associated period of independence as a single adult is a time when a woman's identity is largely defined by her roles as student and employed worker. Women today, then, are more likely to continue nonfamilial roles, even during periods of high family demands, because of earlier investments and commitments to activities outside of the traditional roles of wife and mother.

At first glance, this trend toward a combination of roles may seem to contradict the trend described above of delaying age at marriage and motherhood as a result of increased schooling. The separation of schooling from family formation emphasizes the constraints of family responsibilities on completing education, while the combination of roles suggests that these constraints have become less significant in recent years. We believe, however, that in fact it is the attainment of a higher level of education prior to the assumption of family responsibilities that encourages multiple roles over the life course. Education creates both tastes and opportunities for roles outside the home. The increased association between higher educational levels and employment is indicative of this effect.

4

Marriage and Divorce

From the perspective of the individual woman, the creation of a family through marriage is a major event. It changes her relationship to the family from which she came and provides her with a new set of roles, responsibilities, commitments, and expectations. It is a significant transition in the life course, one that has historically marked the entry into adulthood.

Marriage is equally significant from the perspective of society. The seemingly private decision regarding marriage is, in fact, so important that it is regulated by every known society in the world. The numbers of people who marry, the age at which they marry, and the duration of their marriages are all factors having a direct impact on every other social institution. Marriage behavior affects fertility, the size and nature of the labor force, the consumption of goods and services, and the shape of public policy. A change of one year in the average age at marriage may seem trivial at the individual level, but it has enormous implications for the social system.

The marital behavior of American women has significantly changed in recent decades, and this change has signaled a shift in the relationship of individual women to the family as a social institution and in the way women organize their lives. To begin with, changes in marital behavior since the 1950s point to a significant decline in the importance of marriage in the lives of American women. This decline is being met with a rise in the importance of the primary individual. More women are expected to remain single throughout their lives, those who do marry are marrying later, and marriages are more likely to end in divorce. Consequently, women are spending a smaller proportion of their lives married.

The main reason for the decline of marriage is that, relative to the other options available to women of today, marriage is not as attractive as it once was. In particular, the option of economic independence has changed the way women evaluate decisions regarding whether or not to marry, when to marry, and if already married, whether or not to divorce.

The decline in marriage as a social institution is closely related to recent changes in living arrangements. The rising divorce rate has dramatically increased the number of households headed by unmarried women with dependent children. Likewise, delayed marriage is related to the increasing numbers of young women living alone.

In the following sections of this chapter, we describe the demographic changes in marriage, divorce, remarriage, and cohabitation; present a series of explanations for the changes; and then summarize implications of those changes for the lives of American women.

As a starting point, data on the marital status of the female population between 1890 and 1983 are shown in Figure 4.1. The changing height of the bars represents population growth during the period. The most significant conclusions to be drawn from the data in this figure are the following:

1. The never-married population grew at a constant rate between 1890 and 1940. Throughout this period about 30 percent of the female population over age 15 was single. In absolute numbers, the never-married population reached 13.9 million in 1940. With the boom in marriages and births following World War II, the absolute numbers of single women fell to 11.1 million in 1950 and rose to 12.3 million in 1960. Between 1940 and 1970, the never-married population fell from 27.6 to 22.1 percent of the female population over 15 years old.

2. The separated and divorced female population over age 15 grew very slowly until 1930 when it reached a half million, then increased slowly through 1960 when it began to grow rapidly. The number of separated and divorced women grew from 3.0 million in 1960 to 9.6 million in 1983. In 1983, 10.3 percent of the female population over age 15 was divorced compared to 4.6 percent in 1960.

3. Since 1970, there has been a large increase in the size of the never-married population, from 17.0 million to 21.3 million by 1983,

FIGURE 4.1

Marital Status of the Female Population Aged 15 and over, 1890–1983

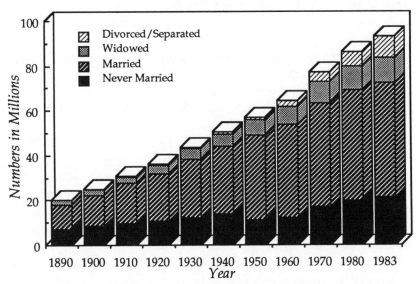

Sources: U.S. Bureau of the Census, Current Population Reports, ser. P-20, no. 35, "Population Characteristics" (1951); ser. P-25, no. 805, "Projections of the Number of Households and Families: 1979–1995" (1979); ser. P-20, no. 389, "Marital Status and Living Arrangements" (1983); Statistical Abstracts of the United States, 1984 (1983).

a growth of 25 percent in just thirteen years. This illustrates the consequences of several major trends. It reflects changes in marital behavior, including declining propensity to marry, rising age at first marriage, increased cohabitation, shorter duration of first marriage, fluctuations in the rate of remarriage, and changes in the age structure of the female population. In the following section we examine these trends in more detail.

CHANGES IN MARITAL PATTERNS

Declining Marital Rates

With a few exceptions, marriage rates during the first four decades of this century were relatively steady. There was a brief surge in rates at the end of World War I and a steep decline associated with the depression (Thornton and Freedman 1983). Between 1940 and 1945 the marriage rate was stable at about 130 marriages per 1,000 unmarried women aged 15–44, which represented about 1.5 million marriages. The end of World War II caused the number of marriages to rise again, but this time the increase was more dramatic and sustained. The marriage rate jumped from 138 per 1,000 unmarried women in 1945 to 199 per 1,000 in 1946, and the number of marriages broke the 2 million mark for the first time in 1946, with 2.3 million marriages taking place (U.S. National Center for Health Statistics 1985a). During the marriage boom of the 1950s this marriage rate remained at relatively high levels of between 150 and 167 per 1,000.

In 1970, this high marriage rate began to decline and has declined steadily ever since, although the actual number of marriages has increased every year since 1975 and has been setting new records every year since 1978, when the large baby-boom cohort began to reach the prime marriage ages. Thus, the number of marriages was increasing even as the propensity to marry was declining (U.S. National Center for Health Statistics 1984a).

Marriage rates at present are similar to those at the beginning of the century. For example, about 90 percent of white women born in 1954 are expected to marry by the age of 44 (Rodgers and Thornton 1985), which compares to 89 to 92 percent for women born around the turn of the century (Shoen et al. 1985). If we focus our attention on marital patterns over the course of the twentieth century, we see a period of relative stability during the first part of the century, followed by a dramatic marriage boom after World War II and a subsequent return to the earlier marital patterns.

Delay of First Marriage

The timing of first marriage has changed in a fashion similar to marriage rates. Historical data indicate that for the marriage cohort of 1890, the median age of women at first marriage was 22. From this point, the median age remained relatively constant until after World War II when it began to fall, reaching an all-time low of 20.1 years of age for the marriage cohort of 1956. Since that year, the median age at first marriage has risen, increasing one full year during the eight-year span from 1970 to 1978 and increasing another full year in the five-year period from 1978 to 1983. This represents a return to me-

FIGURE 4.2

Never-Married Women as a Percentage of the Total Female Population by Age, 1890–1983

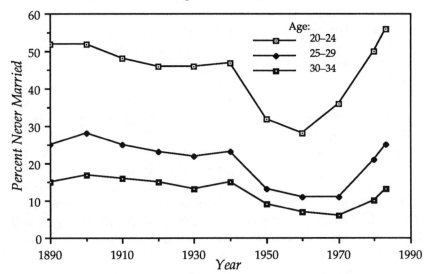

Sources: U.S. National Center for Health Statistics 1985a and 1985b.

dian ages equal to, or slightly higher than, the ages characterizing the first half of this century.

One of the ways to consider changes in marital behavior is to examine marriage over the life course of women born during the same period and then compare the results with those from different groups or "birth cohorts." This approach has the advantage of following a group of women as they age and allows the comparison of their marital behavior at various ages. When viewed from this perspective, the marital patterns of women born during the 1930s and 1940s and marrying during the 1950s can be seen as substantially different from the patterns of both earlier and later cohorts. Women born in the 1930s and 1940s married at younger ages and in greater numbers. While about 11 percent of white women born during the 1880s had not married by age 45, only about 3 percent of those born in the late 1930s were still single at that age (Thornton and Freedman 1983). Data reported by Schoen et al. (1985) also support the atypical nature of this cohort. They found that 97 percent of women born during the 1930–40 decade eventually married, compared to 92 percent of women born between 1890 and 1900. Similarly, Rodgers and Thornton (1985) report that over 96 percent of the birth cohort of 1934 were married by age 44, an all-time high, while about 89 percent of the birth cohort of 1900 married by this age.

Through an examination of these historical patterns of first marriage, Rodgers and Thornton (1985) were able to construct age-specific first-marriage rates for a wide range of birth cohorts. For the marriage boom of the 1950s, they found that the large increase in marriage rates was not consistent across all age groups. Teenage rates increased until about 1956 and then declined sharply, while for those aged 19–23, marriage rates remained high throughout the 1950s and 1960s. During this same period, marriage rates declined steadily for those 24–28 and 29–33. These differences show that the high marriage probabilities observed for women of the 1950s were the result of high marital rates among younger people (Rodgers and Thornton 1985). The decline of marriage rates in the 1970s was also inconsistent across all age groups; like the boom of the 1950s, it was much greater among the younger ones.

Changes in the Propensity to Marry

The general pattern of a return to former marital behavior can be illustrated with data on the percentage of women never married at various ages. Census data from 1890 to 1983 for three age groups are presented in Figure 4.2. For all groups, the period between 1890 and 1940 was relatively stable. Between 1940 and 1960, these groups began to marry at a greater rate, particularly the group aged 20–24, the prime marriage ages. But since 1970, there has been a return to the pre-1940 levels. In 1970 about 36 percent of women in their early twenties had not yet married. By 1980 that figure had risen to 50 percent, and in 1984 to 57 percent. The trends for women aged 25–29 are even more dramatic. Over the same time period, the percentage of never-married women in this age group more than doubled. Specifically, in 1970 about 10.5 percent of these women had never married, by 1980 the figure rose to 20 percent, and in 1984, 26 percent had never married.

Thus, in terms of the proportion of women never marrying, the relatively brief period of decline during the baby boom was a departure from a long-term pattern, the same conclusion we drew from data on age at first marriage and marriage rates. However, projections of the future behavior of currently single women indicate that average age at marriage may stabilize at current levels, but the proportion of the female population that will never marry is expected to continue to increase beyond the levels typical of the first half of the twentieth century (Rodgers and Thornton 1985; Bloom and Bennett 1985).

Using previously unpublished data from the Current Population Survey, Glick (1984) projects that dramatically larger numbers of those currently aged 25–29 may never marry, about 12 percent of women. If these projections are correct, it would mean that three times as many current young adults will spend their lives as single persons than did members of their parents' generation. Other researchers also find an increasing tendency toward singlehood as a permanent lifestyle, not just delayed marriage (Masnick and Bane 1980; Schoen et al. 1985; Rodgers and Thornton 1985; Thornton and Freedman 1983).

CHANGES IN THE PROPENSITY TO DIVORCE

Climbing Divorce Rates

Over the last century, divorce rates have generally risen, but there have been several sharp deviations from this trend. During the early 1900s, the incidence of divorce increased steadily, averaging around 175,000 divorces per year, and peaking in 1929 with 206,000 divorces reported. This translates to a rate of 8 divorces per 1,000 married women aged 15 and over. Because of the economic conditions of the time, the number of divorces dropped to a low point of 164,000 in 1932 and then resumed a steady climb through World War II. Following the war, the divorce rate declined again, remaining low during the baby boom of the 1950s. The rapid increase in divorce beginning in the mid-1960s alarmed many social observers, particularly when compared to the exceptionally low rates of the 1950s.

Figure 4.3 illustrates in more detail the erratic pattern of divorce since 1940. In 1946, at the same time the United States was experiencing its highest marriage rates ever, the divorce rate was also

FIGURE 4.3
Marriage and Divorce Rates, 1940–1982

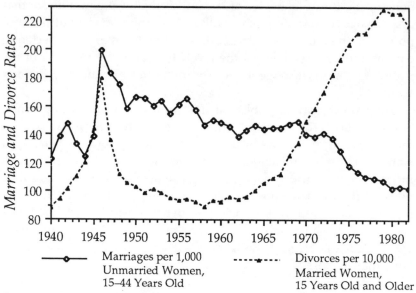

Marriages per 1,000 Unmarried Women, 15–44 Years Old

Divorces per 10,000 Married Women, 15 Years Old and Older

Sources: U.S. Bureau of the Census 1975, 1983, and 1984e.

reaching new highs with a record of 610,000 divorces recorded for that year, or a divorce rate of 17.9 per 1,000 married women 15 and older. (In order to put both rates on the same scale, the divorce rate was multiplied by ten for Figure 4.3.)

The high rates of marriage and fertility associated with the baby-boom period were accompanied by low divorce rates. There were approximately 370,000 divorces per year during the 1950s, including the low point of 368,000 divorces in 1958, a rate of 8.9 per 1,000 women 15 and older. This trend proved to be only temporary, and divorce rates again climbed upward during the 1960s and 1970s. This steady climb from the 1958 low was dramatic. In 1965, 479,000 divorces were registered; in 1970, 708,000; and in 1981, a new peak of 1,036,000 divorces was reached. Recent divorce rates have been around 22 per 1,000 married women 15 years of age and older (U.S. National Center for Health Statistics 1983a, 1985b; U.S. Bureau of the Census 1983).

The Dramatic Increase in Divorce since 1960

The upturn in divorce since 1960 has occurred primarily among women married after 1962. With each succeeding year, the proportion of divorces among women marrying after 1962 is greater than among those marrying earlier (Plateris 1979). This is true for marriages of all durations. For example, a larger proportion of women married in 1964 will be divorced by any given wedding anniversary than women married in 1963, while a smaller proportion of women married in 1964 will divorce than women married in 1965. The marriage and divorce data are presented in Figure 4.3 to illustrate the simultaneous changes in marriage and divorce rates, which followed a similar pattern during the postwar years until about 1963 when the divorce rate began a steady climb. Shortly afterwards, about 1968, the marriage rate began to fall and has declined ever since.

Since half of all divorces now occur within seven years of marriage (U.S. National Center for Health Statistics 1985b), large numbers of divorces are most likely to occur during years immediately following an increase in the number of marriages. Recent statistics show a slight decline in marriage rates and a corresponding leveling off of divorce rates since 1980. Starting in 1962, when the divorce rate per 10,000 married women aged 15 years and older was 9.4, the rate rose every year until it peaked at 22.8 in 1979 and then dropped to 22.6 in 1980 and 21.7 in 1982. The number of divorces also dropped slightly in 1982, from a historic high in 1981 of 1,213,000 to 1,170,000 in 1982. This represents the first decline in the number of divorces in twenty years. Preliminary data showed the number of divorces in 1983–85 to be declining also, but these declines were largely due to previous declines in marriages (U.S. National Center for Health Statistics 1984a, 1983b, 1985a).

THE JOINT EFFECTS OF CHANGES IN MARRIAGE AND DIVORCE

When considered together, the recent trends in marriage and divorce have profound implications for the roles of marriage and the family in the lives of women. In short, the lower rates of marriage, the rise in age at first marriage, the increased proportions of the population remaining single, and the increased divorce rates all point to a decline in the importance of marriage for shaping women's lives. The proportion of women's lives spent married has declined during recent decades while the years spent single and divorced have increased.

A wide range of factors influences the number of years that the average woman belongs to a particular marital status. These include life expectancy, age at first marriage, marriage rates, divorce rates, the average length of time after marriage that divorce occurs, the rates of remarriage, the duration of second marriages, and the probability of a marriage's ending with the death of the spouse. This latter factor is affected by differences in life expectancy and differences in age at marriage between men and women. The impact of all these factors can be summarized in marital-status life tables.

Marital-Status Life Tables

Marital-status life tables by Schoen et al. (1985) and Espenshade (1985) have been used to illustrate the impact of recent changes in marital behavior on the proportion of their lives that women spend single, married, separated or divorced, and widowed. Schoen et al. estimated that the duration of marriage for cohorts born just before the turn of the century was approximately 28.8 years. Average duration of first marriage rose gradually, peaking at 31.1 years with the birth cohort of 1928–32. This familiar group of women was part of the generation that gave birth to the baby boom—women who married young and stayed married for longer periods of time. Duration of marriage for the daughters of this generation has steadily decreased and has even fallen below the figures experienced by birth cohorts before 1900. Current estimates of marital duration are approximately 24 years (Schoen et al. 1985).

Figures 4.4 and 4.5 chart the data of two sets of marital-status tables constructed for black and white women between 1940 and 1980 (Espenshade 1985). The height of the bars in these figures represents average life expectancy. Each bar is then partitioned to show how that average life expectancy is divided among the various marital statuses. For both racial groups, the number of years women spend married has declined significantly, but the decline has been much more dramatic for blacks. The primary factors accounting for

FIGURE 4.4

Distribution of White Female Life Expectancy by Marital Status,
1940–1980

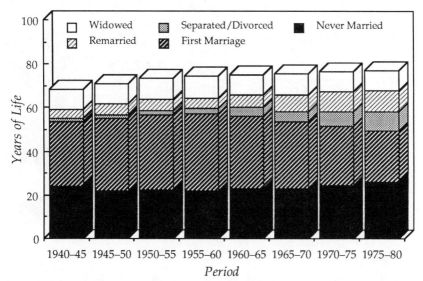

Source: The Urban Institute, as cited by Espenshade 1985.

the declines experienced by both groups are the rise in age at marriage, increases in the proportion never marrying, and the increased incidence of divorce. The duration of separation or divorce has increased for both blacks and whites, as has the duration of remarriage for white women. Only widowhood has remained constant. As divorce rates increase, relatively more marriages are ended by divorce, reducing the average number of years women spend widowed; but this trend has been balanced by increases in the life expectancy of women, which increases the number of years they spend as widows. The result has been no change in the proportion of life women spend widowed. Weed (1980) estimated that if death were the only source of marital dissolution, marriages contracted in 1976–77 could be expected to last 39.1 years. Divorce reduces the average length of these marriages to 23.2 years.

Considering the data on marriage and divorce, there can be little question that marriage as a social institution is declining. Women are marrying later, more women are avoiding marriage altogether, and the proportion of life they spend married is declining, as is the dura-

FIGURE 4.5

Distribution of Black Female Life Expectancy by Marital Status, 1940–1980

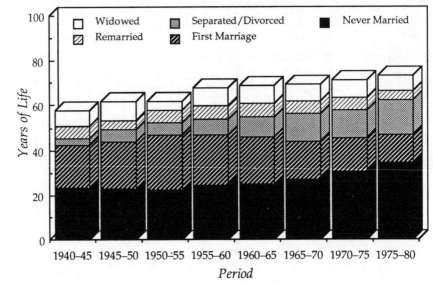

Source: The Urban Institute, as cited by Espenshade 1985.

tion of the average marriage. This is not to say that women no longer value marriage and the family as a central part of their lives. In fact, many studies directly asking about attitudes and beliefs regarding the family find a strong attachment to the traditional family. In terms of behavior, however, the meaning of marriage is clearly changing; it is losing many of its previous functions. In the following section we consider the sources of this change.

THE DECLINE OF MARRIAGE AS A SOCIAL INSTITUTION

Evidence supporting the conclusion that marriage is declining as a social institution can be found not just in marriage and divorce statistics, but also in data on the rise in premarital intercourse and unmarried parenthood, the decline in the proportion of children who are raised in two-parent families, and the increase in the proportion of the population cohabiting (living together in a sexual relationship), living in nonfamily households, or living alone, which are among the fastest-growing types of living arrangements. All of these changes point to a decline in the family's control over those aspects of day-to-day life that have traditionally been the primary functions of the family unit: the regulation of sexual behavior, the socialization of children, and the determination of living arrangements.

There are a number of theoretical explanations for this change in the place of the family within our society and within the life course of women. These explanations are of two basic types, cyclical and linear. Cyclical explanations link changes in marital behavior to cyclical external conditions such as the size of birth cohorts and swings in economic conditions. Changes in marriage, divorce, and fertility are also expected to be cyclical. Linear explanations tie changes in marriage behavior to long-term social change and attempt to extrapolate future changes in marriage from other social trends.

The Relative-Income Hypothesis

The most widely accepted and most fully developed cyclical theory of marriage and fertility behavior is that of Easterlin (1980). Easterlin's thesis is frequently labeled the "relative-income hypothesis" because the income of the members of a cohort relative to the income they experienced as children is the central element of his argument. According to Easterlin, people's material aspirations are formed while they are children living with their parents. If the economic conditions prevailing at the time people are making marriage and fertility decisions are more favorable than what existed during their childhood, it will be relatively easy for them to achieve the level of living they want, and they will then be able to marry early, have a larger number of children, maintain the household with one earner, and remain married. When economic conditions are less favorable than they were during childhood, people will have difficulty achieving the desired level of material well-being and will postpone or avoid marriage, have fewer children, require two incomes, and be more likely to divorce as a result of economic stress.

Cohort size is a critical factor in determining economic conditions and relative income. Individuals born during the depression of the 1930s were members of a very small birth cohort. They were also children during an economically depressed period and consequently developed relatively low material aspirations. When this birth cohort reached adulthood in the 1950s there was a high demand for labor because of the growing economy, but the supply of labor was low because of the size of the 1930s birth cohort and immigration restrictions. Consequently, this group found it easy to achieve the level of material well-being they felt was adequate, and they were able to marry early, have large families, and avoid the high levels of economic stress that are often linked to high divorce rates.

The birth cohorts of the 1950s and 1960s were raised during times of economic prosperity and now face a more difficult economic situation. The economy has not sustained high growth rates, and the size of the baby-boom cohort has increased competition for jobs and depressed growth in wages. Members of this cohort have found it more difficult to achieve the level of living they desire. They have adapted to these circumstances by delaying marriage, having fewer children, and increasing the labor force participation of wives.

Projections from Cyclical Theories

When extended to the future, Easterlin's cyclical theory would predict that today's smaller cohorts will experience relative economic prosperity and will return to earlier marriage, larger families, reduced women's labor force participation, and reduced divorce. While Easterlin's relative-income hypothesis is an appealing explanation of the patterns in the demographic behavior of women after World War II, we do not expect a return to the 1950s levels of marriage, fertility, divorce, and women's labor force participation. The critical point of departure between our reading of the demographic changes and Easterlin's thesis is his implicit assumption that norms regarding marriage and the family have not changed. He argues that when economic circumstances permit, cohorts with high relative incomes favor family life: they marry at high rates and at early ages, remain married throughout most of adult life, have large families, and maintain the traditional division of labor between the sexes. Our position is that the changes in the life course of women documented in this and the following chapters represent fundamental shifts in the roles of women that carry with them changes in the norms and expectations women have for their economic and family roles. We return to this point following a brief description of the exchange-relationship theories regarding changes in marital behavior.

Exchange-Relationship Theories

Almost all of the linear explanations for the decline of marriage and the family in the United States begin by considering the family as a marketplace of sorts in which husbands and wives exchange services. When individuals elect to marry, they agree to enter into a trade relationship in which both parties believe they will be better off than they would be if they remained single. Traditionally, this exchange has been based on a division of labor in which the male participated in the labor market and the female specialized in what economists call "home production" (child care, child socialization, housework, and meal preparation). Descriptions of the family as an exchange relationship vary widely depending on the discipline of the theorist, but the basic concept of individuals trading goods and services is common to economic, sociological, and social-psychological theories.

Given this exchange-relationship, many theorists have argued that several basic social changes have altered the relative position of men and women such that marriage is less attractive. As described by the major economic theory of marriage (Becker 1981), the "gains from marriage" for women have declined as a consequence of several external events, the most important of which is the increased labor force participation and earning power of women. As indicated in the previous chapter, women have made substantial gains in education, permitting them access to higher-paying jobs and the potential for a long-term career commitment. With these gains in earning potential, the "costs" of their not being employed are greater and the traditional division of labor in which the male performs market work and the female performs household tasks is much less attractive to women. Similarly, divorce becomes more attractive as the gains from marriage decline.

Empirical evidence to support this claim can be found in a substantial body of literature indicating that as women increase their ability to be economically independent, they are more likely to delay marriage or never marry, and once married are more likely to divorce. In addition, women in nontraditional occupations are more likely to divorce than women in traditional jobs (Philliber and Hiller 1983). Even among lower-income women, the provision of a guaranteed income in the Seattle-Denver Income Maintenance Experiments was found to significantly increase the probability of divorce (SRI International 1983).

Although most economists point to women's increased labor force participation as the primary factor that has lessened the "gains from marriage," there are other external changes that make marriage less attractive to women. Some researchers believe that the welfare system in the United States and, in particular, the Aid to Families with Dependent Children (AFDC) program lower the costs of illegitimacy and encourage divorce since they provide a guaranteed source of income to single mothers. However, this assertion remains widely debated because it has not been well established that either divorce rates or illegitimacy rates are linked to changes in AFDC payments (Duncan 1983).

The Marriage Squeeze

Some scholars maintain that another external condition has significantly affected the marriage exchange: the ratio of marriageable males to marriageable females. In the United States, women typically marry men who are older than themselves and who are of the same race and of equal or higher educational attainment. When fertility rates vary dramatically, as they did around the beginning of the baby boom, the ratio of males to females becomes unbalanced. For example, twenty-five years after a period of sharp increases in fertility, the number of females aged 22 years will be much greater than the number of men aged 24. This demographic imbalance, the "marriage squeeze," has been designated as the cause of many recent demographic changes, including increased age at marriage, declining fertility, and increased levels of female employment (Guttentag and Secord 1983).

An empirical analysis of the United States marriage market showed some evidence that this type of marriage squeeze affected women born during the early years of the baby boom as they reached the prime ages for marriage. However, the availability of potential partners for young women has been fairly consistent and high over time;

older women are the ones having difficulty finding partners. Data from 1970 and 1980 show that although over 100 suitable men were available for 100 women aged 20–24 (Goldman et al. 1984), the number of available men decreased dramatically as women passed age 25. Women's preference for older partners and men's taste for younger women, combined with higher survival rates among women, make it increasingly difficult for a woman to find a partner as she ages.

Thus, variations in fertility play a much smaller role in the marriage squeeze than do norms for relative age of brides and grooms. Young women typically have not and will not have much difficulty finding a partner. It is the reduced size of the group of men available to older women that causes a squeeze. The marriage squeeze caused by age may be exacerbated as baby-boom women over age 25 who have postponed marriage seek first mates and those who have previously been married seek new mates. However, it is primarily the age of women seeking mates, rather than the number of women seeking mates, that determines how tight the marriage squeeze will be.

Premarital Intercourse and Cohabitation

Other factors that affect the marriage market are social changes that are frequently seen as indicators of a decline in the family. These include increases in premarital intercourse and in cohabitation.

Dramatic changes in sexual behavior are documented in the following chapter. The number of unmarried couples cohabiting more than tripled between 1970 and 1982, making this nonmarital, presumably less permanent, living arrangement more visible. As the family loses control over the regulation of sexual behavior and living arrangements, the value and need for formal marriage is reduced. However, it is important to note that as of 1982 there were only 1.8 million such nonmarital households (4 percent of all couples). Furthermore, the number of women cohabiting at any given time is much smaller than the number of women who experience this living arrangement at some point in their lives. Cohabitation is thus demographically trivial, but it represents a new, rapidly growing lifestyle consistent with the general theme of a decline in dependence on marriage and the family.

MARRIAGE AND LIVING ARRANGEMENTS

One of the most fundamental consequences of the decline in marriage as a social institution is the change in the distribution of the population among various types of living arrangements. As American women spend less time married and more time either never married or previously married (separated, divorced, or widowed), they are much more likely to be classified as head of household, either as individuals living alone or as the heads of families. The major changes in household structure in the United States reflect these trends in the life course of women.

Married-couple households have declined as a proportion of all households. In fact, married-couple households with children under age 18 have declined in absolute numbers since 1970. In 1970 these "traditional family households" represented 40 percent of all households. By 1980 they had declined to 22 percent, and by 1984 they represented only 18 percent. In absolute numbers, this represents a decline of 1.2 million married-couple households—from 25.5 million in 1970 to 24.3 million in 1984. This decline took place while the total number of all households grew from 63.4 million to 85.4 million, an increase of 35 percent. Single women living alone and previously married women with children were household types that exhibited particularly rapid growth (U.S. Bureau of the Census 1984i). Thus, in general, changes in household structure have paralleled changes in marital behavior.

These changes in living arrangements have significant implications for the lifestyle of American women and for the goods and services they buy. In fact, all consumer purchases made at the household level are dependent upon the number and types of households in the population. The recent changes in marriage and divorce and the resulting changes in living arrangements are, therefore, central parts of any description of the changing life course of women.

In the following sections we examine in greater detail changes in household structure and their relationship to marriage and divorce trends. The first section considers the general decline in household size in the United States and the next two sections deal with those living alone and the rise in female-headed households.

The Decline of Household Size

The distribution of the population among various household types is a key index of a society's family structure. The size of households and the number of people who head households reflect the role of family in determining living arrangements. Household composition determines the social context of many aspects of day-to-day life, such as the performance of domestic functions and the availability of primary group ties.

In the United States, average household size has been declining continuously throughout the twentieth century. Explanations for this decline fall into two categories: demographic explanations and explanations based on the increased "propensity" of individuals to form separate or smaller households. The primary demographic factors accounting for the decline in household size in the United States are declines in fertility and mortality. Lower fertility reduces the size of families and lower mortality increases the number of years that couples or surviving parents live after their children are grown. The major effect of lower fertility has been to reduce the number of very large households, and reduced mortality has increased the number of small households (Kobrin 1976a).

Several studies have shown that these two demographic factors, fertility and mortality, account for all of the decline in household size in the United States between 1890 and 1950, because the propensity of individuals to live in smaller households did not change throughout this period (Beresford and Rivlin 1966; Burch et al. 1983). Until 1950, the basic social process governing the distribution of individuals into household units did not change in the United States, nor did it change in other developed countries (Beresford and Rivlin 1966).

After 1950 the demographic explanations were no longer able to account for the continuing decline in household size. The propensity to form separate living arrangements began to increase after World War II and continued to increase through at least 1980. This post-1950 pattern represents a significant cultural shift in the preferences and behaviors of individuals concerning the process by which they establish households, the basic units of consumption. The change has been characterized as a decline in the tolerance of family members for living with kin other than the nuclear family, an increased demand for privacy, and a general rise in the prominence of the "primary individual" (Kobrin 1976a).

In a recent study, Sweet (1984) attempted to explain the sources of the increase in the number of households in the United States between 1970 and 1980. In particular, he wanted to determine what part of this increase was due to demographic factors (population size, age structure, and marital status) and what part was due to a change in the propensity to form separate households. He found that growth in the number of households between 1970 and 1980 was concentrated among the young, never married, and those formerly married who were under the age of 65. Overall demographic factors accounted for two-thirds of the increase in the number of households and increased propensity accounted for one-third of the increase. The rise in age at marriage and the rise in the divorce rate caused these two segments of the population to experience considerable growth. However, even after this growth is taken into account, there was a substantial increase in propensity. In other words, one-third fewer households would have been formed between 1970 and 1980 if there had not been a change in propensity to form separate households.

This dramatic departure from a period of constant levels of propensity is consistent with the conclusion that the life course of American women has changed dramatically since 1950 and that the period following World War II was a turning point for many demographic trends. Since the distribution of various types of households is so closely linked to the distribution of the population among stages of the life course, it is not surprising to find that living arrangements also began to evidence significant change at the same time.

Beyond the general decline in household size, there are two primary changes in the living arrangements of women. The first is a rapid increase in the number of women living alone (a primary reason for declines in household size) and the second is a rapid increase in the proportion of households with children under age 18 that are headed by women. The following sections consider these two changes in more detail.

Change in the Propensity to Live Alone

Between the 1970 and 1980 U.S. censuses, the population living alone increased by 51 percent for females (7.3 million to 11.0 million). The largest growth occurred among women under age 35 for whom there was a 200 percent increase in living alone (U.S. Bureau of the Census 1980a).

Beresford and Rivlin (1966) were the first to draw attention to the apparently sudden change in the propensity to live alone in the United States. They provided evidence for the speculation that the rise in the population living alone subsequent to 1950 was due to a *combination* of a rise in income and an increased taste for privacy, which resulted in a willingness to use income to purchase privacy. Rising income alone was not considered an adequate explanation because pre-1950 gains in income were not linked to increases in living alone. Since the Beresford and Rivlin paper, the majority of the research and debate has centered on the issue of income versus taste for privacy as the causal factors explaining the increase in the population living alone.

Kobrin (1973, 1976a, 1976b) gave income-versus-taste questions a more detailed examination. By suggesting that any rise in living alone is due partly to demographic changes and partly to propensity, she was able to conclude that, after 1950, propensity was the major factor. Increases in propensity were far more important between 1950 and 1974 than changes in the size, age, or marital status of the population. Although Kobrin's explanations focused on normative changes in the value placed on privacy, she linked these changes to increases in the number of older women (over 55) relative to the number of women in their daughters' generation. In short, she argued that the decline in the normative living arrangement of older parents living with their children was related to gains in life expectancy, which increased the number of elderly widows relative to the number of women in their daughters' generation. The "uncompromising nuclearity" of the family was, according to Kobrin, a response to the increasing pressure for extended-family living arrangements.

Although the relationship between income and living alone has been well established (Beresford and Rivlin 1966; Carliner 1975), the first empirical analysis specifically directed at changes in the *propensity* to live alone was reported by Michael et al. (1980). Using state-level data, they examined the relationship between living alone and income level. They found income to be a powerful predictor of living alone and concluded that it began to have an effect only after 1950 because of the logistic, or S-shaped, form of the relationship. In other words, after 1950 income levels reached a threshold beyond which further increases were used to purchase privacy. This is essentially a rejection of the "change in taste" hypothesis of Kobrin, Beresford, and Rivlin in favor of an "income-threshold" hypothesis.

Since the publication of Michael et al. (1980), several papers have challenged the income-threshold hypothesis. The best of these is by Pampel (1983). Unlike Michael et al., he set up the problem at the individual level of analysis and suggested that if the income-threshold hypothesis were true, then increases in average income of individuals over time would account for the increases in living alone. Pampel used the 1960 and 1970 Public Use Samples of the U.S. Census and found that changes in levels of income did not, by themselves, explain the increase in living alone between 1960 and 1970. Thus, income is an important determinant of living alone but there is evidence, after controlling for increases in income, that the propensity to live alone has increased.

In a recently completed study, McLaughlin, Grady, and Landale (1985) analyzed the increase in the population living alone between 1973 and 1979. One objective of their research was to isolate the role of propensity in explaining this increase. The data were analyzed according to the separate categories of race, sex, and marital status. The group for which propensity played the largest role in explaining the increase was made up of white, never-married women. In general, males showed very little evidence of an increase in propensity to live alone. Among the separated and divorced population, white, younger women had significant gains in propensity. Thus, the increases in preference for living alone and for the lifestyle that goes with that living arrangement are concentrated among women—more specifically, among young, unmarried women. It is important to note that these are the categories of women expected to grow in the future because of the changing patterns of marriage and divorce. When the expected growth in this population is combined with an increase in the proportion expected to live alone, it is apparent that this segment will have significant impact on the marketplace.

Changes in the Number of Female-Headed Households

Households comprising an unmarried woman and her dependent children have grown more rapidly in recent years than any other type (U.S. Bureau of the Census 1980a). Between 1970 and 1979, the number of families in the United States increased by 12 percent, whereas the number of female-headed families with children under the age of 18 increased by 81 percent. Because of the magnitude of this increase, female-headed families constituted about 17 percent of all families in 1985, up from 11 percent in 1970. Reasons for this include the increase in unmarried parenthood, the rise in the rate of marital dissolution, and the growth in preference among single mothers for establishing a separate residence as opposed to living with parents.

Prior to 1950 the percentage of all families headed by women was roughly as high as it is currently, but these were primarily older women who became heads of their families through widowhood rather than unmarried parenthood. The rapid growth in female-headed families with young children is of concern because they are much more likely to be poor. In fact, the concentration of poverty in this growing population has come to be called the "feminization of poverty."

Change in the number of households headed by women has obvious implications for lifestyle and consumer behavior. Women who head households not only have different demands but also have to make major purchase decisions on their own. Although this is not the place to analyze in detail the impact of changes in household structure on consumer behavior (see McLaughlin and Zimmerle 1987), we can offer some final thoughts on evolving family and marriage patterns by looking at how different living arrangements may affect the use of income for major purchases.

THE IMPACT OF CHANGES IN LIVING
ARRANGEMENTS ON CONSUMER BEHAVIOR

Traditional and Contemporary Dual-Earner Households

Among two-earner households (typically, married couples or cohabitants), consumption patterns are likely to be governed by the woman's level of attachment to the labor force and her earnings. In the case where the woman's attachment is temporary or sporadic and earnings are low, it is likely that the household will exhibit consumption patterns very similar to those of households with only one earner, because there is very little difference in the amount of income available for family purchases in the long term, and the amount of time available for leisure is similar. In these households the wife's income is considered transitory and is often designated for large one-time purchases.

The greatest difference in patterns is likely to be between those households exhibiting traditional family organization and those households where both the husband and wife are employed full-time outside the home and exhibit substantial lifetime attachment to their jobs. In this situation the incomes of both the husband and the wife are considered permanent income. When wives' earnings are substantial as well as permanent, we expect to see important differences in consumer behavior. Wives' incomes would be factored into major housing decisions as well as into budgets for monthly expenditures. Further, it is reasonable to expect that wives' income would be designated for goods and services to minimize household labor (e.g., restaurant meals, cleaning services), thus maximizing leisure. However, it is important to remember that many women establish full-time careers only later in life. Thus, we would expect consumer patterns to differ among two-earner households as a function of the age of the wife. Only as younger married women increase the permanency of their attachment to the labor force can we expect substantial changes in the consumption patterns of their households.

Single-Parent Families

Single-parent families are increasingly dominated by divorced women with children. These women typically have significantly less money than two-parent families because there is only one earner and women are often employed in low-paying occupations. Surprisingly, there is very little evidence regarding the changes in expenditure patterns as a consequence of divorce. It seems reasonable to expect, however, that consumer patterns would change for those items for which demand is most sensitive to income. The degree to which work-related and/or child-care expenses increase is not known. Moreover, research is ambiguous about both the short- and long-term housing choices following a divorce. Clearly, substantial research must be done to anticipate future changes in consumption patterns of these households as their number changes over time. One important point to remember is that the large majority of women in this category do remarry and many do so in a very short time. Thus, consumption patterns of divorced women may be shaped by their expectations concerning the amount of time they will be unmarried.

Never-Married Women

Younger women living alone are expected to exhibit consumption patterns very similar to those of men their age. Individuals in this category typically earn lower wages as a function of age and stage in career, but there are few household constraints beyond income in terms of influencing consumer choices. Further, at least in the past, never-married women were a largely transitory group. All of these factors suggest that younger single women are likely to be very flexible (and variable) in their consumer choices for both durable and nondurable goods. It is recognized, however, that the number of never-married women is growing significantly. As never-married women remain single for longer periods of time and the composition of the group becomes more stable, distinct consumption patterns may emerge. In the future women in this group may be less mobile and may more often purchase single-family homes.

5

Premarital Sexual Behavior

While there is a great deal of societal diversity in human sexual practices, all societies regulate the sexual behavior of their members in some way in order to control reproduction. In the United States, the transition to sexual intercourse has traditionally been viewed as a major life-course event that should only follow marriage. In discussing changes in American women's sexual behavior in recent years, we will focus on a description of change in this sequence. Attention will be given to premarital coitus in the United States, which has reached an all-time high.

Our analysis of this aspect of women's life course will begin by showing how rates of premarital intercourse have been increasing since the turn of the century. Among white women born in the 1920s, 7 percent of those who married at age 20 or later had premarital intercourse compared to 45 percent for those born in the 1950s. Among black females, the rates are 61 percent for the 1920s birth cohort and 85 percent for the 1950s cohort. In the late 1960s and 1970s, the rate of increase was especially rapid for white females. By 1979, 65 percent of 19-year-old single white females had had intercourse. Among black females the comparable proportion was 89 percent.

As we shall see, since 1970 rates of premarital sexual intercourse have increased more rapidly for women than for men such that the difference between the sexes has attenuated. The racial difference in premarital intercourse has also converged. Black females, however, remain more likely to have had premarital intercourse than white females.

In 1982, the most recent date for which national data are available, there was some indication that the incidence of premarital intercourse may have stabilized for white females and even declined for black females. It is not currently known whether these 1982 results signal the beginning of a long-term trend toward stable or declining rates.

Sources of Data

Any discussion of change in the incidence of premarital coitus must first be qualified with the statement that we have not been rigorously monitoring or collecting data on this behavior decade after decade. In fact, the first major study of sexual behavior in this country did not appear until after World War II when Kinsey et al. published *Sexual Behavior in the Human Male* (1948) and, a few years later, *Sexual Behavior in the Human Female* (1953). This latter study was based on a sample of approximately 6,000 white females born in four successive decades: before 1900, 1900–1909, 1910–19, and 1920–29. Between 1953 and 1970, there were no studies documenting the incidence of premarital coitus among different birth cohorts that were widely representative of American women. However, Udry et al. (1975) reported rates of premarital coitus for cohorts of women born in 1920–29 and 1950–59. These results were based on samples of ever-married black and white women (i.e., women who are married or were married at one time) living in sixteen selected United States cities, who were aged 15–44 when interviewed in 1969–70 and 1973–74. Given the general representativeness of the sample, the findings generated from this study may be viewed as an update of the earlier birth-cohort analyses of Kinsey et al.

An important source of sexual behavior data for more recent years is the Zelnik and Kantner studies. This source permits documentation of changes in *adolescent* premarital sexual behavior at the national level. In 1971, 1976, and 1979, interviews were conducted with nationally representative samples of white and black females aged 15–19. The 1979 study also included a sample of males aged 17–21. The reason for the two-year age difference between the samples of males and females is that the researchers determined from the two earlier studies that females' sex partners were on average approximately two years older. Another difference in the 1979 survey is that only adolescents living in metropolitan areas were interviewed (Zelnik and Kantner 1980). The most recent source of premarital coitus data at the national level is the National Survey of Family Growth, Cycle III (hereafter referred to as NSFG). This survey consists of a representative sample of approximately 8,000 black and white women aged 15–44 who were interviewed between August 1982 and February 1983 (Pratt et al. 1984).

PREMARITAL SEX: 1900 TO 1982

Findings from the above-noted studies can be pieced together to yield a general picture showing an exponential increase in the incidence of premarital coitus in the United States from 1900 to 1982. Kinsey et al. (1953) showed that although the three cohorts of white women born in the decades of 1900, 1910, and 1920 (i.e., those who would have experienced premarital coitus between approximately 1915 and 1940) had similar rates of premarital coitus, they experienced higher rates than white women born prior to 1900. Between 18 and 23 percent of the women in the former three birth cohorts were sexually active before marriage by age 20. Only 8 percent of white females born prior to 1900 reported having experienced premarital intercourse by age 20.

Udry et al. (1975) provide lower estimates of premarital coitus than Kinsey et al. (1953) for the birth cohorts that were studied by both research groups. This is partially accounted for by differences in methodology: Kinsey et al. asked respondents directly about premarital intercourse, whereas Udry et al. inferred it by comparing reported age at first intercourse and age at first marriage. Udry et al.'s approach excluded from the premarital sex category anyone whose age at first intercourse and age at first marriage were the same. Nevertheless, findings from this study reveal that premarital coitus increased among women born in the 1930s (i.e., those who would have been sexually active immediately following World War II) and again among those born in the 1940s. Among whites, the proportion of respondents married by age 20 or later who reported intercourse at an earlier age was 18 percent for the 1930s cohort (up from 7 percent for the 1920s cohort) and 26 percent for the 1940s cohort. Among blacks, the comparable proportion was 70 percent for the 1930s cohort (up from 61 percent for the 1920s cohort) and 76 percent for the 1940s cohort. Udry et al.'s findings reveal not only an increase in the rate of premarital intercourse over time but also a very large differential by race.

The largest increase in the rate of premarital coitus between cohorts for which Udry et al. had data was between women born in the 1940s and those born in the 1950s. Among whites, the percentage of respondents who were married by age 20 or later and who reported intercourse at an earlier age climbed to 45 percent for the 1950s cohort. Among black women born in the 1950s, the rate climbed to 85 percent. As reported by Udry et al., "For each race, the line for women born in the 1950s is as much higher than the line for women born in the 1940s as the line for the 1940s is higher than the line for the 1920s, indicating the rapid increase in sexual experience for those who were between 15 and 19 in the late 1960s" (1975, p. 785). Moreover, the researchers report that this pattern of increasing rates of premarital coitus "does not appear to be due to more permissive reporting during later time periods, or changes in educational or occupational distributions of the population" (Udry et al. 1975, pp. 786–87).

Changes in premarital coitus among the most recent cohorts of women can be noted by comparing the findings from the Zelnik and Kantner studies in 1971, 1976, and 1979. Since the women in these surveys were aged 15–19 at the time of interview, they were born in approximately 1952–56, 1957–61, and 1960–64 for each respective survey year. Thus, there is some overlap with the birth years of women analyzed by Udry et al. Moreover, while the rates previously reported from Udry et al. cannot be directly compared with those of Zelnik and Kantner reported below, the former estimates of premarital coitus at given ages for cohorts born in specific years are similar to those reported in the 1971 Zelnik and Kantner survey (Udry et al. 1975).

Table 5.1 presents the percentage of women aged 15–19 who ever had intercourse before marriage, by marital status and race, for each of the three Zelnik and Kantner survey years. For the sake of consistency, since the 1979 study was confined to those women living in metropolitan areas, the data obtained from the 1971 and 1976 surveys that are presented in the table also pertain only to metropolitan residents. The table shows that the percentage reporting premarital

TABLE 5.1

Percentage of Women Aged 15–19 Who Ever Had Intercourse before Marriage, by Marital Status and Race

Marital Status and Age	1979			1976			1971		
	Total	White	Black	Total	White	Black	Total	White	Black
All									
%	49.8	46.6	66.2	43.4	38.3	66.3	30.4	26.4	53.7
(N)	(1,717)	(1,034)	(683)	(1,452)	(881)	(571)	(2,739)	(1,758)	(981)
Ever-Married[a]									
%	86.7	86.2	91.2	86.3	85.0	93.9	55.0	53.2	72.7
(N)	(146)	(106)	(40)	(154)	(121)	(33)	(227)	(174)	(53)
Never-Married									
Total	46.0	42.3	64.8	39.2	33.6	64.3	27.6	23.2	52.4
15	22.5	18.3	41.4	18.6	13.8	38.9	14.4	11.3	31.2
16	37.8	35.4	50.4	28.9	23.7	55.1	20.9	17.0	44.4
17	48.5	44.1	73.3	42.9	36.1	71.0	26.1	20.2	58.9
18	56.9	52.6	76.3	51.4	46.0	76.2	39.7	35.6	60.2
19	69.0	64.9	88.5	59.5	53.6	83.9	46.4	40.7	78.3
Age at First Intercourse (All)									
Mean	16.2	16.4	15.5	16.1	16.3	15.6	16.4	16.6	15.9
(N)	(933)	(478)	(455)	(726)	(350)	(376)	(936)	(435)	(501)

Source: Zelnik and Kantner 1980, p. 231.
[a]I.e., currently married or married at one time.

intercourse increased from 30 in 1971 to 43 in 1976 to 50 in 1979. Among whites, the percentage increased from 26 in 1971 to 38 in 1976 to 47 in 1979. Among blacks, the percentage increased from 54 in 1971 to 66 in 1976 and then remained stable. This racial difference in the patterns of increase over time indicates that while blacks are still more likely to experience premarital intercourse than whites, the racial differential has attenuated. Not surprisingly, for all survey years and both races, ever-married women aged 15–19 were more likely to have experienced premarital intercourse than never-married teenage women.

Table 5.1 also shows that age is positively associated with the probability of having premarital intercourse. As noted earlier, according to Udry et al., the proportion of members of the 1950s cohort who married by age 20 or later and who reported intercourse at an earlier age was 45 percent for whites and 85 percent for blacks. Although not strictly comparable, these percentages may be roughly compared to the percentages in Table 5.1 of never-married 19-year-olds who reported having intercourse. For whites, the proportion rose from 41 percent in 1971 to 54 percent in 1976 to 65 percent in 1979. For blacks, the proportion rose from 78 percent in 1971 to 84 percent in 1976 to 89 in 1979. Thus, the proportion of young women who experienced premarital intercourse continued to climb throughout the 1970s.

The bottom panel of Table 5.1 reports changes for each of the survey years in the mean age at first intercourse among those who had experienced premarital coitus. These mean ages must be interpreted cautiously since they are a function of the restricted age range (15–19) of the samples. The table shows that for both whites and blacks the mean age at first intercourse declined between 1971 and 1976 and then remained virtually unchanged between 1976 and 1979.

Data from the NSFG reveal that in 1982, 40 percent of white, never-married females aged 15–19 had had sexual intercourse compared to 58 percent of black, never-married females in the same age group. The proportion of never-married 19-year-olds who reported having intercourse in this 1982 survey was 63 percent for whites and 81 percent for blacks. Comparing these rates to those reported by Zelnik and Kantner for 1979, Pratt et al. (1984, p. 13) concluded that the "NSFG data suggest that the steep rise in premarital sexual intercourse among teenagers documented at least for the 1970s may be abating for whites and even reversing for blacks." We will return to this point later.

Before summarizing changes in the incidence of premarital coitus among American women, a brief consideration of the rate of premarital coitus among males is in order. Historically, data for males have been less complete than for females. In general, however, the available evidence suggests that prior to the 1970s the incidence of premarital intercourse for males was approximately double that for females (Darling et al. 1984). For example, while Kinsey et al. reported a rate of 18 to 23 percent for females born in the decades 1900 through 1930, the comparable rate for males ranged between 49 and 53 percent. However, this difference between sexes has changed since the period covered by the Kinsey reports. Table 5.2, derived from the 1979 Zelnik and Kantner survey, shows the percentage of males aged 17–21 who had intercourse before marriage, by marital status and race. If these rates (70 percent for white males and 75 percent for black males) are compared to the 1979 rates for females aged 15–19 (47 percent for white females and 66 percent for black females) on the grounds that females have sex partners who on average are two years older than themselves, then it appears that the sex difference has attenuated over time. Comparing age-specific rates reported for the never-married sample in Tables 5.1 and 5.2 yields the same inference: the premarital intercourse rates for males are no longer double those of females. This attenuation of differences by sex has resulted from a faster rate of increase over time for females than for males.

CHANGES IN THE IDEOLOGY OF SEXUAL BEHAVIOR

The popular literature often plays up the recent development of a sexual revolution. However, if this is meant to convey the idea that there has been an overnight outburst of premarital coitus, then the term "sexual revolution" seems unwarranted. The current rather high rates of premarital intercourse are perhaps more accurately viewed as a continuation of a trend toward increasing rates that began at the turn of the century, albeit a trend that for women is best described by an exponential curve in which the rate of the increase

TABLE 5.2

Percentage of Men Aged 17–21 Who Ever Had Intercourse before Marriage, by Marital Status and Race, 1979

Marital Status and Age	Total	White	Black
All			
%	70.3	69.6	74.6
(N)	(917)	(567)	(350)
Ever-Married			
%	82.7	83.3	72.8
(N)	(74)	(58)	(16)
Never-Married[a]			
Total	68.9	67.8	74.7
17	55.7	54.5	60.3
18	66.0	63.6	79.8
19	77.5	77.1	79.9
20	81.2	80.7	85.7
21	71.2	68.0	89.4

Source: Zelnik and Kantner 1980, p. 231.
[a]N = 33 for each age-race cell among the never-married.

accelerated rather dramatically during the late 1960s (i.e., for those women born in the early 1950s). Premarital coitus among males also appears to have increased over time, but the increase has been far less dramatic. While males still exhibit higher rates of premarital coitus than females, the rates for males and females have converged. Finally, for both males and females, premarital intercourse now appears to be "statistically normative" (Darling et al. 1984)—that is, the majority of men and women today experience premarital coitus.

Social scientists view the trend toward increasing rates of premarital coitus among females as a function of major shifts in the norms governing sexual behavior. Darling et al. (1984, pp. 393–94) provide an interesting typology of the standards that have operated during this century:

Three general eras, characterized by different sexual standards, have been identified. The first, which lasted until the late 1940s or early 1950s, was the era of the double standard, in which [premarital and extramarital] sexual behavior was permitted for males and prohibited for females. In the second, the era of "permissiveness with affection" (Reiss 1967), premarital intercourse was allowable as long as it was in a love relationship and the relationship was expected to lead to marriage. This era lasted until approximately 1970. In the recent era, which began about 1970, intercourse is a natural and expected part of a love relationship for both males and females, without an expectation that the relationship will lead to marriage. Under this standard, while intercourse is also acceptable for both males and females in a nonaffectual relationship, physical or emotional exploitation of the sexual partner is not.

In 1977 Udry posited that "an *ideology of sexual behavior* is now a potent social force transforming the sexual behavior of Americans" and that this ideology, a product of changes in social structure, is itself currently "acting to transform the courtship and family institutions toward forms which correspond to the new ideology." This new value system is based on the following premises:

1. Individual sexual fulfillment is healthy and very important.
2. Institutions that impede sexual satisfaction need to be changed so that they do not.
3. Society has an obligation to encourage sexual satisfaction, not impede it.
4. Other values that formerly had precedence over sexual fulfillment need to be placed in a less prominent position in the social value system.
5. There are many different ways in which individuals may achieve sexual fulfillment. No one should punish or judge the sexual behavior of others. Social norms defining boundaries of permissible or desirable sexual behavior are restrictive of individual freedom, and therefore bad. Sexual norms are conceptualized as the explicit rules for the application of general sexual values to specific social situations. [Udry 1977, p. 9]

These changes in norms are themselves products of changes in the social structure that have been documented elsewhere in this report. For example, Kinsey et al. (1953) accounted for the increase in premarital coitus among birth cohorts of the early decades of this century by the increase in urbanization and its accompanying lifestyle, the increase in contraceptive knowledge, and changes in women's roles and the destruction of the nineteenth-century ideal of feminine purity during the Roaring Twenties. Kinsey et al. also attributed the increases to World War I, when Americans came into contact with more sexually permissive cultures. Similarly, Darling et al. (1984) noted that the more recent increases in premarital coitus were correlated with rising levels of female education, increased economic prosperity and the consequent exploration of new lifestyles during the 1960s and 1970s, and increased female labor force participation and the resulting development of greater economic and social emancipation for women.

CONCLUSION

Given the most recent findings from the 1982 NSFG indicating that rates of premarital intercourse between 1979 and 1982 leveled off for white females and declined for black females, we must ponder whether Udry's ideology of sexual behavior outlined above is still a potent social force. The 1982 figures may signal the beginning of a trend toward stable or declining rates, reflecting a change toward greater conservatism with regard to sexual behavior and attitudes. Perhaps an increased recognition of the risk of contracting sexually transmitted diseases such as herpes or AIDS is also responsible for the recent stabilization of the rates. Alternatively, the 1982 figures may simply represent a momentary dip in the incidence of premarital coitus or reflect an upper boundary above which the rates of premarital coitus will not go.

While it is difficult to draw valid inferences from the 1982 NSFG results and predict what future rates of premarital coitus will be, a few recent findings can be brought to bear on this problem. A Gallup Poll taken in April 1985 indicates that for the first time the majority of adults in the United States are accepting of premarital intercourse. Among those with an opinion, 58 percent of adults aged 18 and over responded that it is not "wrong for a man and a woman to have [sexual] relations before marriage." This represents an increased acceptance of premarital intercourse, from 24 percent in 1969 and 47 percent in 1973 (Gallup 1985). It therefore appears that a movement toward greater conservatism with regard to attitudes about sexual behavior has not occurred. At the present time there is also little evidence to support the notion that fear of contracting sexually transmitted diseases has precipitated a stabilization or reversal in premarital coitus rates. In a study of 232 college students who were interviewed about their attitudes toward herpes, AIDS, and toxic shock syndrome, Simkins and Eberhage (1984) found that concern over AIDS and herpes has had little effect on the respondents' sexual behavior.

Future studies will be required both to document a trend toward lower or stable rates of premarital coitus and to analyze the factors responsible for the decline or stabilization. Given the already relatively large proportion of females who are engaging in premarital intercourse, it is unlikely that we will witness increases in the 1980s of the same magnitude as those of the 1960s and 1970s. In the long term, the rate of increase must decline as the proportion who are sexually active approaches 100 percent. Given that available evidence suggests that we have not entered a period of sexual conservatism and that fear of sexually transmitted diseases has not affected sexual behavior, it is also unlikely that a significant decline will occur in the near future. Our best prediction of future levels of premarital coitus, then, is moderate fluctuations around the current levels.

6

Labor Force Participation

The current trends in the labor force participation of women, especially married women, represent a fundamental shift from patterns established by the Industrial Revolution. When the United States was primarily an agricultural economy, the family—wife, husband, children—was the unit of both production and consumption. As described in Chapter 2, industrialization and urbanization moved the production function outside the family to factories, and city life precluded much of the domestic production of food, clothing, and household goods that had occurred on farms. Men assumed responsibility for exchanging labor for wages, and the family became primarily a consumer unit in which women were responsible for managing the household.

In the emerging postindustrial economy, women are once again central figures in the production process. As they increase their labor force participation, compete with males in the labor market, and combine employment with parental and spousal responsibilities, women are revising many aspects of traditional family life and expanding the range of roles they play. Less dependent on family status for identity and economic well-being, women are increasingly asserting their individual needs rather than organizing their lives to accommodate the needs of their families. As primary individuals, whether or not they live within a family, women are assuming more responsibility for making decisions, especially those concerning major purchases.

Before we turn to the data that document the major changes in women's labor force participation, several points should be high-lighted:

1. The most significant change in the life course of American women has been the dramatic increase in the number who remain employed *throughout* their adult years, until they are of retirement age. Prior to World War II women held jobs almost exclusively before they were married and had children. Beginning in the mid-1940s, women with grown and school-age children began entering the labor force in substantial numbers. Recently women have become less likely to interrupt employment for child-rearing, and they therefore hold jobs for a much longer period of their lives than in the past. Today, almost two-thirds of women aged 20–54 and half of mothers with children under age 4 are in the labor force.

2. Although little progress was made between 1900 and 1970 in reducing the extent to which women worked in female-dominated occupations, women are now entering traditionally male occupations (e.g., managerial positions and the professions) in much greater numbers. It must be recognized, however, that the proportion of women in the labor force who are working in these occupations remains relatively small.

3. These changes in labor force participation and occupational patterns, in combination with educational gains, have resulted in considerable increases in women's earnings during the postwar period. This increase in income is enabling women to become economically independent and has reduced the likelihood of poverty for a given female-headed family despite the overall "feminization of poverty." This trend is highlighted below in our discussion of women's earnings.

4. Contrary to the widely held belief that women have made no gains in closing the "earnings gap," the wages of women have increased considerably relative to men's in recent years. These gains are primarily due to the increase in skills—gained through education and work experience—of women relative to men. Since these trends are likely to continue, the earnings gap is expected to decline in the future.

Despite the substantial rise in women's labor force participation in the past century, very little is known about the changes that women have experienced as they incorporate employment into their life course. In this chapter we look at several important features of the labor force participation patterns of women as well as the causes of those patterns and their consequences. We first consider the major changes in women's timing of labor force participation and some of the reasons for these changes. Next we examine important changes in women's occupational characteristics and employment patterns. We then describe the growth in women's earnings over time, the extent to which women have improved their earnings position relative to men's, and their contribution to family economic well-being. The chapter concludes with a discussion of the interrelationships between labor force participation and other major demographic changes and the likely implications of these changes for how American women will lead their lives in the future.

A Note on Terminology

Not surprisingly, it is common practice to refer to labor force participation by the term "work." The consequence, however, is to suggest that women—especially married women—who do not hold jobs outside the home are not engaged in any meaningful form of work. But being a homemaker and raising children can naturally require a woman to devote herself to an occupation bearing most of the characteristics of "work" except that of receiving a specified wage. The implied derogation of the so-called nonworking woman who serves as a provider of care to her husband and children is reinforced within sociological literature by some of the classic theorists, including Marx, Weber, and Durkheim, who defined "work" as market or paid work. As a result, women's daily work in the household has remained largely unanalyzed and unconceptualized.

To the extent possible, we have sought to designate paid or market work as "labor force participation," "employment," "work outside the home," or, indeed, as "paid work." Nevertheless, in the following pages we do at times use the shorthand terms "work," "working," and "worker" with reference to employed women and their activity in the labor force. It remains the case that the bulk of the literature dealing with labor force participation identifies women who hold jobs as "working women" or "working wives." In time, however, as more and more women seek employment and pursue careers, it should become apparent that the household is (and has always been) a domain of work; because in the absence of wives or mothers in the role of homemaker, services to maintain the home and to care for children have to be purchased by a broader spectrum of the population and supplied by members of the labor force.

CHANGES IN THE TIMING OF
LABOR FORCE PARTICIPATION

As noted earlier, the Industrial Revolution was instrumental in dividing market and domestic labor along sex lines, so that it became the norm for women to give priority to family obligations while men focused on their economic responsibilities. The causes and consequences of this division of labor have been extensively studied by sociologists (Merton 1968; Parsons 1937; Goode 1963; Parsons and Bales 1955; Fogarty et al. 1971; Myrdal and Klein 1956). A prevalent explanation for women's limited labor force involvement has been role conflict. This perspective views work and family obligations as incompatible, as they truly were at the beginning of industrialism, when economic production and domestic duties became physically separate and could no longer be overlapped to save time.

An economic explanation of women's limited involvement in the labor force is also, in part, rooted in normative expectations. Because their primary responsibility was traditionally the family, women did not invest time in acquiring the skills needed to compete in the labor market. As a result, the wages they could earn were so low that their time was better spent on homemaking activities. In addition, discrimination routinely caused married women to be paid less than single women. It is estimated that by 1900 their wages were 30 percent less than those of comparable single women (Smith and Ward 1984).

The normative division of labor was instrumental in determining the timing of women's labor force participation. Before 1940, if women were to work outside the home at all, the dominant pattern was for them to do so before marrying and having children.

Nevertheless, since the turn of the century, women have become an increasingly significant segment of the total labor force. Nearly 20 percent of the labor force was female in 1900, but this figure had changed to 29 percent by 1950 and to 43 percent by 1983 (U.S. Bureau of the Census 1975; U.S. Department of Labor 1983). In absolute terms, the size of the female labor force increased 150 percent, from 18 to 45 million, between 1950 and 1980, while the size of the female population of employment age (16–64) increased only 60 percent, from 54 million to 86 million (U.S. Bureau of the Census 1975). It should be noted, however, that summarizing changes in women's labor force participation rates with a single number disguises the extent and nature of actual changes. The large increases in participation rates say nothing about the types of women who are more likely to work outside the home now than in the past. As we describe below, the expansion of the female labor force involved large changes in the marital, parental, and age characteristics of working women.

Married Women in the Labor Force

The growth in the female segment of the total labor force has been due primarily to the growing work involvement of married women. As Figure 6.1 shows, the proportion of the labor force composed of single women remained nearly constant between 1890 and 1980, averaging between 13 and 17 percent, whereas the proportion of married women in the total labor force has grown from 2 percent in 1890 to 25 percent in 1980.

Table 6.1 provides additional evidence of the convergence in labor force participation rates of married and single women since 1950, when married women were less than half as likely as single women to work. By 1980, however, the labor force participation rate of married women was 82 percent of the rate for single women. The change is even more pronounced for women aged 25–34, those most likely to have small children. In 1950 married women aged 25–34 were less than one-third as likely to work as were single women aged 25–34. However, the labor force participation rates of the two groups converged over the following thirty years such that by 1980, wives aged 25–34 were 70 percent as likely to work as their single counterparts. Thus, while the labor force participation rates for all women increased considerably during this period, married women's involvement in the labor force accelerated at a much greater rate.

FIGURE 6.1

Women as a Percentage of the Total Civilian Labor Force, by Marital Status,
1890–1980

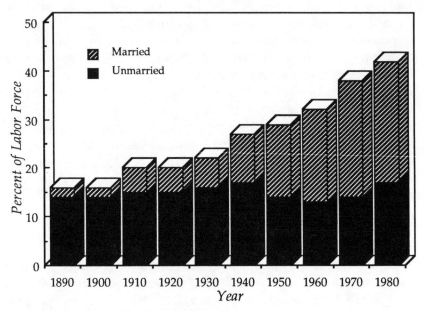

Sources: U.S. Bureau of the Census 1949 and 1984i.

Mothers in the Labor Force

The impact of the family on female labor force participation is illustrated by the effect of family composition on the employment of married women. The presence of preschool-age children and larger numbers of children has been shown to reduce labor force participation of married women (Bowen and Finegan 1969; Nye and Hoffman 1963; Tsuchigane and Dodge 1974; Sweet 1973; Gwartney and Stroup 1973; Fuchs 1974; Heckman 1974; Rosen 1976; Smith and Ward 1984; Johnson and Pencavel 1984). Several of these studies also conclude that the presence of preschool-age children considerably reduces the annual hours worked by married women, and there is additional evidence that the presence of preschoolers limits the labor force participation of single women in the same manner as that of married women (Johnson and Pencavel 1984).

TABLE 6.1

Ratio of Married to Single Women's Labor Force Participation Rates

Year	$\text{LFPR}_M/\text{LFPR}_S$	$\text{LFPR}_{M25}/\text{LFPR}_{S25}$
1950	.432	.281
1960	.692	.347
1970	.761	.487
1980	.820	.704

Sources: Michael 1985; U.S. Bureau of the Census 1984i.
Note: LFPR_M = Labor force participation rate of all married women. LFPR_S = Labor force participation rate of all single women. LFPR_{M25} = Labor force participation rate of married women aged 25–34. LFPR_{S25} = Labor force participation rate of single women aged 25–34.

However, the current trend toward combination, rather than sequencing, of family and wage-earning responsibilities is apparent in the large increases in labor force participation rates for mothers. In 1950 the labor force participation rate of women with preschool-age children was 11.9 percent, and the rate for women with children aged 6–17 was 28.3 percent (see Michael 1985; Hayghe 1984). By 1980, however, these rates had increased to 45 percent for those with preschool-age children and to 62 percent for those with older children. These changes represent increases in labor force participation of nearly 300 percent for women with young children and over 100 percent for women with older children during the thirty-year period.

The tremendous increase in labor force participation by mothers of preschoolers is underscored by comparing their rates with the participation rates of married childless women (see Table 6.2). In 1950 wives with preschool-age children were employed at a rate 39 percent that of married women without children. By 1980 the rates at which these two groups participated in the labor force were essentially identical (Michael 1985). Thus, the rates for mothers and non-mothers have also converged in a manner similar to that of single and married women.

TABLE 6.2

Ratio of Labor Force Participation: Rate of Married Women with Preschool Children to the Rate for Married Childless Women

Year	$LFPR_{PC}/LFPR_{NC}$
1950	.39
1960	.54
1970	.72
1980	.98

Sources: Michael 1985; Hayghe 1984.
Note: $LFPR_{PC}$ = Labor force participation rate of married women with preschool children. $LFPR_{NC}$ = Labor force participation rate of married women with no children.

Changes in the Age of Women in the Labor Force

In the early twentieth century, if a woman was employed outside the home, she usually held a job before she was married or had children. For example, at the turn of the century 5 million women—20 percent of the female population—were working outside the home. Decomposing this figure by age categories illustrates the negative effect of family obligations on labor force activity. As women entered their prime marriage and childbearing ages, fewer worked. In 1900, 27 percent of women aged 16–19 and 32 percent of women aged 20–24 were employed. However, less than 18 percent of women aged 25–44 worked outside the home and only 14 percent of women aged 45–64 were in the labor force (see Appendix A).

By 1940 women's labor force participation rates had gradually increased, and all women over 20 were increasingly likely to be employed. Female labor force participation during World War II was marked by sharp, rapid increases as women of all age groups filled the demand for wartime workers. Between 1940 and 1945, labor force participation rates increased by 20 percent for women aged 16–19 and by 10 percent for women aged 20–24 and 25–44. By 1945, 39 percent of women aged 25–44 were in the work force, as compared to only 18 percent in 1900. This increase in the labor force participation of women aged 25–44 during the war and the immediate postwar period was fueled primarily by the influx of married women who had raised their families, indicating a major change in the sequencing of labor force participation over the life course. The bimodal pattern of lifetime labor force participation—employment before childbearing, exit from the labor force to rear children, and return to employment after children are grown—has now become a familiar one. Women work outside the home when their children are older and require less time and attention so that the normative-role conflict created by holding a job is minimal. However, this pattern is again changing as more women continue to be employed even while parenting duties are the most time-consuming.

Figure 6.2 summarizes changes in women's labor force participation rates by birth cohort and age group. It reveals that for women born between 1916 and 1940 most of the increase in labor force participation occurred as older women filled the postwar demand for female workers, with women over age 35 being the first to respond. As documented in the chapters on marital patterns and fertility, younger women were marrying and having babies at record rates during the 1950s. Thus, they did not participate heavily in this first surge in female employment. Women born since 1940 have participated in the labor force at ages under 25 at rates significantly greater than women born between 1916 and 1940.

Women born before 1940 largely followed the traditional life course of marriage and child-rearing without outside work, followed by a return to the labor force at about age 35 after the lessening of family responsibilities. The 1960s marked the beginning of a shift away from the traditional sequencing of family and employment roles. Women born since 1940 have continued their labor force participation even while between the ages of 25 and 35, when family obligations are typically high. Not surprisingly, therefore, Figure 6.2 indicates that the bimodal distribution of female labor force participation has flattened somewhat (Schoen and Woodrow 1980; Smith and Ward 1984, 1985). The highly educated women of the baby-boom cohort are more committed to having a career and are less likely to interrupt their employment experience for child-rearing than were their mothers. Women are trading the strictly sequenced life course of 30 years ago for one in which they continuously combine familial and nonfamilial roles.

FIGURE 6.2

Labor Force Participation Rates of Female Birth Cohorts by
Five-Year Age Groups

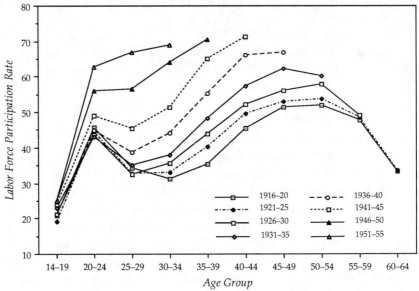

Sources: Masnick and Bane 1980; U.S. Department of Labor, Bureau of Labor
Statistics, 1981 and 1985.

EXPLANATIONS FOR INCREASED
LABOR FORCE PARTICIPATION OF WOMEN

Labor Supply and Demand

As stated above, the typical working woman in the 1950s was either
very young and single or married and over 45. She left the labor
force when she married and returned, if at all, only after her children
were grown. The contemporary female employee is well educated
and more likely to be committed to long-term labor force participation regardless of her age and marital status (Waite 1981; Michael
1985). A comprehensive explanation for the increase in the participation rates of married women is provided by Oppenheimer's economic supply-and-demand model (1970, 1973). Demand factors are

labor-market variables that affect the number of workers needed to fill available jobs; supply factors are worker characteristics thought to either encourage or discourage labor force participation. Labor demand is influenced by the nature of the job and the type of worker that employers desire to fill openings.

Economists and sociologists have long recognized that the labor market is divided into segments and that all potential employees are not in direct competition with each other for all jobs. There are geographic, educational, and social boundaries that prevent competition among employees for some jobs and prevent competition among employers for some employees (Reynolds 1974; Phelps 1967; Caplow 1954; Taylor 1968). Oppenheimer argues that one important segmentation of the labor force is along sex lines. The existence of well-defined norms concerning the appropriateness of one or the other sex for many occupations serves to create noncompetitive male and female labor markets. The notion of a sex-typed labor market makes it possible to argue that an increase in demand for sex-specific labor may account for part of the dramatic rise in female labor force participation.

The gradual shift from agriculture to manufacturing and service industries, along with the growth of nonmanual occupations, influenced the occupational distributions of both women and men (Kaplan and Casey 1958; Bancroft, 1958). However, the shift toward service and nonmanual employment occurred after many of these occupations had become identified as jobs for females. Thus, the demand for female workers grew between 1940 and 1960 as a consequence of industrial transformation.

The interaction of supply and demand characteristics provides an explanation for the tremendous surge in married women's labor force participation at a time when the domestic burdens related to child-rearing were at extremely high levels. The supply of young single women declined between 1940 and 1960 because women were marrying earlier and having their first children sooner. In order to meet the increasing demand for workers in jobs previously defined as "female," employers began turning to the married segments of the female population, eventually including married women with children. These new labor force participants were attracted to work by increased wages.

Increased Wage Rates

Smith and Ward (1984) found that the overall growth in women's labor force participation in the twentieth century is due primarily to rising real wages for women. The increased wage rates are in turn a result of the increased demand for workers in female-dominated occupations and increased levels of education and experience among women. Their model predicts that women have higher employment rates as wages increase, in part because the rewards from employment are greater (or alternatively, the cost of not being employed is higher) and because higher women's wages discourage larger families. Like Mincer (1962), they found that women are less likely to hold a job as their husbands' wages increase, but the negative effects of husbands' increased wages on the labor force participation of wives are offset by the positive effects of women's increased wages. They conclude that 60 percent of the total growth in the labor force participation of women from 1950 to 1980 is due to the rising wages of women. Although this may appear surprising, it is in part because Smith and Ward also found that the wage growth for women has been much larger than is commonly believed, a point we discuss in detail later in this chapter.

Increased Educational Attainment

Education is another supply factor that contributes to the continued expansion of the female labor force (Smith and Ward 1984). Educational attainment above the high school level is associated with increased probabilities of labor force participation. The educational gains of women born since 1940, described in Chapter 3, have contributed to recent increases in labor force participation and a long-term attachment to the work force. Thus, as more recent, highly educated cohorts of women marry and have children, they are less likely than previous generations to sever ties with the world of employment.

CHANGES IN OCCUPATIONAL
CHARACTERISTICS

Between 1900 and 1970, there was little change in the extent to which women were segregated into female-dominated occupations (England 1981). For the most part, women remained limited to clerical and service occupations, and men continued to dominate most other occupational classes. Although various studies indicated some sporadic declines in occupational sex segregation during this period, the consensus among researchers is that the decreases did not contribute to the integration of occupations, and that occupational sex typing remained stable (Gross 1968; Williams 1979).

Female-Dominated Occupations

Female-dominated occupations are typified by a lack of authority, vicarious rather than direct achievement, nurturant duties, and supervision by men (Smith 1979a). For example, male administrators supervise female teachers, secretaries help keep male executives organized, and nurses care for the ill and assist doctors. Perhaps because support and nurturance are ideals to which women are socialized, these occupations continue to attract large numbers of women (Treiman and Hartman 1981).

Women's competing role obligations also influence their choice of occupations and industries in which to work. Women are overrepresented in eating establishments and service industries in general, and as operatives in the manufacture of nondurable goods, particularly textiles. Women are underrepresented in durable goods manufacturing, construction, transportation, and mining. For most jobs in which women are overrepresented the training demands and requirements are low, and those employed are easily replaced (Coser and Rokoff 1971). Because of family responsibilities, women have traditionally been unable or unwilling to invest large amounts of time in specific vocational preparation, and employers have not been willing to invest in training for a woman likely to leave the labor force or to move with her husband. Women who prefer part-time or seasonal work, or desire to work only sporadically, are confined to occupations that can accommodate this flexibility. Family obligations thus make it difficult for women to participate in occupations that require total commitment, whereas men are expected to be committed to their work regardless of family demands. Not surprisingly, therefore, the "sorting" of male and female workers has contributed to the maintenance of a stable, highly segregated occupational structure consisting of male- and female-dominated occupations. However, as we describe in the next section, women's occupations have changed in recent years.

Declines in Occupational Sex Segregation

Starting in 1970, after several decades of stability, occupational sex segregation began to decline (Beller 1985). In 1970 about 68 percent of women in the labor force would have had to change jobs to equalize the distribution of men and women among occupations. By 1980 this figure had dropped to 62 percent. Almost 80 percent of the decline in segregation came from changes in the sex composition *within* occupations. As is illustrated in Table 6.3, most of the change took place within white-collar occupations. During this decade women's relative entry increased substantially in the traditionally male professional, technical, and managerial occupations. While decreases in sex segregation have been significant, and growing numbers of women work in nontraditional fields, most women still work in female-dominated occupations. It should be noted that men made no changes in their occupational choices during this period; all moves toward occupational integration were due to shifts in female employment (Bianchi and Rytina 1984).

The changing nature of women's occupational choices reflects their increased attachment to the labor force and a relative shift in work versus family priorities. Growing numbers of women in the baby-boom cohort are investing in their own human capital—through extended periods of education, delayed family formation, and continued labor force participation during the childbearing years—in order to gain access to and achieve success in traditionally male occupations (Shaw 1985). Although most women continue to work in traditionally female occupations, a trend away from occupational sex segregation is emerging.

TABLE 6.3

Occupational Distribution of Employed Women, 1970–1982

Occupation	1970	1975	1982
White Collar	60.5%	62.9%	66.5%
Professional and Technical	14.5	15.7	17.7
Teachers (except College Teachers)	5.9	6.3	5.3
Managers and Administrators	4.5	5.2	7.4
Salesworkers	7.0	6.9	6.9
Retail Trade	6.3	5.7	4.8
Clerical Workers	34.5	35.1	34.4
Blue Collar	16.1	14.1	12.8
Crafts Workers	1.1	1.5	2.0
Operatives, Including Transport			
Equipment Operators	14.5	11.5	9.6
Non-farm Laborers	.5	1.1	1.2
Service	21.7	21.6	19.7
Farm	1.8	1.4	1.1
	100.0[a]	100.0	100.0[a]
Total	(29,688)	(33,989)	(43,256)

Source: U.S. Bureau of the Census, *Statistical Abstracts of the United States, 1984* (1983).
[a]Because of a rounding error, the total for this column exceeds 100.0%.

PATTERNS OF WOMEN'S
LABOR FORCE PARTICIPATION

As described above, women are entering traditionally male occupations, and a larger proportion of them are working outside the home. However, this does not mean that all women who hold jobs pursue full-time, lifelong careers. Women are increasingly employed for longer periods of their lives, but many women, especially those who are married, work part time and/or intermittently in order to accommodate the other roles they play, such as student, mother, and wife. Thus, while women are expanding their labor force activity,

FIGURE 6.3

Female Work-Life Expectancy at Ages 16, 25, and 35

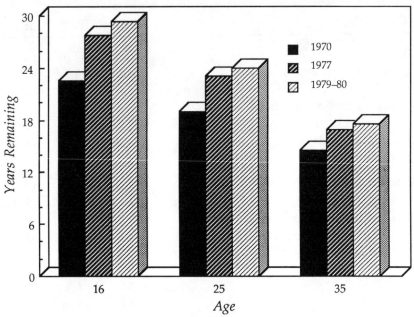

Sources: Smith and Horvath 1984; U.S. Department of Labor, Bureau of Labor
Statistics, 1982.

family responsibilities continue to affect the nature of that participation. This section describes the expanding length of women's employment experience and provides a closer examination of the nature of women's labor force participation.

Working-Life Expectancy

Another way to describe changes in the employment behavior of women is to estimate how much of the average woman's lifetime is spent in the labor force. This has to be done with working-life tables based on past rates of labor force participation. A woman born in 1900 could expect to live about 48 years and be employed 6. By 1980 women were likely to be employed 29 years of their nearly 78-year life expectancies (U.S. Department of Labor 1982; Smith and Horvath 1984). As shown in Figure 6.3, the proportion of life women spend in the labor force has increased tremendously in a period of ten years.

In 1970, a 16-year-old woman could expect to spend 37 percent of her adult life being employed, a total of 22.5 years. Only ten years later, a 16-year-old was likely to be in the labor force 46 percent, or 29.3 years, of her adult life (U.S. Department of Labor 1982; Smith and Horvath 1984).

Labor Force Attachment

Though labor force participation among more recent cohorts has increased, not all these women are employed at the same rates or exhibit the same levels of labor force attachment. Women's labor force participation and attachment to the work force depend on several factors, including age, marital status, parental status, previous employment experience, and educational attainment. However, women continue to modify their labor force participation largely to accommodate the needs of their families. During the five-year period from 1972 to 1976, 30 percent of women were not in the labor force, 23 percent worked full time with no interruptions, and 47 percent worked full time and/or part time, but intermittently (Moen 1985).

Married women are less likely to have a history of uninterrupted employment experience than are never-married or previously married women. This is at least in part because, unlike nonmarried women, they have an additional source of income—namely, a spouse's income. The family obligations of married women, especially mothers, also make their labor force participation problematic. Between 1972 and 1976, 52 percent of married women worked intermittently at either part-time or full-time jobs, 29 percent did not work outside the home at all, and only 19 percent were employed full-time with no interruptions (Moen 1985). More recent cohorts continue to limit their labor force involvement when family demands are great, such as during child-rearing.

While their family obligations are no less than those of married mothers, previously married women with children are more likely to hold a job than married women. They are typically the sole economic support of their families. Nearly half of divorced women were employed full time during the five-year period of Moen's study (1985). Thus, while women have expanded their labor force participation and work more continuously than in the past, this increase does not apply to all women equally.

WOMEN'S EARNINGS

The primary consequence of the increased labor force participation patterns and shifts toward traditionally male occupations documented above is an increase in family money income. As indicated in Table 6.4, the median income of year-round, full-time employed women increased considerably from 1955 to 1980. Income in current (unadjusted) dollars increased from $2,700 to over $11,000 during this period, and even after adjustment for inflation, real income increased by over $3,000 (or nearly 40 percent). For women as for men, all of the increase in inflation-adjusted real income during this period occurred by 1970. From 1970 to 1980, a slow-growing economy, coupled with relatively high inflation rates, prevented increases in money income from translating into gains in real purchasing power. Since 1980, however, there has been a rapid rise in the wages of employed women (Smith and Ward 1984, 1985). The long-term increase in income, coupled with more recent rapid increases in women's wages, is an important factor in enabling women to become economically independent.

As employment, choices of occupation, and income have expanded for women, extensive attention has been focused on two less positive observations: (1) the increased feminization of poverty and (2) the persistent gap between male and female wages. In Table 6.5, we illustrate how the population in poverty changed from 1960 to 1980. As the third column indicates, being in poverty is becoming considerably more "feminized." In particular, from 1960 to 1980 the percentage of families in poverty that are headed by women doubled to nearly one-half, even though women head only 15 percent of all families. On the other hand, it is important to note that the likelihood of a given female-headed family's being in poverty declined considerably from 1960 to 1970 (consistent with the increase in real income achieved during this period), although it has remained fairly constant since then. Thus, although female-headed families are a growing percentage of the families in poverty, a given female-headed family is considerably less likely to be in poverty today than it was in the 1960s.

TABLE 6.4
Median Income of Year-Round, Full-Time Working Women

Year	Income (In Current Dollars)	Income (1980 Dollars)
1955	$ 2,735	$ 8,418
1960	3,296	9,169
1965	3,816	9,967
1970	5,440	11,544
1975	7,719	11,818
1980	11,591	11,591

Sources: U.S. Bureau of the Census, *Current Population Reports*, Consumer Income Series P-60, nos. 23, 37, 51, 80, 105, 132 (1957, 1962, 1967, 1972, 1977, 1982).

The Earnings Gap

That women's earnings have historically been much lower than men's is well documented, and the reasons underlying this earnings differential have been studied extensively. Of major concern is the fact that women's wages have remained approximately 60 percent of men's wages throughout the postwar period, with the disconcerting implication that women have made no gains in closing the earnings gap. As we describe below, most studies have found that much of the male/female earnings gap is due to differences in human capital, occupational segregation, and discrimination. Below, we discuss the results of some recent studies on this important issue.

The Increase in Women's Human Capital

According to human capital theory, relative wages depend primarily on relative job skills. Members of the labor force continue to acquire job skills and other characteristics that enhance productivity as long as they can expect additional investment to yield a return in the form of higher wages. Thus, women's expectations of minimal labor force participation may in the past have caused them to invest less in edu-

TABLE 6.5

Poverty Status of Families by Family Status

Year	Percent of Female-Headed Families in Poverty	Percent of Male-Headed Families in Poverty	Percent of Families in Poverty Headed by Females
1960	42.4	15.4	23.7
1965	38.4	11.1	28.5
1970	32.5	7.1	37.1
1975	32.5	6.2	44.6
1980	32.7	6.3	47.3

Sources: U.S. Bureau of the Census 1976b, 1977, and 1982.

cation and job training than men. And because they had lower levels of human capital investment, women's lower wages were, in part, a reflection of their lower value in the labor market (Treiman and Hartman 1981).

In the postwar years, the education and job experience of women in general have increased considerably, yet the earnings gap appears to have remained constant. This constancy of the earnings gap in light of improved skills has properly occupied a large segment of media attention and has been the subject of much analysis. If we look, for example, at the data charted in Figure 6.4, showing the long-term labor force participation rate of women and the ratio of their earnings to the earnings of men, it becomes vividly apparent that women have made almost no gains in wages.[1]

The graph of these indicators of women's earnings is derived from recent studies by Smith and Ward (1984, 1985), who contend that the seemingly smooth labor force participation curve and the flat earnings ratio disguise a great deal of variation in the kinds of women who have been employed, which, in turn, has had a significant im-

1. Since data on the earnings of full-time workers were not available over the long time-span portrayed in Figure 6.4a, it was necessary to utilize average earnings of all workers. This resulted in a somewhat lower ratio than the more familiar .59, which is based on full-time workers. See Smith and Ward (1984) for a more detailed explanation of these calculations.

FIGURE 6.4

*Proportion of Women in the Labor Force and the Ratio of Female to Male
Earnings, 1900–1980*

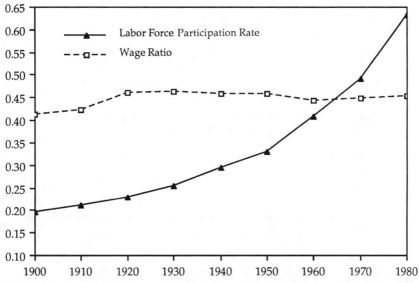

Source: Data are from Tables 1 and 8 in Smith and Ward 1984.

pact on their relative earnings. The gradual increase in women's labor force participation that took place through 1920 was primarily
fueled by young, unmarried women. Young married women began
entering the labor force in significant numbers between 1920 and
1940, primarily in response to the growth of clerical jobs and a corresponding increase in the relative wages offered for these jobs. After
1940, older, less well educated women began to be dominant among
the new labor entrants because the younger cohorts were remaining
out of the labor force while they took part in the unprecedented
"baby boom" as well as the accompanying "marriage boom." Between 1940 and 1960 the percentage of women under age 35 who
were in the labor force declined and the number of women over 35
entering the labor force increased dramatically. After 1960, and continuing today, this pattern has been reversed and younger, more
highly educated women are entering the labor force in greater numbers. In addition, the post-1960 cohorts are accumulating experience
at a much more rapid rate. The result is that both the education and

FIGURE 6.5

Labor Force Participation Rates by Education Levels and Age (20–24)

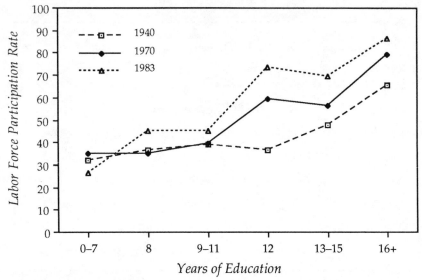

Sources: Decennial Census of the U.S. for 1940 and 1970; U.S. Bureau of the Census, "Educational Attainment of Workers," Special Labor Force Report (March 1983).

experience levels of the female labor force have begun to increase at a faster rate than they have for the male labor force.

The magnitude of the changing impact of education on labor force participation of younger women is illustrated in Figures 6.5 and 6.6. For both age groups, women 20–24 and 25–34, labor force participation increased with higher levels of education much more rapidly in 1983 than in either 1940 or 1970. All women with at least an eighth-grade education were more likely to work in 1970 than in 1940, but the effect of education on work increased much more dramatically in the thirteen years between 1970 and 1983 than it did over the thirty-year period between 1940 and 1970. This pattern is most striking among women aged 25–34 with at least a high school education. Over 70 percent of women in this age group with some college education held jobs in 1983 compared to only 45 percent of similarly educated women in 1970 and 40 percent in 1940. The result is that, since 1970, the basic character of the female labor force has become much more highly educated.

In the case of labor force experience, there are very recent in-

FIGURE 6.6

Labor Force Participation Rates by Education Levels and Age (25–34)

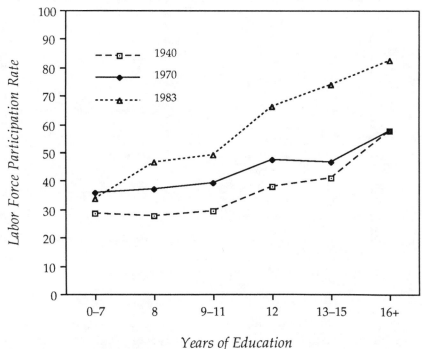

Years of Education

Sources: Decennial Census of the U.S. for 1940 and 1970; U.S. Bureau of the Census, "Educational Attainment of Workers," Special Labor Force Report (March 1983).

creases in the average experience held by women of specific ages. Based on extrapolations of data presented in Smith and Ward (1984), Figure 6.7 presents average levels of experience held by three age groups of women from 1910 to the year 2000. Given the conservative assumption that future cohorts will continue to work at current rates, this figure demonstrates that after seventy years of relatively constant experience levels, future cohorts of working women will make enormous gains in the amount of experience they acquire. The impetus behind these increases is the fact that women entering the labor force today are doing so before marriage and are remaining employed after marriage and after the birth of the first child. As a result, their employment experience is becoming almost as continuous as that of male workers.

These historical swings in the types of women entering the labor

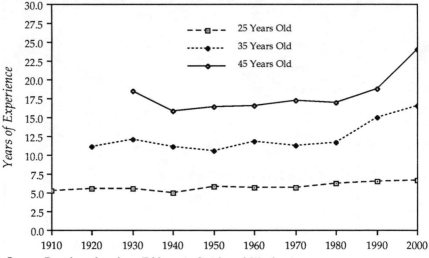

Source: Based on data from Table 32 in Smith and Ward 1984.

force caused the mix of skills (education and experience) to change over time. Thus, beginning in 1940, the average skill levels (as measured by education and experience) of the female labor force declined relative to those of the male labor force. The decline in the relative "quality" of the female labor force tended to force wages down while the growing demand for female labor during and after World War II forced wages up. These two factors were of roughly equal magnitude, causing the wage ratio to remain constant.

This pattern of declining quality of the female labor force in terms of both education and experience continued until 1970. After 1970 the pattern reversed itself, and younger, more highly educated women entered the labor force at a rapid pace. In addition, since 1970 the experience of these women was growing much more rapidly than the experience of the male labor force. Consequently, the quality of the female labor force has been growing faster than the quality of the male labor force.

This change in the relative quality of the female versus male labor force has, very recently, been reflected in a narrowing of the male/female earnings gap. From 1960 to 1980, average hourly wages of full-time women workers remained at approximately 60 percent of male hourly wages.[2] By 1983 the ratio of hourly wages had increased to 64 percent, and by 1986 the ratio based on weekly earnings of full-time workers had increased to 70 percent (Bureau of Labor Statistics 1987). Younger women are closing the gap at a much faster rate than older women, demonstrating the importance of higher educational levels for commanding higher wages. In 1986 the ratio of weekly earnings for full-time women workers relative to men in the same age group were 86 percent for ages 20–24, 78 percent for ages 25–34, 64 percent for ages 35–44, and 61 percent for ages 45–54 (Bureau of Labor Statistics 1987). This trend should continue through the year 2000 as the female labor force becomes increasingly more educated and experienced.

Occupational Segregation

Whether employed full time or part time, women have worked in the same types of occupations through much of the twentieth century (Gross 1968; Williams 1979). Even during the years after World War II when the growth of the female labor force was accelerating, the jobs held by women were jobs that were already identified as "women's work" (Oppenheimer 1970). Since these jobs normally do not pay well, have no clear promotion ladders, and demand little investment by either the worker or the employer, a significant part of the male-female wage gap can be attributed to occupational segregation.[3]

However, as we saw earlier, women have made substantial gains in white-collar occupations since the late 1970s, particularly in the male-dominated professions such as law and in managerial occupations (Bianchi and Rytina 1984). In 1970 about 60 percent of all women in the labor force were in occupations in which women were at least an 80 percent majority; by 1980 only 46 percent of women workers were in occupations in which at least 80 percent of the workers were women. During this period, the percentage of women in

2. Note that this more familiar 60 percent wage ratio is based on the full-time labor force and consequently differs from the historical data presented in Figure 6.4.

3. Actual estimates of the amount of the male-female wage gap that can be attributed to occupational segregation range from 18 to 23 percent. The remainder is due to pay differences within occupations (Reskin and Hartmann 1986).

occupations that were not sex-typed (having from 30 to 60 percent female workers) doubled from 11 percent to 22 percent (Bianchi and Rytina 1984).

This change in occupational segregation occurred during the same time that significant changes were taking place in the educational achievements of women, particularly their rapid entry into traditionally male-dominated fields of study. The change in educational fields appears to be a necessary precursor to changing the sex-typed occupational world. Since it is the new entrants to the labor force that are creating the change, a transformation of the occupational system will take considerable time. Nevertheless, the trend should persist given the continued movement of women into educational fields formerly dominated by men.

If occupational segregation continues to diminish, the future may include a labor force in which, for the first time, males and females compete for jobs and for wages. The long-term separation of work into male and female jobs has prohibited any real competition between the sexes throughout the period after World War II when women were entering the labor force in unprecedented numbers. Although the exact effect of competition on the wage gap remains to be seen, Tan and Ward (1985) estimate that competition between women and men in the labor market will lead to lower growth in male wages. Specifically, their model predicts that the wages of new male labor market entrants and experienced male workers will increase at lower rates than would occur if women were not competing with men in the labor market. The optimistic projections regarding the wages of the generation of Americans following the baby-boom cohort into the labor force may have to be revised downward under a scenario of increased participation by women in a labor market with diminished occupational segregation.

Unexplained Wage Differences

Unfortunately, a large proportion of wage differences between women and men cannot be explained by occupation, education, or experience. Corcoran et al. (1984) estimated that two-thirds of the wage differences between white women and white men and three-quarters of the difference between black women and white men could not be explained by human capital factors. Therefore, discrimination probably contributes to the earnings gap in the 1980s, but its magnitude is difficult to quantify. The reasons behind women's occupational choices and the differential remuneration for workers in female- and male-typed occupations must be more closely examined to identify their specific contributions to male-female wage differentials.

WOMEN'S CONTRIBUTION TO HOUSEHOLD INCOME

The impact of the earnings of employed women on the household's demand for goods and services depends on the type of household and the amount of other income available to it. Here we focus on the impact of the earnings of women in households in which there are two earners because these are the households most profoundly affected by the increase in women's employment. The relative contribution of women's earnings in other household types (for example, married couples with one earner or female-headed households) is unchanged by women's increased labor force participation.

Wives who are employed contribute from 23 to 28 percent of household income. This basic ratio has not changed since 1950 and is even stable across various levels of total household income. For example, in 1972 employed wives in the lowest quintile of household income contributed 29 percent of the total income and employed wives in the highest quintile of household income provided 28 percent of the total household income (Vickery 1979). Among wives with full-time jobs outside the home, the contribution to total household income is roughly 40 percent.

The most obvious effect of a wife's employment is an increase in the family's income. What is not so obvious is the effect of her employment on real income. The wife's time that would otherwise be spent doing work in the home is difficult to value, as are the increased expenses associated with her employment. One effort to estimate the real income benefits of the wife's employment was reported by Lazear and Michael (1980). They compared the expenditures of two-person families (a husband and a wife with no children) when both the wife and the husband were employed with expenditures when only the husband was in the labor force. Based on data from the 1972–73 Consumer Expenditure Survey, they found that the income of families with an employed wife was 35 percent higher than the income of families in which the wife did not hold a job. Income taxes reduced the income advantage to 17 percent. If the additional expenses associated with the wife's employment (such as meals at restaurants, transportation, and office clothes) are subtracted from the remaining income gain, the net benefit is only 5 percent.

This is an admittedly rough calculation based on data that are now over fifteen years old. Nevertheless, the fact remains that the actual income benefits of the wife's employment were quite small during the years when married women were entering the labor force at unprecedented rates. This suggests that there might be other motivations that play an important part in the decision to be employed. These motivations might include a preference for purchasing services—such as child care, food preparation, and house cleaning—as opposed to performing them oneself, and the nonincome rewards of employment. In addition, the desire for economic independence suggested by our concept of the rising importance of women as primary individuals is a significant factor. The security provided by a full-time job is a form of insurance against the loss of the husband's income through death, disability, or divorce. The wife's power to make decisions within the family is also greater when she holds a job and thereby serves as a breadwinner.

Despite the fact that, in the past, real household income was not substantially affected by the wife's employment, there are recent indications that women's income is an increasingly important component of household income. Between 1970 and 1982, mean income for two-earner families (families in which both wife and husband are labor force participants) has remained about 25 percent higher than the mean income for one-earner families (families in which the wife is a full-time homemaker). However, the gap between these two family types has widened in recent years. Figure 6.8 illustrates this gap using 1984 constant dollars. In 1970 two-earner families had a mean income $6,800 greater than that of one-earner families, and by 1984 the gap was nearly $9,500. This recent widening of the income gap between two-earner and one-earner families can be attributed, at least in part, to real increases in women's wages. To the extent that women's wages continue to catch up with those of men, the household income gap between these two types of families will continue to grow.

Figure 6.8 also shows the mean income difference between married-couple, one-earner families and female-headed families. Female-headed families had a 1970 mean income which was $12,200 less than married-couple, one-earner families and $19,000 less than two-earner families. In 1984 the difference in mean incomes between two-earner families and female-headed families had increased to $22,000, but to only $12,600 between female-headed families and married-couple, one-earner families. This evidence that the relative position of female-headed families compared to married-couple, one-earner families has remained steady while becoming less positive compared to two-earner families is another indication that improved female wages are making an increasingly substantial contribution to household income.

The nonmonetary advantages of the wife's employment mentioned above, such as the ability to purchase services and increased power and security, are all consistent with the values and lifestyle we have described as part of the emergence of women as primary individuals and appear to drive the continuing increases in the number of two-earner households. As employed women begin to close the earnings gap and continue to make gains in the reduction of occupational segregation, increases in real family income can be added to the list of factors that will cause future increases in the employment of married women.

LINKS WITH CHANGES IN EDUCATION, MARRIAGE, AND FERTILITY

The shift in the timing of labor force participation from exclusively before marriage to a more continuous segment of life has been associated with changes in educational, marital, and fertility trends. As discussed in Chapter 3, changes in women's labor force participation have, in part, resulted from increased levels of education among women and a strengthening of the positive relationship between educational attainment and labor force participation. Throughout the century, women with college educations have been more likely to work than less-educated women, but in the past twenty years wom-

FIGURE 6.8

Mean Incomes for Three Family Types

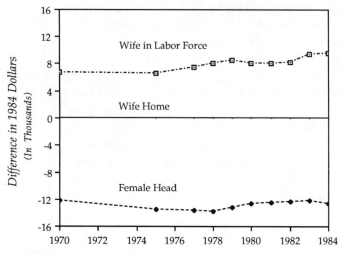

Sources: U.S. Bureau of the Census, Current Population Reports, ser. P-20, nos. 80, 113, 118, 128, 129, 132, 137, 142, 146, and 151 (1970, 1977–84).

en with college degrees have increased the rate at which they work more rapidly than have women with less education (Smith and Ward 1985). In addition, college-educated women are increasingly attached to the labor force and work more continuously than in the past. This increased labor force attachment is partly due to the movement of women into traditionally male occupations, which require higher levels of career commitment than do many female-typed jobs but also provide a better return on the required human capital investment in education.

Higher levels of labor force participation and career commitment are also related to changes in the composition of the female population with regard to marital status. Young, highly educated women are investing time in career development before marriage, effectively raising the typical age at first marriage among recent marriage cohorts. Cherlin (1980) found that young women aged 20–24 who expected to be employed at age 35 had lower probabilities of marriage in their early twenties than women who expected to be homemakers at age 35. Thus, later age at first marriage is one implication of increased female labor force participation.

Another factor influencing female labor force participation is the recent increase in divorce rates. Since divorced women can no longer rely on a husband's income, they generally must work to provide economic support for themselves and their children. It is important to note that actual or anticipated labor force participation can make divorce easier for women. With the knowledge that their economic future is secure, women are more likely to leave an unsatisfactory marriage (Booth et al. 1984; Hannan et al. 1978). In effect, labor force participation lowers the threshold of dissatisfaction at which marital disruption occurs. The combination of marriage and career may create role strain such that women with a high level of career commitment may divorce in order to reduce that strain (Houseknecht et al. 1984). Higher career priority indicates that work is a legitimate alternative to marriage and parenthood, an alternative from which women can derive their identities.

As we describe in Chapter 7, there is also a strong relationship between labor force participation and fertility. Although there is some degree of mutual causation, it appears that fertility negatively influences labor force participation in the short term but that long-term plans for work have a negative effect on the number of children a woman expects to bear (Waite and Stolzenberg 1976; Stolzenberg and Waite 1977; Smith-Lovin and Tickamyer 1978; Cramer 1980). Delayed childbearing, smaller families, and permanent childlessness limit the parenting responsibilities of women, allowing women who choose to work more time for labor force participation (Tsui 1984).

Aside from demographic changes in education, marriage, and fertility, economic and social changes also play an important part in explaining women's increased labor force participation. Although definitions of need have changed over time, the most prevalent reason for employment among women remains economic necessity; in 1975 two-thirds of women in the labor force worked for economic reasons (Barrett 1979). Increased demand for female labor due to the rapid growth of female-dominated clerical and service occupations and higher wage rates have also contributed to increased female labor force participation. In the past, existing social pressure inhibited labor force participation, particularly for married women, but prevailing attitudes now encourage women to work (Smith 1979a).

FIGURE 6.9

Labor Force Participation Rates for Married Women Aged 25–34 with and without Children, 1950–1990

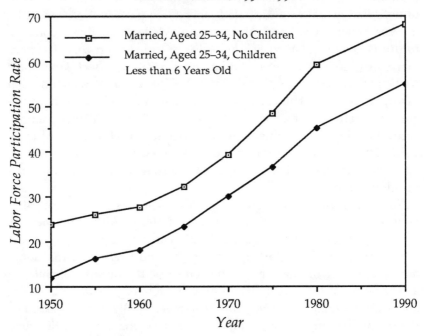

Sources: Michael 1985; Smith 1979b.

Projections for Women's Labor Force Participation

Smith's (1979b) projections for women's labor force participation in 1990, illustrated in Figure 6.9, show continuing participation increases among married women. While the participation rates of married mothers are not expected to equal those of single childless women, it is projected that married women with children will work in increasing numbers. According to Smith (1979b), the presence of children, especially under age 6, will become less of an obstacle to women's labor force participation. The growing acceptability of combining family responsibilities and market work will contribute to this change. However, the dual demands of home and family continue to be borne primarily by wives and, for some, the benefits of market work will never outweigh the costs of devoting less time and effort to the role of mother and homemaker.

The greater labor force participation of women of the baby-boom generation than that of previous generations has important implications for future work trends. In particular, these women are less likely than their mothers and grandmothers to leave the labor force when they marry or have children, a fundamental change in the nature of women's work involvement. Women of the baby boom are investing more time in work, and the resulting additional labor force experience and higher wages make them more likely to continue working. Ultimately one side effect of their work commitment will be the aging of the labor force.

Implications of Women's Labor Force Participation

Changes in female labor force participation are fundamental to the alteration of women's relationship to the family and the economy. No longer limited to the roles of wife and mother, women are more likely to marry later or never marry and limit the size of their families and the period during which they have children. Their increased involvement in the role of economic producer has been associated with an increased commitment to work outside the home and greater interest in career development.

These trends suggest that women's family and work priorities may be becoming similar to men's. However, the relationship of most women to work and the family continues to differ significantly from that of men. While men have always combined work with family life, they continue to consider their roles as fathers and husbands to be secondary to their role as providers, whereas family and work remain a problematic combination for women. Because women continue to bear most of the responsibility for daily household functioning and child-rearing, their economic activity may precipitate changes in traditional family structure.

Delayed marriage, permanent singlehood, and divorce are trends associated with the rise of women as primary individuals and increasing female labor force participation: with their family responsibilities reduced through these trends, women may more easily accommodate work. While it is not likely to occur soon, married women who work may combine work and family by dividing household responsibilities with their spouses. It seems probable that, given the inadequacy of current child-care facilities, continued and increased female labor force participation will influence the availability and nature of nonfamily day-care facilities or alternative child-care arrangements within the family; for although trends toward lower fertility have been associated with higher labor force participation, most women who work are not childless.

We have shown that labor force participation has a significant impact on the course that women choose to follow in their lives. Employment opportunities influence marital and reproductive decisions, and current trends in these decisions show that women are shaping their lives very differently from the way their mothers and grandmothers shaped theirs. Market work is a socially acceptable alternative to domesticity in providing women with a means of identity. Rather than structuring their lives to accommodate family needs and priorities, women increasingly choose a life course that maximizes their individual potential, inside and outside the family.

7

Childbearing

Throughout most of United States history, there has been a gradual decline in childbearing. Like women in developed European countries, American women in each successive generation have had fewer children. Women who were in their childbearing years in the early 1800s had an average of 7 or 8 children. In the late nineteenth century, average family size dropped to 4 children, and by the early 1900s it declined to 3 children. A low point in fertility was reached during the depression years, when the average family size dipped to 2.3 children. However, during the 1950s an aberrant upsurge in fertility occurred, with the average number of births per woman rising to over 3. So dramatic and unexpected was this reversal in fertility levels that this period has been commonly labeled the baby boom. The trend of declining fertility resumed in the late 1960s and the total fertility rate fell from 2.6 to 1.8 in 1976. Since then the average number of children per woman has stabilized around 1.8—the lowest fertility rate ever experienced in the United States.

Among the notable changes in childbearing behavior that we discuss in this chapter are the following trends:

1. Women are entering motherhood at later ages now than they have in the past thirty years. Members of the baby-boom generation are postponing childbearing, on average, until they are almost 23, older than their mothers, who typically had their first births between the ages of 21 and 22. Furthermore, there has been a sharp rise in women who delay births to after age 30; the proportion of these births tripled from the 1970s to the 1980s. However, such late births

123

are not common; only 11 percent of all births in 1982 were to women aged 30 or over.

2. While most women have a child at some point in their lives, there has been a recent increase in the proportion of young women remaining childless. One out of six women aged 25–29 had no children in 1970, compared to one out of eight women in this age group in 1960.

3. Women are waiting longer after marriage before having their first child. Women now are typically married approximately two years before having a child, compared to slightly over one year in the past.

4. In the last twenty years there has been little change in the incidence of contraceptive use. Approximately two-thirds of married couples use some method of contraception. What has changed is the use of the most effective methods—sterilization, the pill, and the IUD. Among married couples using some form of contraception, reliance on one of these three birth-control methods almost doubled from slightly over one-third in 1965 to two-thirds in 1982.

5. There has been a tremendous rise in the number of illegitimate births in recent years, due both to the large increase in the number of unmarried women and to an increase in the rate at which unmarried women bear children.

6. More highly educated women and employed women continue to have fewer children and to have these children at later ages. Delaying and reducing fertility facilitates the continuous employment pattern that is becoming more common for educated women.

7. The dramatic drop in overall fertility and the later age at first birth means that women in general are devoting less of their lives to childbearing and child-rearing. In addition, they are taking on the responsibilities of motherhood after spending more time as independent single adults and more time married without children.

Trends in childbearing have important implications both for the population of the nation and the course women's lives follow. In terms of population, the size of a birth cohort affects the demands placed upon the economy and social institutions. For example, the cohort born during the depression was relatively small, and ample resources were available for its education and consumption. The baby-boom cohort, however, has placed and will continue to place heavy demands on various social institutions because of its sheer size. In particular, the educational system was forced to expand rapidly as large classes passed through each stage of the educational process. This surge was followed by cutbacks and school closings. When this large segment of the population retires, the Social Security retirement program and private retirement programs will be affected. Moreover, the return to lower fertility levels means that a smaller working population will bear the cost of baby-boom retirement.

Since women have traditionally had primary responsibility for child-rearing, fertility also has implications for the course that women's lives follow—that is, the number and spacing of children have impinged upon women's other roles. As we have noted in earlier chapters, female labor force participation, in particular, has historically revolved around parental responsibility. Women once earned money to support their families at jobs that allowed them to remain with their children. Piece-rate garment manufacturing was common among immigrant mothers, who chose to do paid work at home. Seasonal agricultural jobs allowed mothers and children to work together. Taking in boarders was another way mothers could earn money yet remain at home. During the "clerical revolution," many women of childbearing age did not enter the labor force because it meant greater separation from the home when children were present, so women who had not yet married or who had finished raising families were the ones who entered the labor force at this time (Michael 1985). However, over the past twenty years women have been combining their family roles with their nonfamilial roles in ways never seen before. Instead of occupying these roles sequentially, women are workers, students, wives, and mothers simultaneously.

Before we can meaningfully examine the interaction of women's roles with respect to their fertility, it is necessary for us to discuss in greater detail the trends in family size and the timing and sequencing of childbearing.

TRENDS IN FAMILY SIZE

Changes in Fertility Rates

Trends in fertility may suitably be measured by the total fertility rate. The total fertility rate is obtained by calculating the average number of births per women of a particular age group (e.g., 15–19, 20–24 . . . 45–49) for a given year and summing these averages. The resulting figure may be interpreted as the average number of children a woman would have during her lifetime if she had the same number of children in each period of her life (i.e, between the ages of 15 and 19, etc.) as the average women in that age range was having during the given year (Westoff and Westoff 1971). The total fertility rate is unaffected by changes in the age composition of the female population, since it is based on the sums of average fertility for women of specific age groups. As such, it provides more meaningful comparisons of fertility levels at different points in time. A total fertility rate of 2.1 signifies replacement-level fertility. Because some children die before reaching adulthood, each woman must have an average of 2.1 children during her lifetime in order for the population to remain constant (i.e., to provide replacements for herself and her husband).

Figure 7.1 illustrates changes in the total fertility rate over the past sixty years. These variations in family size have been influenced by historical events and economic conditions. During the depression, in response to unfavorable economic conditions, families were smaller and more women remained childless than at any other time in this century. The total fertility rate of 2.3 for the 1930s was significantly lower than for previous years.

After World War II the United States experienced a time of economic prosperity. During the period 1945–64, the baby-boom era, the fertility rate exceeded 3.0, peaking at 3.7 in 1957. It is important to note that this sharp rise in the fertility level was not primarily due to a return to large families. Ryder explains the baby boom by comparing women who had children during the 1930s with those who had children during the 1950s: "What actually happened was that the proportion of women having at least two children rose from 55 percent to 85 percent, whereas the average number of children those women had only increased from 3.63 to 3.78. The low fertility of the earlier period occurred mainly because a very large proportion of

FIGURE 7.1
Total Fertility Rate in the United States, 1922–1982

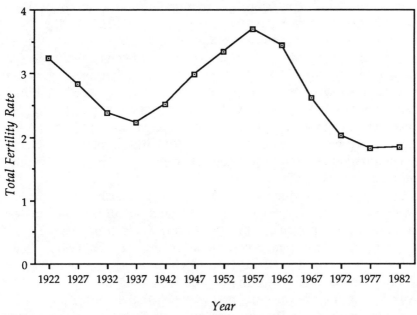

Sources: For the period 1920–78, U.S. Bureau of the Census, "Population Profile of the United States, 1980," Current Population Reports, ser. P-20, no. 363 (1981); for the period 1979–82, U.S. Bureau of the Census, "Population Profile of the United States, 1982," Current Population Reports, ser. P-23, no. 130 (1983).

women had either no children or only one child. . . . The principal change in the later period was that only a small proportion of women had fewer than two children" (Ryder 1973, p. 60).

Economic Prosperity and the Baby Boom

One explanation for the phenomenal increase in fertility levels during the 1950s and early 1960s is economic, and it is based on Easterlin's (1962, 1966, 1973, 1978) relative-income hypothesis. (See also the discussion of the relative-income hypothesis in Chapter 4.) According to Easterlin, marriage and fertility patterns are influenced by people's assessments of their current economic prospects relative to those that prevailed in their families. Goods and services of all kinds were in high demand during the postwar period, but the labor necessary to produce them was in exceptionally short supply. There were few young people entering the labor force as a result of low fertility during the depression, and immigration restrictions prevented the importation of an alternative labor supply. Therefore, this small number of workers had the advantage of competing for a large number of well-paying jobs. The new availability of consumer credit for mortgages and durable goods also contributed to an optimistic economic atmosphere. As a result, comfortable homes in which children could grow were widely available. Implementation of public and private social insurance programs such as the minimum wage, Social Security retirement and survivor benefits, and employer-provided benefits packages removed economic barriers to marriage and family formation.

This generation, which was now experiencing economic prosperity, had grown up when many families could not afford much material comfort, first because of the depression and later because of wartime rationing. Therefore, according to Easterlin, they developed few tastes for material goods and instead chose to invest their relative economic gains in children. In addition, many teenage males had to work during the prewar years because their fathers either could not find employment or were away from home. It has been suggested that paternal deprivation caused this generation of young men to desire families that fit their ideal image of a husband supporting his wife and children (Cherlin 1981). The economic security and optimism of the postwar years, coupled with this generation's desire for children rather than material goods, resulted in a pronatalist society that could afford unplanned and planned births (Westoff and Westoff 1971).

Return to Low Fertility Rates

Total fertility rates spiraled downward from their high in the second half of the 1950s to a record low of 1.77 in 1976. While fertility rates have increased slightly since this low, they appear to be leveling off near 1.8. Some of this decline was due to the young ages of childbearing during the 1950s and early 1960s—that is, these women completed their childbearing at very young ages and had few babies after age 30. Thus the decreases were due in part to women's having already had children who might otherwise have been born in the late 1960s and 1970s.

Another factor that is contributing to the recent low fertility rates is a return to "depression-style" childbearing. According to a contemporary application of the Easterlin hypothesis, current low fertility levels can be explained by the baby-boomers' tastes for material goods and the pessimistic economic environment. This generation grew up during a period of prosperity and became accustomed to possessing many material goods. Yet they entered the labor market at a time of economic recession, and the large size of this cohort generated increased competition for jobs. This competition was probably intensified by the labor force participation of young women, which did not occur during the 1950s boom period. Faced by economic uncertainty, and forced to choose between spending their incomes on children and buying material goods, many young women and men have opted for employment and purchasing power rather than marriage and families.

The trend in United States fertility over this century may therefore be characterized as a continuation of a decline that began at least one hundred years earlier. However, just as the 1950s decade was an atypical period in United States history with regard to marriage and divorce rates (see Chapter 4), so too was it unusual with respect to fertility rates. There was a surge in fertility immediately following World War II that did not abate until the mid-1960s. In the late 1960s, fertility rates continued their downward spiral, reaching levels that currently are even lower than the rate during the depression.

Fertility and Population Size

As noted above, the current total fertility rate, which hovers around 1.8, is below the 2.1 level needed for replacement. This, however, does not imply that the United States population has stopped growing or is beginning to decline. Fertility rates below the replacement level would have to be maintained for several generations before a noticeable decline in population size would occur. At present, the population of the United States continues to grow. In fact, until very recently the number of births had been increasing. In 1973 there were approximately 3.2 million registered live births in the United

States. This number increased during the following years until 1982, when 3.7 million live births were recorded. Provisional data for 1983 indicate that there was a decline of about 2 percent in the total number of births from 1982 (U.S. National Center for Health Statistics 1984).

The apparent anomaly between total fertility rates that remain relatively stable and below replacement level and increasing absolute numbers of births is due to the built-in momentum of the population structure. As a consequence of the baby boom, there are a large number of women of childbearing age. While the daughters of the baby boom are having fewer children than are necessary to replace themselves and their spouses, the sheer size of their cohorts prevents population decrease.

Changes in the Proportion of Childless Women

The preceding sections have highlighted changes in fertility rates over this century. Much of the change in these rates can be accounted for by changes in couples' propensities to remain childless. Indeed, the total fertility rate and the percent who remain childless are generally inversely related during any given period. That is, in periods when fertility rates have been high, the percent childless has been low and, conversely, periods of low fertility have been associated with high rates of childlessness.

Table 7.1 presents the percent childless among ever-married white women, by age in 1970 and by birth cohort. In this table, childless women are defined as those who were without children at age 35 (Mattessich 1979). Women born between 1896 and 1910 were of childbearing age during the depression. As can be seen from the table, during this period of low fertility 17 to 19 percent of women remained childless. Immediately prior to and following the depression, between 10 and 17 percent of women remained childless. Women born between 1926 and 1940 were of childbearing age during the baby boom. At this time childlessness became relatively rare; roughly 8 percent of women never had children.

The childless percentages for the 1941–45, 1946–50 and 1951–55 birth cohorts reported in Table 7.1 are misleading because these women have not necessarily completed childbearing. Nevertheless, some indication of the most recent trends in childlessness can be

TABLE 7.1

Percent Childless for Birth Cohorts of Ever-Married White Women, 1970

Cohort	Age in 1970	Percent Childless
1951–1955	15–19	53.7
1946–1950	20–24	37.7
1941–1945	25–29	16.1
1936–1940	30–34	8.1
1931–1935	35–39	7.1
1926–1930	40–44	8.1
1921–1925	45–49	10.1
1916–1920	50–54	13.1
1911–1915	55–59	16.8
1906–1910	60–64	19.0
1901–1905	65–69	19.0
1896–1900	70–74	17.2
1891–1895	75–79	15.7
1886–1890	80–84	14.8

Source: Mattessich 1979.

obtained by comparing past and present age-specific rates for women in the younger age groups. Among the 1941–45 birth cohort, aged 25–29 in 1970, 16.1 percent were childless. When the 1931–35 birth cohort was aged 25–29 in 1960, only 12.3 percent were childless. Similarly, the 37.7 childlessness rate for those aged 20–24 in 1970 can be compared to the 25.0 rate for those aged 20–24 in 1960, and the 53.7 rate for those aged 15–19 in 1970 can be compared to the 46.4 rate among those of the same age in 1960 (Mattessich 1979). In short, over the last ten years there has been an increase in the rates of childlessness among the younger age groups. "The younger cohorts of women (those beginning their childbearing years in 1965, 1970, and 1975) . . . have significantly higher rates of childlessness at each age than any of the older cohorts at similar stages in the reproductive cycle" (Poston and Gotard 1977).

It should be noted that the trends in childlessness for nonwhites have not been the same as those reported above for whites. Historically, nonwhites (the majority of whom are black) have had higher rates of childlessness than whites because of involuntary causes such as malnutrition, poor health, and venereal disease. More recently, improved health conditions have contributed to declines in childlessness among nonwhites, although this decline has been partially offset by increases in the use of effective birth control methods. The net effect of these two opposing forces has been that among nonwhites there is no difference in the rates of childlessness between those who began their childbearing years in 1965, 1970, and 1975 and those who began prior to 1965 (Poston and Gotard 1977).

While the percentage of childlessness has fluctuated considerably over this century, it is important to clarify that for the last one hundred years 80 to 90 percent of all ever-married women have had at least one child. Although Blake (1979) notes that childlessness will probably never become predominant, over the past several years rates of childlessness among the young cohorts of women have increased. This may ultimately result in smaller completed family sizes and more permanent childlessness (Morgan and Rindfuss 1982).

Bloom and Trussell (1984) have demonstrated that low fertility levels in the 1970s were due to delayed childbearing and increased levels of permanent childlessness, fertility patterns similar to those during the depression. As discussed earlier, this return to depression-style childbearing may be associated with the poor economic conditions of the 1970s. However, women may choose not to have children because children's social value has diminished, rather than not having children because of the economic costs involved. This may be especially true for certain groups of women. For example, childlessness has been associated with above-average age at marriage, high education levels, labor force participation, and low income (Mosher and Bachrach 1982). Historically, those women who remained childless had one or more of these characteristics (Mattessich 1979). This indicates that levels of childlessness may continue to rise as women delay marriage, attend college, and work outside the home in increasing numbers. The relationship between female labor force participation and fertility is discussed in greater detail in a subsequent section.

Changes in the Proportion of One-Child Families

In addition to the effects of childlessness documented above, it is likely that changes in families' propensities to have only one child have contributed to the changes in overall fertility rates. Documentation on trends in one-child families, however, is less complete than that available for childlessness. We do know that one-child families have become more common after being nearly nonexistent during the baby boom. Among women aged 30–34, 12 percent had only one child in 1970, but by 1978, 18 percent of this age group had only one child. In 1982, the proportion of women aged 30–34 with just one child had risen to 21 percent (Blake 1981; U.S. Bureau of the Census 1984d). Thus, it appears that the trend in one-child families has closely paralleled that of childlessness.

Tsui (1984) predicts that childless and one-child families will be more common as women who postpone parenthood miss opportunities to have children because of lower levels of fertility due to age and the risk of divorce as well as female work patterns and preferences. As discussed in a subsequent section on changes in contraceptive practices among American couples, childlessness and the one-child family have become largely voluntary. "For the first time motherhood itself is fully a matter for rational evaluation. Obviously childbearing roles offer much that is rewarding, but these rewards are not likely to be experienced equally by all women. . . . [Motherhood has become a competitor] with other social roles" (Bumpass 1973). Underscoring the devaluation of motherhood as the sole role for women and contributing to the weakening of the two-child family norm is recent evidence that "only children" are not disadvantaged or maladjusted (Blake 1981). In fact, Blake shows that only children have numerous advantages over children from multiple-child families, especially in terms of educational opportunities. As more women become aware of these advantages, one-child families are likely to become more prevalent.

Changes in Fertility by Race, Religion, and Education

Having discussed the general trend in fertility during this century, we now focus briefly on those characteristics that have historically distinguished individuals' fertility behavior and document recent changes in these fertility differentials. Three such characteristics are race, religion, and education. Changes in fertility brought about by female labor force participation are discussed in a subsequent section of this chapter.

Black women have traditionally had larger completed family sizes than white women. Some of this difference is associated with lower socioeconomic status: with lower incomes and less education, many blacks are more likely to have unwanted births because they have less access to family-planning services and use contraceptive methods less effectively. Even when the component of unwanted fertility is taken into account, however, blacks continue to have slightly larger completed family sizes than whites. Demographers typically attribute this remaining difference to subcultural differences in the value and rewards attached to childbearing. Over the last decade the average number of children ever born declined more for ever-married blacks than whites, and the absolute difference between races therefore attenuated slightly. In 1973 the average number of children ever born to whites was 2.16 compared to 2.90 to blacks. In 1982 the rates were 1.84 and 2.49 for whites and blacks, respectively (Pratt et al. 1984).

Historically, Catholics have had higher fertility than non-Catholics. "In the 1960s, religious affiliation was labeled 'the strongest of all major social influences on fertility,' but the differences between Catholic and Protestant fertility recorded in the national surveys of the 1950s and 1960s have narrowed considerably" (Pratt et al. 1984). This attenuation can be largely attributed to Catholics' adoption of contraceptive-use patterns similar to those of non-Catholics. Although the Roman Catholic church officially forbids the use of contraceptives, it appears to have lost its influence on attitudes and behaviors related to family planning. Over the last decade, the religious differential continued to narrow. In 1973 the average number of children ever born to Catholics was 2.37, and the comparable rate for Protestants was 2.23. By 1982 the average number of children ever born was 1.96 and 1.92 for Catholics and Protestants, respectively (Pratt et al. 1984).

Just as there has been a convergence in family size between races and between religious groups, the family sizes of women with different levels of education have also converged. In 1973 the average number of children ever born to women with less than a twelve-year education was 2.95. For those with twelve years of education, it was 2.08, and for those with thirteen or more years of education it was 1.68. By 1982 the average number of children ever born to women of the low-, medium-, and high-education groups was 2.51, 1.90, and 1.61, respectively. Thus, although the family-size differential has declined over the last decade, substantial effects of education remain. As noted by Pratt et al. (1984), "Differences in fertility by education reflect such factors as delayed childbearing by women who continue education beyond high school and better-educated women's greater opportunities to pursue activities other than motherhood." We will return to this point in our later discussion of delayed childbearing.

TRENDS IN THE TIMING OF CHILDBEARING

There are a number of ways to depict changes in the timing of childbearing, two of which are the assessment of change in age at first birth and change in the length of birth intervals. We will now look at trends in these two measures and demonstrate how they are related to the changes in fertility rates previously discussed. We can then discuss the current phenomenon of delayed childbearing in the United States.

Changes in Age at First Birth

Table 7.2 shows that a recent shift toward older age at first birth is restoring the median age at first birth to levels not seen since before the baby boom. The 1900–1909 and 1910–19 birth cohorts of women had their first births during the depression and were about 23 years old when they became mothers. Age at first birth of mothers during the baby boom (the 1930–39 and 1940–49 birth cohorts of women) was under 22. The baby-boomers themselves (1950–59 birth cohort) are postponing childbearing, and the age at first birth is again climbing to near 23. It should be noted that a one-year increase in mean age at first birth is quite sizable, having a very large impact on fertility levels recorded for any given period.

The trend toward later childbearing can also be seen by comparing the proportions of birth cohorts of women who have their first child by a particular age (see Table 7.3). Postponement of first birth has

TABLE 7.2

Median Age at Birth of First Child for Birth Cohorts of Women

Birth Cohort	Median Age in Years
1880–1889	23.0
1890–1899	22.9
1900–1909	22.8
1910–1919	23.5
1920–1929	22.7
1930–1939	21.4
1940–1949	21.8
1950–1959	22.7

Source: U.S. Bureau of the Census 1978a.

occurred with increasing frequency among women born since 1945. After atypical timing of the first birth during the baby boom (the 1935–39 and 1940–44 birth cohorts of women), we see a return to patterns of timing existing before World War II. By age 20, 16 to 17 percent of the depression mothers had had their first child. This figure climbed to 20 percent following the depression. During the baby boom, 27 percent of women were mothers by age 20, but only 22 to 23 percent of their daughters were parents by the same age. While almost 70 percent of baby-boom mothers had their first child by the time they were 25, just over half of their daughters (the 1950–54 birth cohort) did. Only 44 to 47 percent of depression mothers had their first child by the time they were 25.

These trends in age at first birth tend to parallel trends in fertility rates. The completed fertility rate for depression mothers (who were older at the birth of their first child) at age 40 was 2.1. Baby-boom mothers (who were younger at the birth of their first child) had a completed fertility rate of 3.0 at age 40, whereas lifetime births for the baby-boom generation are predicted to be 2.1 (U.S. Bureau of the Census 1984d). This parallelism between the depression and the baby-boom generation is due primarily to the greater years of potential childbearing of women who begin having children at young ages.

TABLE 7.3

Percentage of Women Having a First Child, by Successive Ages, for Birth Cohorts from 1905–1909 to 1955–1959

Birth Cohort	18 years	20 years	23 years	25 years	28 years	30 years	40 years
1955–1959	9.4	22.0	—	—	—	—	—
1950–1954	8.9	23.0	42.1	52.6	—	—	—
1945–1949	8.1	23.3	47.6	60.0	72.3	77.0	—
1940–1944	9.7	27.7	56.2	68.7	79.6	83.5	—
1935–1939	9.8	27.2	56.2	69.6	80.9	84.2	89.6
1930–1934	9.5	24.2	52.1	67.1	79.0	83.1	89.0
1925–1929	7.1	20.3	46.4	61.1	74.6	79.9	87.9
1920–1924	6.9	17.3	40.4	55.3	71.2	76.5	84.6
1915–1919	6.6	16.3	35.9	46.9	61.5	68.4	80.5
1910–1914	7.7	17.7	33.9	43.7	56.9	63.0	75.9
1905–1909	7.4	17.1	37.3	47.2	59.0	65.0	75.3

Source: U.S. Bureau of the Census 1984a.

This additional exposure to childbearing is due to both biological factors (i.e., fecundity, the higher capacity to bear children at younger ages) and social factors (i.e., development of alternative, conflicting roles to motherhood as childbearing is delayed).

Changes in the Length of Birth Intervals

In a period of high fertility like the 1950s, women are more likely to have a child within the first year of marriage than in periods of low fertility like the 1930s and 1970s. As age at marriage has increased, the pace at which women have children has slowed. As shown in Table 7.4, 40 percent of women who married between 1960 and 1964 had their first child within one year of marriage (upper panel) and 30 percent had two within three years (lower panel). In contrast, only 33 percent of the 1970–74 marriage cohort had their first child before their first wedding anniversary and 17 percent had a second child by their third anniversary. The child-spacing pattern of the 1970–74 marriage cohort is similar to that of the 1935–39 and 1940–44 cohorts, of whom about 25 percent had their first child before their first wed-

TABLE 7.4

Interval between First Marriage and First and Second Births, by Year of First Marriage: June 1980

	Period of first marriage							
	1970–1974	1965–1969	1960–1964	1955–1959	1950–1954	1945–1949	1940–1944	1935–1939[a]
Number of Women (Thousands)	7,999	7,351	6,442	6,039	5,817	6,442	5,391	4,338
First Births								
Cumulative percent[b]								
Before first marriage	10.7	9.2	8.5	8.1	6.4	5.5	4.4	5.6
After first marriage								
6 months	18.4	16.4	14.4	12.5	10.1	8.9	7.2	8.7
8 months	24.5	24.1	22.4	18.0	14.7	12.0	10.2	12.1
10 months	28.9	29.6	30.0	25.9	21.9	19.0	16.4	17.6
12 months	32.8	36.0	39.9	35.9	31.5	28.1	23.8	25.5
15 months	37.7	43.0	48.4	46.8	41.8	37.5	32.8	34.4
18 months	41.5	48.3	54.4	54.3	48.1	44.5	39.2	40.6
24 months	48.1	57.1	63.8	63.9	58.8	55.6	49.5	49.5
36 months	58.8	68.2	76.0	75.4	71.3	68.2	62.2	61.4

Cumulative percent

Before first marriage

	3.0	2.6	3.2	2.5	1.9	1.4	1.3	1.6
After first marriage								
12 months	5.1	4.4	5.2	4.5	3.2	2.6	2.1	2.7
24 months	9.0	9.7	13.3	12.1	9.3	7.2	5.4	6.3
36 months	16.5	21.5	29.8	30.6	25.9	20.9	15.6	17.7
48 months	25.4	33.8	43.9	46.2	40.9	33.8	26.8	27.2
60 months	34.2	43.5	55.8	57.8	53.1	44.8	36.8	36.6
84 months	—	58.8	68.9	69.6	67.4	59.9	52.2	50.1
120 months	—	68.6	77.4	76.3	76.3	70.8	64.4	60.7

Source: U.S. Bureau of the Census 1984a.
[a]Due to age restrictions in the survey, data are slightly incomplete for this cohort and may not be comparable for women who first married at age 30 and over.
[b]Births cumulated up to beginning of each month.

ding anniversary and about 17 percent had their second child within three years of marriage.

Another measure of birth spacing, the median length of the first birth interval (i.e., the number of months between marriage and first birth at which half of the women had had their first child), shows similar trends (upper row of Table 7.5). During the depression and World War II, this interval increased from 15.5 months in 1930–34 to 18.1 months in 1940–44, and then decreased in the high-fertility era of the baby boom. By 1955–59, half of all first births occurred within 15.7 months of marriage; toward the end of the boom, in 1960–64, it was only 14.2 months. Lower fertility rates in the 1970s were associated with increased intervals between marriage and first birth: 16.6 in 1970–74 and 23.5 in 1975–79.

The interval between the first and second birth shows the same trend as fertility rates and the interval between marriage and first birth (lower row of Table 7.5). During the period 1945–49, the median interval between first and second birth was 30 months, during 1960–64 the interval was only 26 months, and during 1975–79 it was 36 months.

Delayed Childbearing

The patterns of increases in age at first birth and length of the first and subsequent birth intervals among the more recent cohorts of women signify delayed childbearing for those born during the baby boom. The baby-boom generation of women is more independent and is exposed to more lifestyle choices than were their mothers. A significant number have advanced educations, work outside the home, and remain single for extended periods of their lives. Each of these factors may account for delayed childbearing among the most recent cohorts of women. For example, 84 percent of baby-boom mothers who did not finish high school had their first child by age 25. Sixty-four percent of high school graduates were mothers at age 25, but only 30 percent of college-educated women had their first child by this age (Bloom and Trussell 1984; Morgan 1982). As documented in Chapter 4, there has been a tendency for many members of the baby-boom cohort to postpone marriage. A late age at marriage is associated with a longer interval between marriage and the first child and between the first child and subsequent children (Mar-

TABLE 7.5

Median Interval of First Birth since Marriage and Second Birth since Birth of Previous Child, by Year of Child's Birth: June 1980[a]

	Period of Child's Birth									
	1975–1979	1970–1974	1965–1969	1960–1964	1955–1959	1950–1954	1945–1949	1940–1944[b]	1935–1939[b]	1930–1934[b]
Median Interval of First Birth since Marriage (Months)	23.5	16.6	14.0	14.2	15.7	18.1	18.1	18.5	16.8	15.5
Median Interval of Second Birth since Previous Birth (Months)	36.0	32.8	29.1	26.4	27.8	30.4	30.0	29.7	28.3	27.6

Source: U.S. Bureau of the Census 1984a.
[a]Data limited to women aged 15–75.
[b]Due to age restrictions, data for these cohorts may be relatively incomplete, especially for intervals between higher order births.

ini and Hodson 1981). Thus, the trend toward later age at marriage may also partially account for delayed childbearing among the more recent cohorts of women. Another explanation for this childbearing pattern is the increased labor force participation of female members of the baby-boom cohort. This relationship is discussed at length in a subsequent section of this chapter.

The popular literature often refers to delayed childbearing as the "fertility phenomenon of the 1980s" (Langer 1985). Between 1970 and 1982 the number of first births to women aged 25 and older doubled. The number of first births to women aged 30 and older nearly tripled, from 57,000 in 1970 to 165,000 in 1982 (Langer 1985). This is certainly an impressive increase. However, even though the percent of all first births accounted for by women aged 30 and over almost tripled, from 4 percent in 1970 to 11 percent in 1982, these women's contributions to current childbearing in the United States still remained quite small.

Often reports of an increase in the number of "mature" mothers imply that this phenomenon will have a large impact on subsequent fertility rates. That is, it has been suggested that the current fertility rates are artificially low and that the delayed childbearing of the baby-boomers will ultimately result in larger completed family sizes for members of this cohort than the current fertility rates suggest. This is unlikely because some women who delay childbearing eventually decide never to have children (Morgan 1982) or find they are no longer able to do so: in common parlance, their "biological clocks" run out. In addition, Morgan (1982) has shown that older women and those with fewer children who delayed childbearing are less certain about their intentions for another child, and that uncertainty finally becomes forgone fertility.

TRENDS IN THE SEQUENCING OF CHILDBEARING

Just as there have been changes in the timing of childbearing, so have there been rather dramatic changes in the sequencing of childbearing vis-à-vis other major life-course events. Most childbearing occurs within marriage, as assumed in the previous discussion, but a growing proportion of all births occur before marriage and between marriages. Changes in fertility during remarriage have also taken place. Therefore, some examination of these phenomena is necessary for a complete description of fertility trends and the implications of fertility for women's lives. In addition, we also discuss the complex relationship between fertility and female labor force participation.

Changes in Illegitimacy

Between 1940 and 1960, the illegitimacy rate (number of births per 1,000 unmarried women aged 15–44) tripled from 7.1 to 21.6. However, during the same period the number of unmarried women decreased by about 18 percent, making the denominator upon which the illegitimacy rate is based smaller over time. Thus, the absolute number of illegitimate births increased by 2.5 times from 89,500 in 1940 to 224,300 in 1960 (Ventura 1980). Between 1960 and 1979, the illegitimacy rate did not change a great deal: the 1979 rate of 27.2 was only 1.3 times larger than the 1960 rate of 21.6. However, the number of unmarried women in 1979 was 1.5 times as large as in 1960. This increase in the unmarried female population and the slight increase in the rate of illegitimate births caused the absolute number of illegitimate births to nearly triple, from 224,300 in 1960 to 597,800 in 1979 (Ventura 1980).

In recent years national concern has grown over the proportion of births to teenagers that occur out of wedlock. The rise in such births can be attributed to increased levels of premarital intercourse, less effective use of contraception among teens than among older women, and lower rates of teen marriage either before or after conception. Thus, as evidenced in Table 7.6, the proportion of all births to women under 20 that were illegitimate has increased dramatically. For women born before 1945, less than 20 percent of births at age 20 or younger were illegitimate. After that point the proportion of illegitimate births among teens began to soar. Over one-fourth of women born just after the war—at the start of the baby boom—had illegitimate births, but nearly 40 percent of births experienced by later baby-boomers before they were 20 were illegitimate.

Most of the increase in illegitimate births has been due to rising rates among white teens and younger teens aged 15–17 years old

(Ventura 1980). Of special note is that in 1971 the fertility rate among adolescents (births per 1,000 unmarried females aged 15–19) was nearly ten times higher for blacks than for whites. However, by 1981 the size of this race differential was reduced by half because of a rise in the childbearing rate among unwed white adolescents and a corresponding, although smaller and somewhat erratic, decline among unwed black adolescents.

In order to provide a general explanation for this racial convergence in childbearing rates among unwed adolescents, Billy et al. (1987) estimated the simultaneous net effects of the proximate determinants of unwed-adolescent motherhood by race and for two time periods. The proximate determinants are the proportion of unmarried teenagers that are having sexual intercourse, the rate of conception among sexually active unmarried teenagers, the proportion of these conceptions that are carried to term (i.e., result in a live birth), and the proportion of these live births that occur before marriage. A change in any of these proximate determinants can result in a change in the rate of births to unwed adolescent mothers. Between 1971 and 1982, black unwed adolescent women did not exhibit much change in their childbearing rates, primarily because of the offsetting effects of an increase in the proportion having intercourse and a decrease in the proportion of those having intercourse who also had a conception. In contrast, during the same period, the white unwed-adolescent childbearing rate increased rather dramatically, because of an increase in the proportion having intercourse and the proportion not marrying to legitimize the birth of a child. The increase in white unwed motherhood would have been even higher had it not been for the decline in the proportion of those with a premarital conception who experienced a live birth.

Billy et al. found that having intercourse and not marrying to legitimize the birth were the primary factors responsible for the overall racial convergence in unwed-adolescent motherhood, with whites increasing at a faster rate than blacks on both proximate determinants. Convergence in the proportion of those having premarital intercourse who experience a conception was also partially responsible for the racial convergence in illegitimate-birth rates. Partially offsetting this trend toward convergence, however, was the racial divergence in the proportion of those experiencing a premarital conception who have a live birth. Blacks and whites exhibited similar proportions in 1971, but this proportion subsequently declined at a faster rate among whites than among blacks.

Adolescent childbearing, especially among unwed mothers, has become a growing concern because of the number of undesirable consequences that are associated with it. Among these are health problems for the mother and infant (Menken 1980), more children in rapid succession (Bumpass et al. 1978), resultant larger completed family sizes (Millman and Hendershot 1980), low educational attainment (Furstenberg 1976; Card 1977; Moore and Waite 1977; McLaughlin 1977), low earnings (Hofferth and Moore 1979), welfare dependency (Moore 1978), child abuse and neglect (Herrenkohl and Herrenkohl 1979), low personal efficacy (McLaughlin and Micklin 1983), and high rates of marital disruption (McCarthy and Menken 1979). As such, adolescent childbearing and illegitimate birth precipitate a series of lifelong difficulties both for the mother and child.

Changes in Fertility after Marital Disruption

A relatively neglected aspect of nonmarital fertility is that of formerly married women. Fifty percent of twice-married women sampled in 1965 and 1970 had given birth during the interval between marriages and two-thirds of these births occurred within twelve months of marital disruption (Rindfuss and Bumpass 1977). Although many of these children were conceived during marriage, their mothers were nevertheless unmarried when they were born and were therefore very much like women who had premarital births: economically disadvantaged, young (young women, especially those under 20, are the most likely to have a birth after marital disruption), and poorly educated (Rindfuss and Bumpass 1977; Watkins et al. 1981).

No significant increase has occurred in the incidence of fertility after marital disruption despite the increased duration and incidence of separation and divorce (Watkins et al. 1981). In fact, a decline in fertility after marital disruption has occurred for women 25 and older, perhaps because of more effective use of contraception both immediately prior to and during separation or divorce. However, women under 20 continue to experience rates that parallel premarital motherhood. Differences in fertility after marital disruption among various demographic segments remain similar to the differ-

TABLE 7.6

Percentage of All Births to Unmarried Women under 20

Birth Cohort	Percent
1905–1919	18.7
1920–1929	18.3
1930–1934	19.1
1935–1939	19.7
1940–1944	18.8
1945–1949	27.2
1950–1954	34.3
1955–1959	38.5

Source: U.S. Bureau of the Census 1984a.

ences of the past. Blacks, less-educated women, and younger women continue to have a higher incidence of fertility after marital disruption than other groups (Watkins et al. 1981).

Changes in Fertility during Remarriage

Fertility in remarriage reflects the more general fertility trends previously discussed. Over the past twenty years, as fertility rates in general declined, so too did fertility rates within remarriage. While the probability of a birth within remarriage remains quite high (a 69 percent chance for whites and a 52 percent chance for blacks), such births are less common than during and prior to 1964. Currently, half of these births occur within eighteen months of remarriage. The probability of a birth declines rapidly if a remarried woman's next-oldest child is over two years of age. Young childless women are less likely than in the past to have children if they remarry or marry a man who is five or more years older than they are (Griffith et al. 1985).

Perhaps the most important reason for remarried women to have a child or additional children has been to cement the new marriage, to give it legitimacy as a real family. The decline in births in remarriage may be due to a deemphasis of this rationale because of changes in women's roles and their priorities. Women who worked during their previous marriage may be less likely than in the past to desire a child and extend the childbearing portion of their lives. Having invested more than a few years in the labor force, they may be unwilling to jeopardize that experience by taking time off for child-rearing. Women who began working after their marriages ended may find the worker role more satisfying than similar women in the past because of increased opportunities and rewards afforded to females in the labor force. They may also be less likely to need the role of mother for status or self-definition (Griffith et al. 1985). In short, the overall decrease in births after remarriage may reflect a redefinition of women's roles. It is to this redefinition of roles that we now turn as we discuss the relationship between fertility and female labor force participation.

Labor Force Participation and Fertility

Research has repeatedly documented that working women have smaller completed family sizes than nonworking women, a relationship that has existed for more than thirty years (Pratt and Whelpton 1958; Ridley 1959; Namboodiri 1964; Kupinsky 1971, 1977; Cochrane 1979; Freedman 1961–62; and Hawthorn 1970). However, there is no agreement on the causal factor in this relationship (Bumpass and Westoff 1970; Cramer 1980; Pratt and Whelpton 1958; Ridley 1959; Smith-Lovin and Tickamyer 1978; Waite and Stolzenberg 1976). Some maintain that fertility affects employment; some argue that it is the reverse. Yet others suggest that the variables affect each other simultaneously.[1]

Those maintaining that fertility is the causal variable view the decision about the number of children to bear as preceding the decision to work outside the home (Waite 1975). To the extent that children are valued more than careers, family size will determine whether the mother will be employed (Smith-Lovin and Tickamyer 1978). Others have argued that the age of the youngest child in the family pre-

---

1. Much of the following discussion was adapted from John D. Kasarda, John O. G. Billy, and Kirsten B. West, *Status Enhancement and Fertility: Reproductive Responses to Social Mobility and Educational Opportunity* (New York: Academic Press, 1986).

dicts labor force participation better than the total number of children in the family. Traditionally, having *young* children has reduced the chances that a woman would work outside the home (Gendell 1965; Grossman 1978; Ware 1976).

Those who argue that employment is the causal factor point to findings that women who work outside the home or intend to do so in the future expect to have smaller families than full-time homemakers (Jones 1981; Pratt and Whelpton 1958; Ryder and Westoff 1971a, b). In addition, the duration of a woman's employment is significantly related to the spacing of her children. Length of time employed since marriage and time between marriage and the first birth are positively related. Furthermore, the longer a woman participates in the labor force, the longer the interval between subsequent births, resulting in a smaller completed family size (McLaughlin 1982; Namboodiri 1964).

It is increasingly recognized that a degree of mutual causation exists between female employment and fertility. Using special techniques designed to analyze the simultaneous effects of these two factors, Waite and Stolzenberg (1976) found that while mutual causation is evident, labor force participation plans were more important in affecting fertility expectations than the reverse. Cramer's (1980) findings supported Waite and Stolzenberg's conclusions. Employment plans depressed expected family size, and the reciprocal effect of expected children on labor force participation was trivial. Cramer speculated that in the short run, family size will affect employment more than the other way around, but in the long run, family size will only minimally affect labor force participation. However, Smith-Lovin and Tickamyer (1978) found that although the number of children influenced employment after marriage, postmarriage employment did not alter fertility.

Perhaps the best-known sociological explanation of the inverse relationship between fertility and labor force participation involves the concept of role incompatibility or conflict, which can arise when society disapproves of nonfamilial roles for mothers or when time required in rearing children competes with time required in being employed. The traditional viewpoint maintains that a woman's major roles in life are those of wife, mother, and homemaker (Collver and Langlois 1962), so that even with outside work demands, she is still often held responsible for the successful operation of the household.

Yet at the same time, she is expected not to allow such domestic obligations to interfere with her job performance. With heavy demands on her to be successful at both endeavors, the employed mother finds her roles in conflict. Typically, the more prestigious the job and the more extensive the educational prerequisites for it, the greater the role conflict (Safilios-Rothschild 1972; Weller 1968).

Unless the father increases his domestic participation to parallel the mother's increasing labor force participation, the only way the employed mother can alleviate role conflict is to reduce her competing obligations to manageable proportions. Since occupational demands remain fairly rigid while family size can be modified, women tend to opt for smaller families. This option holds even for women able to purchase child care. The inverse relationship between labor force participation and fertility can thus be largely attributed to incongruity between the roles of mother and paid worker. Furthermore, the greater this incongruity, the greater the differential fertility behavior between employed women and homemakers.

Other explanations for the inverse relationship between fertility and female employment include fecundity (the biological capacity to reproduce), work commitment, and opportunity costs. Some argue that subfecund and involuntarily sterile women are more likely to be employed than fecund women (Freedman et al. 1959). Freedman and his associates found that for all age groups women who work outside the home are more likely to be sterile than women who are not active in the labor force.

Psychological commitment to paid work is another factor used to explain the relationship between female employment and family size. Tien (1965, 1967) proposed that women committed to a career tend to desire and have fewer children than women committed to a familial role. In addition, economists argue that an increase in women's wages decreases the number of children they have (Schultz 1973). To the extent that perceived economic benefits of paid work and opportunity costs of children outweigh the perceived benefits of children, a woman is likely to choose to enter the labor force and restrict her fertility.

While the inverse relationship between fertility and labor force participation remains, there is some evidence that it is abating. Negative societal attitudes regarding employed mothers are rapidly changing. There is increasing acceptance of mothers who work outside the home, even when they have young children. With larger proportions of women obtaining college degrees and with open, extensive discussion of "women's liberation" and equality of opportunity, many women (including mothers) may feel social pressures, or may fundamentally desire, to take on nonfamilial work roles. As documented in Chapter 6, in recent decades the number and proportion of women in the labor force have rapidly increased; since the end of World War II, the number of employed women has more than tripled. This increase has been particularly pronounced for employed mothers. Over half the children in the United States under age 18 now have mothers who work away from home—more than double the proportion and ten times the number recorded in 1945 (Grossman 1983). Moreover, while the relationship between age of the youngest child and female labor force participation still exists, this association has been changing (Mott and Shapiro 1983). Women today are less likely to avoid employment while they have preschool-age children. In 1978, 39 percent of mothers with children under age 6 were in the labor force, compared to over 50 percent in 1982 (Grossman 1983).

In short, many women are no longer conforming to the baby-boom lifestyle of not entering or dropping out of the labor force in order to raise children. Instead, they are opting to occupy the roles of mother and wife simultaneously with that of paid worker. As such, there has been a change in the sequencing of childbearing relative to female labor force participation. Women are combining their family roles with their nonfamilial roles in ways rarely seen before.

TRENDS IN BIRTH CONTROL PRACTICES

In the previous chapter we had occasion to mention changes in the birth-control practices of American women. This topic merits further comment before we sum up our findings on changes in childbearing behavior. Birth control is most accurately viewed as a proximate determinant of fertility; that is, it is a key intermediate variable through which such motivating forces as increased levels of education and female labor force participation, and rising female status in general, operate on fertility. As such, it is the "facilitator" for a woman's or couple's fertility intentions.

A long-term analysis of trends in contraceptive behavior in the United States is not possible because reliable data are only available for the last few decades. Findings from five national sample surveys of fertility in the United States (the 1965 and 1970 National Fertility Studies and the 1973, 1976, and 1982 National Surveys of Family Growth) indicate that the proportions of married couples with wives aged 15–44 currently using any method of contraception were 64, 65, 70, 68, and 68 percent, respectively, for the five survey years (Bachrach 1984; Westoff 1976). Thus, in the last twenty years, there has been little or no change in the incidence of contraceptive use among married couples. However, contraceptive methods have changed dramatically. In 1965, 37 percent of married couples with wives aged 15–44 who were using any contraceptive method were relying on contraceptive sterilization, the pill, or the IUD, which are all highly effective methods. By 1982, the percentage of such couples relying on any of these highly effective methods had climbed to 68 percent (Bachrach 1984; Westoff 1976). The development of such effective methods is an important technological change. It has added to the ability of women to structure their life course with greater certainty to fit lifestyle objectives. Based on the figures cited above, it appears that more and more women are opting for the advantages afforded by the improved technology.

Dramatic changes also occurred between 1973 and 1982 in the use of the contraceptive methods mentioned above. Pill use among currently married women aged 15–44 using any type of method declined sharply from 36 percent in 1973 to 20 percent in 1982, but it continued to be the most popular method among wives aged 15–24. Contraceptive sterilization evidenced a modest increase between 1973 and 1976, from 23.5 percent to 27.4 percent, but rose dramatically to 41 percent in 1982 among all married users aged 15–44. Most of the latter increase was due to the rise in *female* contraceptive sterilization. Among currently married users aged 35–44, 62.7 percent depended on contraceptive sterilization in 1982, making it the leading method of birth control among older women. Use of the IUD declined between 1973 and 1982, with the sharpest drop occurring between 1976 and 1982, from 9.3 percent to 7.1 percent among currently married users aged 15–44 (Bachrach 1984).

Finally, after the 1973 Supreme Court ruling that declared restrictive state abortion laws unconstitutional, the number of reported legal abortions increased, reaching 1.6 million abortions in 1981 (see Table 7.7). The rate of increase in abortions performed, however, has been declining. The abortion rate in column 3 of Table 7.7 indicates that in both 1980 and 1981, 3 percent of women of reproductive age obtained abortions. This compares to less than 2 percent in 1973. Column 4 of the table presents the number of abortions per 1,000 pregnancies. As such, it indicates that in 1973, 19 percent of all pregnancies (excluding miscarriages and stillbirths) were terminated by abortion. In both 1980 and 1981, 30 percent of all pregnancies were terminated by abortion. In each of the years from 1973 to 1981, women who obtained abortions were predominantly the young, white, unmarried, and childless (Henshaw and O'Reilly 1983).

In sum, most American couples practice some means of birth control. This has been the case for at least the last twenty years, with little change in the incidence of contraceptive use. Most dramatic has been the increased reliance on the highly effective methods of birth control, which has permitted women to plan their lives better. As noted in our earlier discussion, childlessness and the one-child family have become largely voluntary. "For the first time motherhood itself is fully a matter for rational evaluation" (Bumpass 1973).

THE DECLINING STATUS OF MOTHERHOOD

In this chapter we have documented trends in the fertility behavior of American women during the twentieth century and have discussed the causes and consequences of these trends. To recapitulate, the general trend throughout United States history has been one of decreasing fertility. Following an aberrant upsurge in fertility levels after World War II, the total fertility rate resumed its downward trend in the 1960s. Current fertility levels are below replacement, hovering around 1.8. To a large extent these low fertility rates are experienced by all groups of women; that is, fertility differences by race, religion, and education have attenuated over the last one or two decades, although sizable differences remain among women with different educational levels.

Accompanying these trends in fertility rates have been changes in the proportions of women remaining childless and having only one child as well as changes in the timing of childbearing. During the

TABLE 7.7

*Number of Reported Legal Abortions, Rate of Abortions
per 1,000 Women Aged 15–44, and Abortion Ratio
per 1,000 Abortions and Live Births: 1969–1981*

	Measure		
Year	No. of Abortions (Thousands)	Abortion Rate	Abortion Ratio per 1,000 Abortions and Live Births
1969	22.7	—	—
1970	193.5	—	—
1971	485.8	—	—
1972	586.8	—	—
1973	744.6	16.6	193
1974	898.6	19.6	220
1975	1034.2	22.1	249
1976	1179.3	24.5	265
1977	1320.3	26.9	286
1978	1409.6	27.7	292
1979	1497.7	28.8	296
1980	1553.9	29.3	300
1981	1577.3	29.3	300

Sources: For 1969–72, Weinstock et al. 1975; for 1973–77, Forrest et al. 1979; for 1978–80, Henshaw and O'Reilly 1983; for 1981, Henshaw et al. 1985.

baby boom, childlessness and one-child families were relatively rare. Age at first birth was low and intervals between births were short. Over the last ten years there has been an increase in the proportions of women who are childless or have only one child. There has also been a recent shift toward older age at first birth and an increase in the interval between marriage and first birth and between first birth and subsequent births.

These changes reflect a pattern of delayed childbearing among the more recent cohorts of women. It is unlikely that this delayed child-bearing will ultimately result in a larger completed family size for members of the baby-boom cohort than current fertility rates suggest. Many women who delay childbearing because they have taken on roles that compete with motherhood eventually never have children, either because they decide against it or because their "biological clocks" run out. Policymakers and planners should be aware, however, that even if these women do not have large families the absolute number of births in the United States will be high owing to the sheer size of this cohort. The increase in the absolute number of births between 1973 and 1982 bears out this logic.

This chapter has also documented trends in the sequencing of childbearing vis-à-vis other major life-course events. Premarital childbearing has risen significantly over the past forty years and has become a national concern as mounting data point to its negative consequences. While no significant increase in fertility after marital disruption has occurred in recent years, women under 20 continue to exhibit postmarital fertility rates that parallel premarital fertility rates. Many of these mothers have low educational levels that contribute to their poverty. Finally, over the past twenty years, there has been a decline in fertility during remarriage that parallels the general fertility decline and may reflect not only a change in women's roles, but also a redefinition of marriage, according to which a man and a woman do not have to have children to fulfill their union as husband and wife.

The change in women's roles can clearly be seen in the relationship between fertility and labor force participation. While an inverse relationship between these two factors continues to exist, there is some evidence that it is abating. There has been a change in the sequencing of childbearing relative to female labor force participation. Many women today are opting to occupy the role of mother simultaneously with that of worker. Improved contraceptive technology and increased reliance on the most highly effective birth-control methods have added to women's ability to plan their lives to meet such goals as additional educational attainment and participation in the labor force.

The return to low fertility rates similar to those seen before World War II may be associated with the poor economic conditions of the 1970s. Easterlin's relative-income hypothesis seems well suited as an explanation for these macrolevel fertility trends. In addition, the current fertility rates, which are even lower than those of the depression era, may also be associated with a change not only in the relative economic value of having children but also in the social value of childbearing. As documented in previous chapters, more women are remaining single or delaying marriage, obtaining advanced levels of education, and entering the labor force. As such, motherhood may indeed have become a "competitor with other social roles." The value of having children declines as children become less important as a means of conferring status on women.

Those forces that have produced low fertility rates may, in turn, be affected by low fertility. Less demanding familial roles associated with smaller family size allow women to avail themselves of other lifestyle options, such as education aimed at developing work skills. As noted in our discussion of the relationship between fertility and labor force participation, women with few or no children are more likely to be employed than women with several children. To the extent that a norm of small family size becomes firmly entrenched in American culture and there is a dissipation of the traditional viewpoint that a woman's major roles in life are those of wife, mother, and homemaker, more women may opt for nonfamilial roles and develop more fully as individuals with the prospect of organizing their lives to meet personal and career objectives.

Part Three
Attitudinal Changes

8

The Demographic Context
for Attitudinal Change

Up to this point we have examined demographic changes, in separate categories such as education, marriage, employment, and childbearing. But it should be apparent that the actual life course of women is affected by all these changes taken together. In order to establish the demographic context for the changes in attitudes and values that are discussed in the next chapter, we turn once again to the life-course perspective as a means of summarizing the impact of the full range of demographic changes on the lives of American women. We then further substantiate and synthesize the demographic observations made in earlier chapters by analyzing two large, nationally representative surveys of ten thousand women for the fifteen-year period from 1967 to 1982.

THE FRAMEWORK FOR THE ANALYSIS

Life-Course Stages

We have developed a set of life-course stages based on four significant roles women play: student, labor force participant, wife, and mother. By using all four roles in defining these life-course stages, we can describe the consequences of changes in the timing, duration, and sequencing of these roles on the distribution of women among the stages.

Each of the roles used to designate life-course stages represents a status that a woman may attain and then leave over the course of her life. Changes in the *rates* of moving into or out of a role (e.g., declines in the marriage rate or increases in the divorce rate), changes in the *timing* of entry (e.g., older age at marriage, delayed childbearing), and changes in the *sequencing* of entry into and exit from these roles (e.g., entrance into the labor force after marriage and after child-rearing) will cause the distribution of the population among life-course stages to change. Using appropriate longitudinal data, we can describe changes in the life course of several cohorts of women by observing shifts in their distribution among life-course stages as they age. Moreover, we can compare the distribution among life-course stages of women of the same age group at different points in time to determine, for example, similarities and differences among women who were teenagers in the 1960s, 1970s, and 1980s.

In order to conduct our analysis we needed to develop life-course stages that were complex enough to account for the many variations in the roles of student, spouse, parent, and labor force participant, yet simple enough to provide a meaningful categorization. To accomplish this we developed a classification scheme based on whether a woman was enrolled in school full time; whether she was single, married, or divorced; whether she was living with her own dependent children (defined as under 18 years old); and whether she was working outside the home (either full time or part time). All possible combinations of these factors yield a total of twenty-four life-course stages. Over 90 percent of the female population, however, can be captured with seven or eight categories (depending on the age group). The categories are:

1. Student: a woman who is enrolled in school full time but is neither married nor employed nor living with a dependent child.
2. Jobholder: a woman who is in the labor force but not married and not living with a dependent child.
3. Wife: a woman who is married but not living with dependent children and not working outside the home.
4. Employed Wife: a woman who is in the labor force and married but has no dependent children living with her.
5. Mother: a woman who is married and living with her dependent children but is not in the labor force.

6. Employed Mother: a woman who is married, living with her dependent children, and working outside the home.
7. Divorced Employed Mother: a woman who is no longer married but is living with her dependent children and working outside the home.
8. Divorced Mother: a woman who is living with her dependent children but is no longer married and is not in the labor force.
9. Other: a miscellany of all combinations not classified above. Examples include never-married mothers in and out of the labor force, previously married nonparents, and respondents who were neither married nor in the labor force nor living with dependent children nor enrolled in school. This category, which is necessary to permit correct population totals and valid representations of the percentage distributions of the other categories, typically is quite small and never exceeds 10 percent of the population.

Life-course stages define individuals in terms of their fundamental life circumstances. Consequently, an individual's membership in a particular life-course stage is not only a factor of the four demographic determinants used to construct the life-course stages but is also tied to attitudes. Formal definitions for the construction of the life-course stages are included in Appendix C.

The National Longitudinal Survey Data

The data sets that formed the basis of our analysis were obtained from two birth cohorts of women surveyed by the National Longitudinal Surveys of Labor Market Experience (NLS) conducted by the U.S. Bureau of Labor Statistics. The NLS is one of a few government-sponsored, national surveys that follow the same individuals over a number of years.

The two birth cohorts comprised one group of five thousand women who were 30–44 years old in 1967 and a second group of five thousand women who were 14–24 years old in 1968. The individuals in both groups were contacted eleven times between 1967 and 1982, the most recent year for which data were available. Women were contacted via face-to-face interviews, mailed questionnaires, and telephone surveys. The schedule and format of the data collection effort are described in more detail in Appendix B (Table B-1).

The NLS included a number of questions that dealt with individuals' values and attitudes toward women's changing relationship to the world of employment. During the fifteen years these women were followed, they were asked questions about their attitudes toward women working outside the home, about their commitment to employment, and, for the younger group, about their plans regarding employment when they reached age 35. The measurement of each of these attitudes is discussed in more detail when the results are described. Appendix B (Table B-3) lists the years when each question was asked of the groups of women.

Advantages of the NLS

We selected the NLS data sets because they represent two of the most demographically important cohorts of women in recent United States history. The older group includes women who reached their twenties after World War II and gave birth to the baby boom. As indicated in earlier chapters, these mothers of the baby boom were unique in many important respects. In addition to being responsible for reversing a long downward trend in fertility, they differed from previous generations in terms of educational attainment, marriage, divorce, and participation in the labor force. The younger group of women is roughly representative of the baby boom. As we have also noted in previous chapters, this baby-boom cohort returned to many of the patterns and trends that were interrupted by their mothers. The baby-boom cohort regained the ground their mothers lost to men in educational attainment, returned to marriage rates and an average age at marriage that were typical of the first half of the twentieth century, and returned to a pattern of declining fertility and increasing divorce rates. But if the women of the baby-boom cohort are returning to former demographic patterns, they are doing so for new reasons. As we have already discussed in detail, the crucial distinguishing feature of the younger generation can be characterized as the rise of women as primary individuals.

We divided the two data sets into four separate five-year birth cohorts. From the sample of the older women, the first group includes those born between 1928 and 1932, and the second group is made up of women born between 1933 and 1937. The younger women were divided into those born between 1944 and 1948 and those born between 1949 and 1953. The oldest cohort, which is among the mothers of the baby boom, reached their primary childbearing ages during the peak of the baby boom, and their members were 35–39 years old when the survey began in 1967. Those from the youngest group of women were born during the baby-boom years of 1949 to 1953 and were between 15 and 19 when their first interview took place in 1968. Our analysis is largely aimed at contrasting these adjacent but dramatically different generations. The remaining middle two cohorts are used to make comparisons of same-aged women at different points in time and to confirm our generational comparisons with an additional set of birth cohorts.

LIFE-COURSE CHANGES AMONG WOMEN: 1960 TO 1980

The Factor of Aging

As a first step in examining changes in the lives of American women we applied the life-course stages to the mothers of the baby boom as they aged from 1967 (when they were 35–39 years old) to 1982 (when they were 50–54 years old), and to the baby-boom cohort as they aged from 1968 (when they were 15–19 years old) to 1982 (when they were 30–33 years old). The results, weighted to provide accurate population estimates for the United States, are displayed in Appendix Table D-1.

Changes in the life-course distributions of these two cohorts between 1967 and 1982 reflect changes that occur in the normal progression of aging. For example, the percentage of the baby-boom cohort in the student category declined as they aged, and the percent in the wife, mother, and jobholder categories increased. For the mothers of the baby boom, the percent in the mother categories declined over time as these women reached their fifties and their youngest child left home.

This process is illustrated in Figures 8.1 and 8.2. Shifts in the four largest life-course stages for the mothers of the baby boom and the baby-boom cohort, respectively, are shown in these two figures. Through their late thirties and early forties, very few mothers of the baby boom were wives or employed wives—the categories without

FIGURE 8.1

Mothers of the Baby Boom: Percent in Four Life-Course Stages, 1967–1982

Source: Appendix Table D-1.

dependent children. As the last child reached age 18, the percent of women who were wives or employed wives increased to about 13 percent of the entire cohort. Similarly, the percent who were mothers declined from 45 percent of the cohort at ages 35–39 to 18 percent by ages 50–54.

For the mothers of the baby boom, the period between 1967 and 1982, when these women reached middle age, represented a time of reduced parental responsibilities and increased involvement in the labor force. Such changes determine much of the character of a woman's life and, as is demonstrated in the next chapter, her orientations toward employment and the family.

The pattern among the baby-boom cohort is quite different. All four categories of married women increased sharply between the group aged 15–19 and those aged 20–24 as these women completed their schooling, married, had children, and entered the labor force.

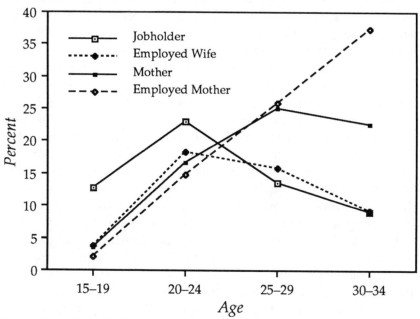

FIGURE 8.2

The Baby-Boom Cohort: Percent in Four Life-Course Stages, 1967–1982

Source: Appendix Table D-1.

The categories of jobholder and employed wife shrank as the majority of these women had their first child. Most striking is the increase in the employed mother category, which continued to grow through the early thirties while the mother category leveled off. At ages 30–34, only 23 percent of the baby-boom cohort were traditional mothers, while 37 percent were combining the roles of wife, mother, and labor force participant.

The most notable aspect of the early adult years of the baby-boom cohort is the continued importance of work outside the home, even though this period involved the assumption of major family roles and responsibilities. By 1982, 81 percent of employed women had married and 71 percent had become mothers. Consistent participation in outside employment, even during the period of family formation, demonstrates again the decreased impact of women's family roles on their relationship to the economy.

Changes in the Life Course among Women in Their Thirties

In order to consider differences in the ways the mothers of the baby boom and the baby-boom cohort organized their lives, we compared the two groups in the years when the women were in their thirties (ages 30–39): 1967 and 1982. Since the two younger cohorts in the NLS reached their thirties by 1982 and the two older cohorts were in their thirties when the survey began in 1967, it is possible to make a fifteen-year comparison. As a rule, that would be regarded as too short a time to reveal significant demographic change. In this case, however, change was so rapid that women who were in their thirties in 1967 can be shown to have led lives markedly different from the lives of women in their thirties only fifteen years later. Once again, recall that changes in the timing, sequencing, and duration of major life-course events are the factors that account for change in the life-course stages of women who reach the same age in different years.

The results for all women in their thirties are displayed in Figures 8.3 and 8.4.[1] Figure 8.3 describes the changes in terms of the percentage of women in each life-course stage, and Figure 8.4 presents the same information in terms of absolute numbers of women in each life-course stage. Because the size of the two cohorts changed considerably between 1967 and 1982, percentages are more valuable for assessing the magnitude of the change. However, the absolute number of women in each category is useful in assessing the impact of life-course changes on the demand for public and private services, such as housing and education.

Figure 8.3 demonstrates that most women in their thirties are either mothers or employed mothers. In 1967 almost half of all women in their thirties were mothers, 30 percent were employed mothers, and the remaining 20 percent were distributed among the other five stages. By 1982 the percentage of women in their thirties who were in the "traditional" status of mother (not employed) had *declined* from about half to less than one-fourth. The employed mother category correspondingly increased from 30 percent in 1967 to 41 percent in 1982.

1. The full results of our analysis are presented in Tables D-2 and D-3 of Appendix D. Appendix Table D-2 contains the results for all women in their thirties, while Appendix Table D-3 displays the results for two five-year age groups: 30–34 and 35–39.

FIGURE 8.3

The Life-Course Stages of Women in Their Thirties,
1967–1982

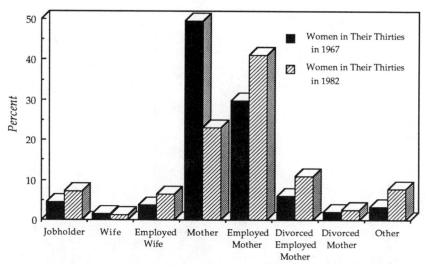

Source: Appendix Table D-2.

How striking are these changes in the life course of women in their thirties? In 1967 there were 11 million women between the ages of 30 and 39 in the United States. But by 1982, as the baby boom was reaching middle adulthood, the number of women in their thirties increased to 16 million. Despite this enormous increase in the size of the population, the absolute number of 30-year-old women in the traditional mother category actually declined, from 5.4 million to 3.7 million. Correspondingly, the population of employed mothers more than doubled, from 3.3 million in 1967 to 6.7 million in 1982.

The divorced employed mother category exhibited another significant change. In 1967 there were six hundred thousand women in this category, representing 6 percent of all women between 30 and 39. Within fifteen years the category tripled in size to 1.8 million women, 11 percent of all women in their thirties. This growth is due to the combined effects of a higher divorce rate and the increased participation of women in the labor force.

FIGURE 8.4

Number of Women by Life-Course Stage: Women in Their Thirties,
1967–1982

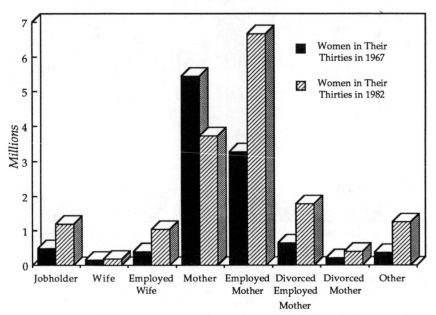

Source: Appendix Table D-2.

The enormous demographic changes discussed in the preceding chapters acquire a dramatic context when we examine shifts in the distribution of women among life-course stages. These shifts imply major alterations in the lives, social roles, and basic character of populations of women. As the magnitude of growth in the number of women who are simultaneously employed, married, and caring for children tells us, the relationship of women to the world of employment has undergone a striking transition. Clearly, work outside the home is no longer limited by traditional obligations of women to their husbands and children. Increasingly, in fact, women entering adulthood are concerned with integrating labor force participation and family responsibilities throughout their lives. Relative to almost any standard of social change, such a shift is both radical and unusually swift. In the next chapter we turn our attention to women's attitudes toward employment and the family in order to understand the implications of life-course changes for these institutions and for women's roles within them.

9

Change and Continuity in Women's Attitudes

The first half of the 1970s, during which the leading edge of the baby-boom cohort became young adults, was clearly a turning-point in the lives of American women. Among the various behavioral changes that were occurring at that time, perhaps none had wider impact than the commitment of women to continuous participation in the labor force during their prime childbearing and child-rearing years. Given the new directions in the life course of women over the last fifteen years, we can expect that women's attitudes toward their appropriate adult roles have also shifted. But the evidence suggests that, for the most part, women modified their attitudes toward work, family, marriage, child-rearing, and other aspects of the life course only *after* they had already established patterns of behavior markedly different from those of previous generations of women.

While women's attitudes changed enormously during the 1970s, becoming more similar to the attitudes that men have held since the 1960s, men's views changed at a much slower pace. The result has been the convergence of women's attitudes with men's in a number of areas. We now detail how this convergence has manifested itself.

CHANGING EMPLOYMENT ORIENTATIONS
DURING THE 1970S

On the threshold of adulthood in the late 1960s and early 1970s, baby-boom women imagined they would lead lives very similar to those their mothers had led. As they aged through their twenties and early thirties, however, their expectations and attitudes regarding family and labor force participation shifted radically.

As shown in Figure 9.1, most young women in the late 1960s expected to be full-time homemakers when they reached their mid-thirties. Among those aged 15–19 in 1968, 65 percent planned on being homemakers, as did 58 percent of women aged 20–24. Over the next five years the proportion of women in both cohorts who held this expectation declined sharply, to 41 percent of the younger group (aged 20–24 in 1973) and 37 percent of the older group (aged 25–29 in 1973). This decline continued through 1978, to approximately 20 percent for both groups, and stabilized at that level in 1982.

Figure 9.2 shows the rapid transition that took place among women in the 1970s. In contrast to the 65 percent of those aged 15–19 who planned to be homemakers in 1968, only 25 percent of this age group in 1979 had this expectation. Older women also had fewer plans to be homemakers. In 1968 over half (58 percent) of women aged 20–24 expected to be homemakers when they reached their mid-thirties compared to only 26 percent of women in this age group in 1978. By the late 1970s, then, most young women had undergone a major shift in attitudes and life plan. No longer content with traditional expectations of becoming homemakers, these women fully intended to work outside the home, even during the period when they would most likely be raising young children.

A study by Parelius (1975) points again to the critical nature of the early 1970s. In research that compared the career plans of college women in 1969 and in 1973, Parelius found, as late as 1969, that the majority of college women expected to stop working outside the home with the birth of their first child and did not plan to return to employment until their youngest child was grown. Only 16 percent planned to work outside the home throughout their adult lives (see Figure 9.3). Four years later, in 1973, the employment orientation of

FIGURE 9.1

Changes in Life-Course Plans of the Baby-Boom Generation, 1968–1982:
Percentage of Women Intending to Be Homemakers at Age 35

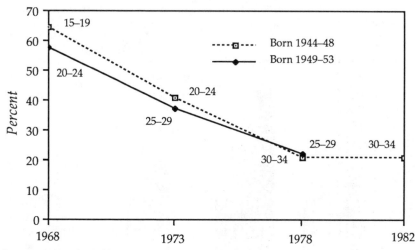

Source: Appendix Table D-4.

college women had changed dramatically. The proportion of women planning to be employed continuously throughout adulthood more than doubled, to 37 percent, and the percentage of college women who planned to devote their entire time to family responsibilities until their children were grown dropped to 37 percent. This substantial change in college women's orientation toward their major adult roles took place in just four years.

Evidence from the late 1960s and early 1970s also shows changing attitudes toward the value and legitimacy of women's employment when it is in competition, and even in conflict, with traditional family responsibilities. The National Longitudinal Survey (described in Chapter 8) asked women to indicate their approval or disapproval of a mother of preschool-aged children who entered full-time employment because of her desire to work outside the home. Two conditions were presented: first, if her husband approved, and second, if he did not. As shown in Figure 9.4, from 1968 to 1978 women of all age groups steadily increased their approval of mothers' working outside the home under both conditions.

In 1968 women in their twenties generally approved of mothers'

FIGURE 9.2

Life-Course Plans of Women by Age Group, 1968–1982: Percentage of Women Intending to Be Homemakers at Age 35

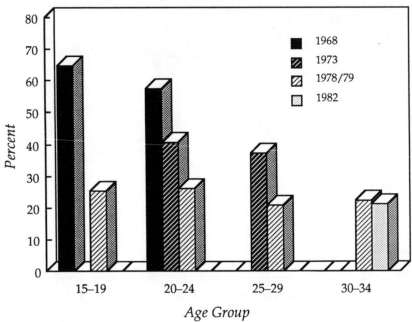

Age Group

Source: Appendix Table D-4.

working outside the home when their children are young if their husbands approved (mean of 3.5 on a 5-point scale from 1 = strongly disapprove to 5 = strongly approve). There was clear-cut disapproval, however, when the husband was not supportive (mean of 1.7). By 1978 women's approval of mothers' working outside the home with husbands' approval increased substantially (mean of 4.5), and the rise in approval was even greater in response to the husbands' disapproval (mean of 3.1 compared to a mean of 1.7 ten years earlier). Women in their thirties and forties showed similar patterns, although younger women adopted nontraditional attitudes more quickly and more extensively than older women. The most rapid period of change for women in their twenties took place between 1968 and 1972, while for women in their thirties the greatest change occurred between 1972 and 1978.

Two significant themes revealed themselves during these years.

FIGURE 9.3
Changes in Employment Plans of College Women, 1969–1973

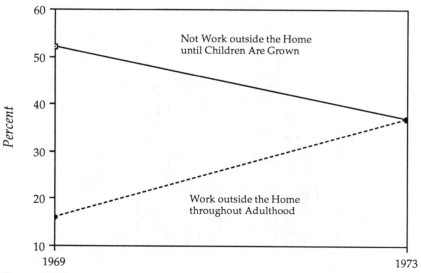

Source: Parelius 1975.

First, women began to find general approval for a substantial work commitment during the period of their greatest family responsibilities. Second, support for a married mother's preference for outside employment—even when her husband disapproved—rose significantly. As women emerged as primary individuals, the legitimacy accorded to decisions they made for their personal lives, even when they conflicted with traditional expectations, also grew.

A comparison of the baby-boom cohort with mothers of the baby boom (Figure 9.5) demonstrates that the baby-boom generation shifted its support earlier and more strongly to women's employment outside the home (even when it conflicted with their husbands' wishes). In 1967 both generations of women disapproved of mothers' working outside the home without their husbands' approval (means ranged from 1.7 to 1.8). By 1972 the mean for the baby-boom cohort had risen to 3.0, while the mean for mothers of the baby boom had risen only to 2.1. By 1978 the gap between the two generations had closed substantially; the mean score for the baby-boom cohort was 3.0 and for the mothers of the baby boom it was 2.5 (and by 1982 the mean for this older group was 2.8).

FIGURE 9.4

Attitude of Women toward Full-Time Employment of Mothers, 1968–1978

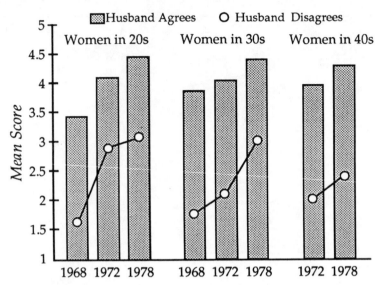

Sources: Appendix Tables D-5 and D-6.
Note: Scaled from 1 to 5, with higher scores indicating a more positive attitude.

But the enormous shift in the legitimacy and importance of work in women's lives came as no gradual trend. During the early 1970s, which stand out as a period of rapid assimilation of new behaviors and attitudes, a substantial number of women began to view commitment to outside employment as a woman's individual prerogative, largely independent of a husband's attitude. This was a change that ranged across all ages, educational levels, and standards of living. As shown in Figure 9.6, even mothers who were not in the labor force significantly increased their support for women's prerogative to choose full-time employment, despite conflict with husbands' wishes (from a mean of 1.6 in 1968 to 2.7 in the early 1970s). The older of the baby-boom cohorts experienced a rapid and radical alteration of the traditional life-course expectations they had generally held at the outset of college, marriage, and employment. The younger cohort, however, reached adulthood with attitudes already in support of a work role for women during the primary years of family building.

FIGURE 9.5

Attitude toward Mother's Working When Husband Disapproves, by Age

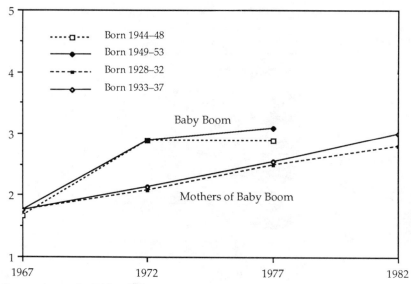

Source: Appendix Table D-6.
Note: Scaled from 1 to 5, with higher scores indicating a more positive attitude.

A Convergence in Attitudes

One important result of women's greater desire for, and participation in, work outside the home has been the steady convergence of their attitudes with those of men. While the employment behavior of women has become more similar to men's (as described in Chapter 6), women's preparation for work and career has also begun to follow the traditional course followed by men.

This shift appears first in changes in women's educational goals. Figure 9.7 shows that during the 1970s women significantly increased their focus on career preparation when asked to give their primary reason for attending college. (Other response choices included obtaining a general education, learning to get along with different types of people, developing social poise, and preparation for participation in community and public affairs.) In 1970, 21 percent of female students (and 31 percent of male students) regarded preparation for a career as the main objective of their college education. In

FIGURE 9.6

*Attitude toward Mother's Working When Husband Disapproves, by
Life-Course Stage, Age, and Year*

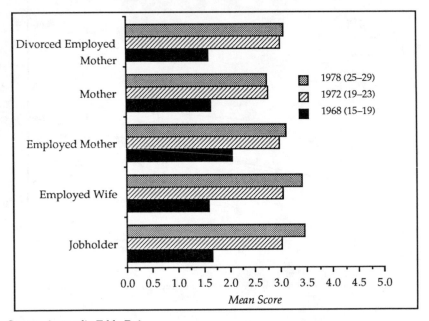

Source: Appendix Table D-6.
Note: Scaled from 1 to 5, with higher scores indicating a more positive attitude.

the same year, 18 percent of the women (versus 10 percent of the men) indicated that preparation for marriage and family was the most important reason for attending college. By 1980, however, almost no women or men (1 percent and 2 percent, respectively) considered family preparation to be an important educational goal. Instead, a plurality of both women (40 percent) and men (43 percent) saw career preparation as the major purpose of higher education (Regan and Roland 1982). From 1970 to 1980, the percentage of female students who saw career goals as primary doubled, while the percentage of male students with the same view grew by only one-fourth. The result, of course, is a convergence of the educational goals of men and women.

A similar pattern of convergence can be found in the beliefs of men and women college students regarding the importance of career and family life. As shown in Figure 9.8, the difference between men

FIGURE 9.7

Primary Reason for College Attendance: Career versus Family Goals of Men and Women, 1970–1980

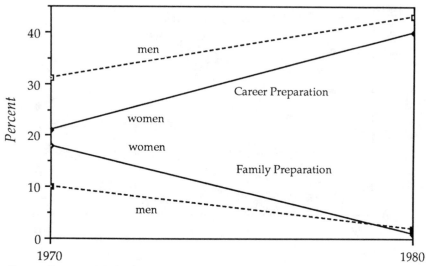

Source: Regan and Roland 1982.

and women was much greater in 1952 than in 1974. This convergence has continued, as evidenced by the trends charted for 1970–80 in Figure 9.8. During both periods (1952–74 and 1970–80), the change in attitude was greater among women than among men (Regan and Roland 1982).

The data from these two surveys of college students suggest that a significant change in orientation toward career and family took place in the early 1970s, and that it was during these years that women's work attitudes and behavior became firmly established in their confluence with men's. In 1970, for example, both women and men gave responses more similar to the 1952 responses than to the 1974 responses. The 1974 findings, which distinctly differ from those of preceding surveys, are almost identical to the 1980 results.

Surveys of entering college students (based on a national sample) from 1967 to 1984 also document convergence between the sexes (American Council on Education 1967, 1969, 1970, 1974, 1977, 1982, 1984). In 1969 women entering college were less oriented toward individual achievement than were men (see Figure 9.9). By 1984, how-

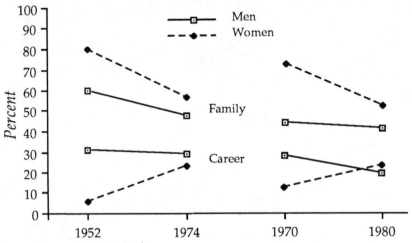

FIGURE 9.8

Percentage of College Women and Men Selecting Career versus Family as Most Important Life Goal

Source: Regan and Roland 1982.

ever, almost no difference could be found between college men and women in the extent to which they valued "having administrative responsibility" (44 percent and 41 percent), "obtaining recognition from colleagues" (56 percent and 54 percent), and "becoming an authority in [one's] field" (75 percent and 72 percent). While both men and women in this period increased their desire for such personal achievement, women, consistent with their changing orientation toward the workplace, changed to a greater extent.

In addition to converging in their personal employment and family goals, female and male college students became increasingly similar in their attitudes toward what they considered appropriate roles for adult women. As shown in Figure 9.10, fully two-thirds of males entering college in 1967 thought married women should restrict their activities to home and family, compared with slightly less than one-half of women entering college (American Council on Education 1967). By 1984 this position was held by a minority of both men and women: only 30 percent of men and 16 percent of women agreed that married women should confine themselves to the home (American Council on Education 1984). While the gap between men's and women's attitudes narrowed slightly during this period, women

FIGURE 9.9

Aspects of Individual Achievement Viewed as Very Important by College Freshmen, 1969–1984

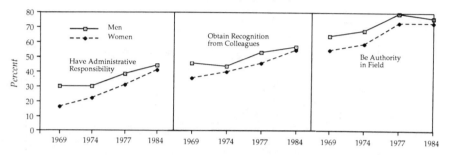

Sources: American Council on Education 1969, 1974, 1977, and 1984.

have been and continue to be less traditional than men. Again, the sharpest changes occurred in the early 1970s; thereafter, traditional attitudes declined more gradually through the late 1970s and early 1980s.

Taken together, these studies indicate that most of the convergence in men's and women's attitudes has been due to the speed with which women have adopted orientations similar to those that men have held. Men's attitudes have changed much more slowly.

CHANGES IN ATTITUDES TO ACCOMMODATE NEW BEHAVIOR

Women's significant transitions over the past two decades—in both their attitudes and their behavior—lead to an important question: Did a major shift in orientations toward women's roles lead to changes in behavior? Or did new ways of behaving begin to influence the attitudes of the time? The sequence of shifts in attitudes toward the role of women in employment and actual changes in the labor force suggest that attitudinal change, particularly regarding married women, lagged behind behavioral change.

As late as 1970, 78 percent of married women under 45 said it was better for a wife to stay at home and her husband to be employed (Oppenheimer 1970); 41 percent of married women were employed

FIGURE 9.10

Percentage of College Freshmen Agreeing That Married Women's Activities Are Best Limited to the Home, 1967–1984

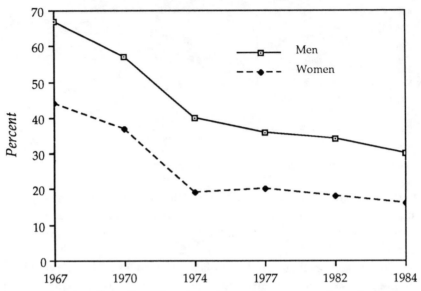

Sources: American Council on Education 1967, 1970, 1974, 1977, 1982, and 1984.

at that time. By 1979 young women's attitudes had become more congruent with women's employment behavior: only 33 percent of women aged 14–21 thought it was better for a woman to be at home (Mott and Mott 1985). In that year 50 percent of all married women and approximately 60 percent of married women aged 20–44 were in the labor force (see Chapter 6).

The more recent entry into the labor force of married women with small children has been followed by a groundswell of approval similar to that following the rapid entry of married women into the labor force during the 1950s. The percentage of women in the labor force with children under 6 increased from 12 percent in 1950 to 19 percent in 1960, 30 percent in 1970, 45 percent in 1980, and 52 percent in 1984 (Hayghe 1984). As late as 1968, approximately one-third of women in their twenties felt that a mother with preschool children should not choose to work outside the home even when her husband agreed and a "trusted relative" was available to care for her children. By 1972 only one-fifth of young women disapproved, and by 1978 there

FIGURE 9.11

Changes in Work Expectations and Employment Behavior of Women,
1968–1982

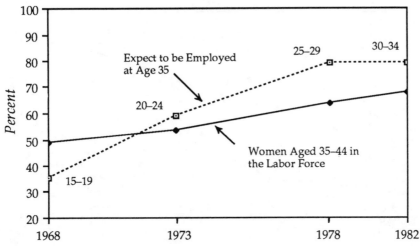

Sources: Appendix Tables D-4 and D-7.

was almost universal approval (94 percent) for the mother's working outside the home under these circumstances (Mott 1982).

In the late 1960s, when only about one-third of baby-boom women aged 15–19 anticipated outside employment when they reached their mid-thirties, about half of women currently in their mid-thirties were in the labor force. In the early 1980s, when baby-boom women entered their thirties, about two-thirds of them were actually in the labor force, double the percentage that had expected to work. The shift to expectations that were more consistent with women's actual employment behavior was completed by the mid-1970s, when the proportion of women planning to work outside the home was similar to employment rates at that time (see Figure 9.11). Employment expectations have now fully caught up with behavior and, in fact, have surpassed current employment levels for women in their thirties.

Attitudes seem to follow behavior in the realm of sexual activity as well as the world of work (see Figure 9.12). From 1960 to 1970 the percentage of women who engaged in premarital intercourse (based on self-report) increased substantially from 26 percent of white women who reached their twenties in the early 1960s to 45

FIGURE 9.12

Percentage of Women Engaging in Premarital Intercourse and Approving of Premarital Intercourse, 1960–1980

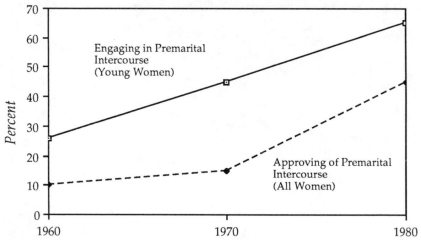

Sources: Gallup 1985; Reiss 1967, p. 27; Udry et al., p. 785; Zelnik and Kantner 1980, p. 231.

percent of white women who reached their twenties in the early 1970s (Udry et al. 1975). But women's attitudes changed little during this period. Approximately 10 percent of women approved of intercourse prior to marriage in the early 1960s (Reiss 1967) compared to approximately 15 percent at the end of the 1960s (Gallup 1985). From 1970 to 1980, the proportion of young women engaging in premarital intercourse rose sharply: by 1979, 65 percent of never-married white women aged 19 reported having had sexual relations (Zelnick and Kantner 1980). During the 1970s, a period of rapid change in other spheres, attitudes finally began to catch up with behavior. The proportion of women who approved of intercourse before marriage tripled, so that by 1985 close to half (45 percent) of all women saw nothing wrong with premarital sexual relationships (Gallup 1985).

The impact of behavior on attitudes is also evident in changes in attitudes toward divorce. One study, for example, followed a group of young women for twenty years. A longitudinal analysis of this group indicated that a woman's attitude toward divorce had no effect on the likelihood of her getting divorced in the future. Undergoing a divorce, however, did make women more approving of divorce in general. In 1962, 51 percent of respondents approved of divorce when the couple did not get along and there were children at home; by 1977 approval had increased to 80 percent, and to 82 percent in 1980 (Thornton 1985). By 1980 these women held virtually the same attitudes as their daughters, who were in their late teens at this time; 83 percent of the daughters also approved of divorce under these conditions.

Attitudes toward women's "proper" place in the family and the world of work—and the lives that today's women actually lead—have changed dramatically over the last fifteen to twenty years. But attitudinal change did not lead to subsequent changes in behavior. Rather, as we have noted in previous chapters, many external factors, including growth in female-dominated occupations in the 1950s and 1960s, helped to set in motion the greater and more extensive participation of wives and mothers in the labor force (Oppenheimer 1970), which, together with the attitudes that shifted to accommodate it, continues to have a far-reaching impact on education, marriage, childbearing, and household arrangements for women and, consequently, for men as well. Men's and women's attitudes thus appear to adapt to the actual behavior and experience of the time. Younger people tend to adopt these new attitudes more quickly than older people. Attitudes, of course, also influence behavior, affecting the plans and commitments both men and women make in preparing for their adult lives. But major external constraints and opportunities have a greater impact on the aggregate behavior of women and men than do the predominant attitudes of a given period.

THE STABILIZING OF ATTITUDES

While members of the baby-boom generation have made striking changes in their work and family roles, they have experienced tension between their new orientations and the largely traditional assumptions with which they formed marriages and began families. Incorporating new roles into the old forms has precipitated its share of struggle.

In contrast to the young women of the 1960s and 1970s, today's young women enter adulthood with a clear vision of the importance of employment in their adult lives. As shown in Figure 9.13, most

FIGURE 9.13

*Employment Behavior of Women and Employment Plans of Female
Teenagers, 1968–1979*

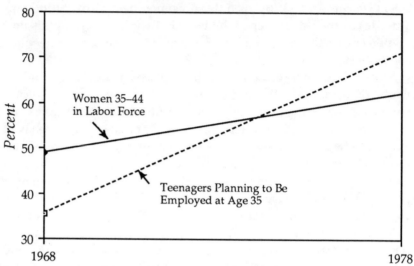

Sources: Appendix Tables D-4 and D-7.

young women in 1979 planned to work outside the home in their prime adult years, an expectation that is consistent with the reality of women's lives today. Women of the 1980s have the advantage of holding attitudes in favor of employment at a time when such attitudes can have an impact on life-course decisions. They are able to acquire the educational credentials necessary for their career objectives, they can delay marriage while accumulating training and employment experience, and they are more able to time the births of their children to minimize their impact on career goals.

Furthermore, the convergence in the personal life goals of men and women, and in men's and women's views concerning appropriate adult roles for women, suggests that women of the 1980s may face less marital conflict over the decision to combine employment and family than did women in the 1970s. This does not suggest, however, that they will actually have eliminated the barriers to combining employment and family responsibilities. Many of the constraints are not family-based but society-based. As is discussed below, institutional change, like attitudinal change, tends to lag behind changing behavior patterns.

Led by the baby-boom generation, the transition in attitudes toward combining employment and family roles is now largely completed. Because of greater congruence between the behavior and attitudes of young women today, women reaching adulthood during the 1980s are not expected to face the massive changes in orientation toward employment that the leading edge of the baby-boom generation experienced. Rather, we expect the 1980s and 1990s to be a period of consolidation and stability after the rapid behavioral and attitudinal changes of the 1970s.

THE CONTINUING COMMITMENT TO FAMILY VALUES

Given the significant demographic and attitudinal changes that have occurred over the last twenty years, can we conclude that today's woman has little use for family life? Marriage rates have declined, women are delaying marriage until they are older, divorce rates are high, living together without marriage is common, and women continue to be more career-oriented, despite conflicts with family responsibilities. But in spite of the overwhelming appearance of a decline in women's commitment to the family, there is little actual evidence that women today are placing any less value on marriage and children.

Changes in women's attitudes toward their roles in the family and toward the value of family life must be considered from two different perspectives: how women feel about their own family aspirations, plans, and objectives (described below), and how they feel about the family roles of others (discussed in the next section). The research provides two quite different pictures of attitude change depending on whether women are asked about their own lives or about the lives of others.

Marriage rates have been falling for over twenty years in the United States and fell most sharply during the early 1970s. If this behavioral change reflected a decline in the perceived value of marriage, we would expect to see declines in the percentage of young women planning to marry sometime during, or shortly after, the actual declines in marriage rates. But no such evidence exists. Drawing on data from two national surveys of high school students, in 1960 and 1980, Thornton and Freedman (1982) examined change in the intentions of adolescent men and women to marry. They found that over 90 percent of young men and women, both in 1960 and in 1980, expected to marry. Thus, while actual marriage rates were declining, the proportion of adolescents expecting to marry remained high.

In 1974 and 1985 the Virginia Slims American Women's Opinion Poll asked women what would give them "personally the most satisfying and interesting life" (Roper 1986). Being married was selected by 96 percent of all women in 1974 and by 94 percent in 1985. This commitment to marriage as an essential element of women's lives holds up across all age groups in the most recent 1985 data. Younger women held the same high regard for marriage as older women. Thus, during the same years that marriage rates declined, women continued to include plans for marriage in their lives.

Marriage is not the only aspect of the "traditional" life that American women continue to value. They also expect to have children. In 1979 less than 1 percent of young women considered having no children as the "ideal family situation," the same response found in 1971 (Borus et al. 1980). When asked about the lifestyle that would offer "the most satisfying and interesting life," 89 percent of the 1985 national sample of women from the Roper (1986) poll included children as part of that life; in 1974 the figure was 90 percent.

Although women today expect and want to have fewer children, this decline is primarily due to a drop in the number of women who plan to have three or more children. The majority of women have come to view the two-child family as ideal, while the number of women who plan to remain childless has risen very slightly.

Even the most career-oriented women, those with high educational aspirations and plans for a lifelong career, show no evidence of rejecting marriage and family for themselves. In fact, career-oriented young women are nearly identical to those with more "traditional" expectations in their desire to raise children. While career-oriented young women are less likely to plan to have three or more children, most do expect to have two children (Borus et al. 1980; Shapiro and Crowley 1983).

Change (or lack of change) in attitudes toward family roles can be effectively examined by surveying young women and men who have not yet taken on adult family roles but who have witnessed the reorganization of the life course described in Chapter 8. At several points

FIGURE 9.14

Percentage of College Freshmen Rating Commitment to Raising a Family as Very Important, 1969–1984

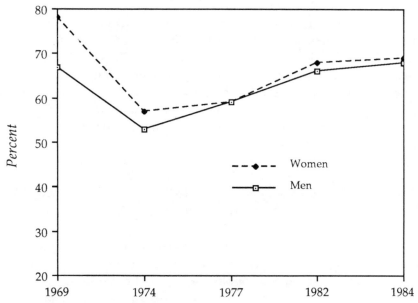

Sources: American Council on Education 1969, 1974, 1977, 1982, and 1984.

between 1969 and 1984, college freshmen rated the importance (for their own lives) of raising a family. The percentage indicating that raising a family was "very important" is shown for both women and men in Figure 9.14.

Figure 9.14 illustrates three important points. First, the overall level of commitment to raising a family is extremely high. The question permitted both "important" and "very important" responses; so the rates of 60 to 80 percent for "very important" responses document the central role that family aspirations played in the life-course plans of women in 1969 and continue to play today.

Second, even this item was modestly affected by the dramatic shifts in attitudes that took place during the early 1970s. Unlike attitudes toward other aspects of women's lives, however, commitment to the family quickly resumed its previous high levels and has demonstrated remarkable stability over the last ten years.

Finally, these data further document the convergence of women's attitudes with men's. In 1969 almost 10 percent more women than men regarded "raising a family" as "very important." Since 1974, however, males and females have responded almost identically to this question.

Here is a clear and consistent picture of the role of the family in the life plans of American women. Getting married and raising children are still essential ingredients in women's projections for a satisfying life. Women have in no way decreased their commitment to the family, despite changes in marriage rates, career aspirations, and work behavior that might suggest otherwise. In the face of the enormous transitions that women have experienced, the core family values remain stable.

INCREASING TOLERANCE FOR THE AUTONOMY OF OTHER WOMEN

As women reassert the importance of marriage and children for their personal happiness, do they insist that others follow their example? In fact, substantial evidence points to just the opposite conclusion: women's tolerance has increased for those who do not choose to have families and for those whose ways of life, in the recent past, were considered inappropriate and illegitimate. This increased respect for the autonomy of others in making life-course decisions is consistent with the rise of women as primary individuals that we have documented in this book. Although most women continue to choose family roles for themselves, for others they clearly view family life as a choice and not a requirement.

In 1957 over half of a sample of American adults were negative and over a third were neutral about an individual who intended never to marry; by 1976 one-third were negative and half were neutral (Thornton and Freedman 1982). In 1985, 72 percent of American women reported believing "a woman could have a complete and happy life if she remained single" (Roper 1986). Similarly, there is more acceptance of the choice of others to remain childless today. In 1962, 84 percent of a sample of mothers agreed that "almost everyone should have children if they can." By 1980, about half of these women had changed their position; only 43 percent agreed with the statement (Thornton and Freedman 1982).

Attitudes toward those who elect to end a marriage have similarly changed. As mentioned earlier, in 1962 almost half (49 percent) of women felt that a couple with children should stay together even though "they don't get along." By 1980, however, 81 percent approved of divorce for such a couple (Thornton 1985).

These figures suggest the emergence of a more individualistic orientation toward the decisions that must inevitably be made when personal and family goals come into conflict. At least partly in response to this, women have decided to delay marriage and to have fewer children. In 1960, for example, 68 percent of 18-year-old women indicated that they expected to be married by age 22. But by 1980, less than half (48 percent) of 18-year-old women expected to be married by that age (Thornton and Freedman 1982). Women's marriage and child-rearing plans must now be integrated with other, more independent, often career-oriented life objectives. Although women have not diminished their desire for family life, they no longer see marriage and child-rearing as priorities in planning and organizing their lives. This reappraisal of family, personal, and career goals also appears in the increased willingness of young women and men to postpone marriage in order to complete school or acquire employment experience. In 1980, 50 percent of 18-year-old women and 60 percent of 18-year-old men said they would postpone marriage by one year rather than reduce full-time school attendance. About half of the 18-year-old men and women thought it was very important to be employed full time for a year before marriage; only 10 to 15 percent felt that employment experience prior to marriage was not important (Thornton and Freedman 1982).

Additional evidence of the extent to which life-course decisions have become more individualistic can be found in the National Longitudinal Survey data concerning the appropriateness of married mothers' working outside the home when the husband approved and when he disapproved. These two questions provide an opportunity to assess change in the impact of the husband's opinion. Women who respond very differently to the two conditions are strongly affected by the husband's opinion, suggesting that, in their view, the appropriateness of a married mother's employment is contingent on the approval of her husband. Those who respond in the same fashion evaluate the proper role of married mothers in the labor force independently of the opinion of the spouse.

By subtracting the response to the "husband disagrees" item from the response to the "husband agrees" item, we estimated the extent to which respondents considered the husband's opinion in their approval or disapproval of a mother's working outside the home. The results indicate a significant decline in the effect of the husband's approval on women's attitudes toward mothers' working outside the home. The choice, apparently, is increasingly seen as belonging to individual women.

CONCLUSION

As we have seen, women's attitudes toward their roles in society changed most dramatically during a comparatively brief span of time, the late 1960s and early 1970s. The leading edge of the baby-boom generation began adulthood with attitudes and expectations very similar to those of their mothers—which would be deemed "traditional" by today's standards. As those first birth cohorts of the baby boom were aging into their twenties and early thirties, they accomplished a remarkable shift in outlook and attitude, which later cohorts of the baby boom took to be firmly established. That is, they were prepared to include both a lifelong commitment to labor force participation and plans for marriage and children in their life-course decisions.

An important conclusion to be drawn from our analysis is that most attitudes among women changed after the associated behavior was already fairly common. For example, women tended to approve of married mothers' working outside the home once the numbers of married mothers in the labor force had significantly increased. Similarly, premarital intercourse was generally viewed as acceptable only after it had become more prevalent. Thus, with regard to basic aspects of family life, behavior has changed first, often in response to external factors; then new attitudes have emerged, serving to accommodate and reflect the newly established patterns of behavior. In many respects, the attitudinal changes described in this chapter reveal more about where American women have been than where they are going.

Another point to be emphasized is that over the last twenty years both women's behavior and their attitudes have begun to converge with those of men. This is most evident in the areas of education and employment, in which the demographic behavior of women has returned to patterns that preceded the baby boom, the difference being that women see a greater possibility of pursuing the kinds of careers that formerly were identified with men. It should not be surprising, then, that women's views about their own involvement in the labor force should be similar to the views that men have typically had about being employed. The convergence in attitudes is primarily due, however, to changes in the way women perceive educational attainment, employment, and family responsibilities; men have changed much less.

The dominant pattern of attitudinal change supports our projection that the demographic behavior of women will be far more stable than it has been in the recent past. The period of transition, in which attitudes were catching up with behavior that was already in place, appears to have been essentially completed. Beginning with the trailing edge of the baby-boom generation, women have entered early adulthood expecting a significant role in the labor force, and they have been able to act on their expectations. As a result, the new normative life course of women includes higher levels of education, more flexible living arrangements, delayed marriage, and delayed motherhood. Women of today assume that employment will be an integral, continuous part of their adult lives.

Part Four
Summary and Outlook

10

Changes across Three Generations of American Women

The previous chapters describe in detail a number of important changes in the life course of American women. The descriptions of behavioral change are arranged in a series of specific demographic topics—educational attainment, marriage rates, fertility, etc.—and then supplemented with an analysis of women's attitudes over the last twenty years. Although the discussion of specific topics in sequence is an effective way to present research findings, it does not provide a concise summary of how demographic and attitudinal changes have affected the way different generations of American women have organized their lives.

Throughout this volume, implicit comparisons are drawn between the experiences of three different groups of women: those born in the late 1920s and 1930s who gave birth to the baby-boom generation in the 1950s; their daughters, the baby-boomers who entered adulthood in the late 1960s and early 1970s; and a new generation of women, the daughters of the baby-boomers who will be reaching adulthood in the late 1980s and the 1990s. For ease of comparison, we refer to each of these groups as a distinct "generation" of women in order to highlight the differences in their life patterns. As described in earlier chapters, the experiences of each generation have differed in the areas of education, employment, marriage, sex, and fertility. The objective of this final chapter is to integrate our findings in these areas by reorganizing them into descriptions of the life course as experienced by each of these three generations.

THE MOTHERS OF THE BABY-BOOM GENERATION

The generation of women born in the 1920s and 1930s differed significantly in their family patterns from both their mothers' and daughters' experiences. In general, the mothers of the baby boom married earlier, had their first child sooner after marriage, and had larger families than the generations of women that immediately preceded and followed them. They also were less likely to divorce than either their mothers or their daughters. During the 1950s, when these women were in their prime adult years, marriage and the family were clearly the dominant forces in the lives of American women.

Because of the family's importance to this generation of women, they were circumscribed by their family commitments to a greater extent than the generations preceding or following them. For the first time in the twentieth century women's educational attainments did not keep pace with those of men, who made rapid advances in the postwar era largely because of GI Bill assistance for college attendance. In terms of employment, the mothers of the baby boom were a major part of the beginning of a rapidly accelerating rate of women's labor force participation. During this period of the 1950s, however, women's employment was largely structured around the demands of their family roles. That is, women for whom continuous employment was not an economic necessity worked before marriage, and to a lesser extent after marriage, withdrawing from the labor force when their first child was born and typically reentering it only after their youngest child was grown. Their employment was almost exclusively in occupations clearly identified as female jobs, mostly in the growing service sector of the economy. The major exception to this pattern was the temporary employment of women in a wider range of occupations during World War II.

In order to understand the behavior of the mothers of the baby boom, it is critical to recognize the historical events they experienced and the probable impact of those events on their lives. Most members of this generation experienced the Great Depression when they were children. The depression had substantial lifelong impacts on basic values and life ambitions of the entire United States population and had a particularly dramatic impact for those who experienced it as children (Elder 1974). The close interdependence between the family's well-being and the well-being of its individual members is heightened during times of adversity. The sudden loss of income from the father caused mothers to assume a more central role in the depression family. Older children sometimes assumed adult roles by taking on partial responsibility for economic support or by providing child care and other household tasks. During this period of family-centered efforts to survive, mother-daughter relationships were often strengthened, and these bonds appeared to encourage women to seek mobility through marriage rather than through labor force participation (Elder 1985).

As these "children of the Great Depression" (Elder 1974) reached adulthood, they encountered World War II, another major historical upheaval with far-reaching implications for marriage, the family, and the economy. With the advent of the war the economy began to grow rapidly and, because of the relatively small birth cohort of the depression years, the wages available to both men and women began to climb. Marriage rates rose sharply. Couples married earlier, had their first child soon after marriage, and had larger families. This was partially motivated by the relative economic prosperity expected and—for the most part—realized by this generation.

THE BABY-BOOM GENERATION

The major consequence of the demographic behavior of the cohort of women described above was the creation of what is now called the baby-boom generation. This cohort of women, typically defined as those born between 1946 and 1964, has long been the subject of study by sociologists, economists, demographers, political scientists, and market researchers. By virtue of their numbers alone, this generation has had profound effects on every social institution in the United States. They have forced a restructuring of the educational system, the political system, the labor force, and the family.

The life course of the baby-boomers has differed more dramatically from that of their mothers than any previous pair of adjacent generations in the twentieth century. This generation is now between 24 and 42 years old, the age range during which their mothers' lives were devoted to raising families.

But baby-boom women have experienced an overwhelming shift toward lives that involve simultaneous participation in marriage, employment, and parenthood. From 1967 to 1982—in just fifteen years —the number of women in their thirties who were married employed mothers doubled from slightly more than 3 million to over 6.5 million. During the same time period, the number of women who were "traditional" mothers declined sharply. In 1967 one-half of all women in their thirties were married mothers and full-time homemakers; by 1982 only one-fourth of women in their thirties held this traditional role.

As women with traditional views added the responsibilities of outside work to those they already shouldered at home, the era of the "super mom" was established. Studies of household and outside work during the late 1960s and early 1970s show that employed wives worked a substantially greater number of total hours than employed husbands (Walker and Woods 1976; Robinson 1977).

The "trailing edge" of the baby boom has departed from the marriage and childbearing patterns of their mothers largely in response to the new array of opportunities for economic independence that has become available to them. Recognizing these opportunities, such women have turned to education, not to become better mothers or wives but to acquire the credentials and skills to succeed in the labor market. The decision to prepare for employment through higher education is a rational one for the women of this group, for there are obvious benefits in the form of increased earning potential. Moreover, given current rates of marital dissolution, the baby-boom woman's acquisition of education and work experience can serve as insurance against the prospect of becoming financially unable to support herself and her children.

The additional time spent acquiring educational credentials has led to a delay in average age at marriage. For some, the educational experience and the prospect of a successful career have led to an avoidance of marriage altogether. The opportunity to be economically independent, in addition to being linked to the timing of marriage, has also fundamentally changed the ground rules within which the decisions to marry and remain married are made. In short, the attractiveness of early marriage, from the perspective of women, has declined as the option of remaining single has become more viable.

Although these data indicate that marriage as a social institution has declined, they must be interpreted cautiously. The fact remains that most baby-boom women have married. There is no evidence of a wholesale rejection of marriage and the family as social institutions. However, relative to their mothers' life course, the life course of women of the baby-boom generation is controlled less by marriage and family and more by the combination of employment with later marriage, fewer children, and larger proportions of their lives spent as single independent adults.

THE DAUGHTERS OF THE BABY-BOOM GENERATION

The daughters of the baby-boom generation are now of school age. Mothers born at the peak of the baby boom (about 1957) have children entering the early grades, and rapid growth in enrollment is already causing a problem. (While their fertility rates are extremely low, the size of the baby-boom cohort has resulted in an increasing absolute number of births.) The way this generation organizes its life course will be a major factor shaping the future of our social institutions. The following discussion of that future is based only on informed speculation; no formal projections or predictive models have been employed.

We anticipate that the recent pattern of the rising importance of the primary individual will continue throughout the lifetime of this generation. We expect that the educational attainments of women, driven by improving opportunities for women in the labor force, will retain their current parity with those of men. We also expect women to continue entering previously male occupations, and, largely because of the opening of occupational doors, we expect more direct competition between the sexes for both jobs and wages. The net result will be a substantial increase in women's wages relative to men's. However, projections that this generation will enjoy a substantial wage advantage over their mothers' generation because of the relatively smaller size of the cohort are expected to fall short because of the direct wage competition between the sexes, which will retard the wage growth of the entire cohort. In other words, the labor force participation of women is expected to continue to increase, which will increase the supply of labor, thereby lowering wages and partially offsetting the advantages of the cohort's smaller size. Because some of the growth in women's labor force participation is expected to take place within male-dominated jobs, wage competition between men and women becomes a real issue. The segregation of males and females into different occupations has precluded a great deal of wage competition among past cohorts of working women and men. As the labor force behavior of this generation becomes more like that of men, the sex of the employee will become less relevant and the male-female wage gap will begin to decline. However, we do not expect that the labor force participation rates of women will equal those of men, nor do we expect that the occupational segregation of the sexes will disappear or that the wage gap will be completely eliminated in the foreseeable future. On the other hand, we do expect to see evidence of trends in this direction during the adult years of the daughters of the baby-boom generation.

As women increase their role in the labor force, we anticipate a continuing erosion in the control exercised by marriage and the family over the life course of women. Sexual behavior outside of formal marriage will continue at its currently high rates, and cohabitation in the form of temporary trial marriages will continue to increase. The proportion of this generation never marrying will continue to increase and will reach record levels. Age at marriage will continue to rise slowly.

Divorce rates are also expected to continue at their currently high levels or perhaps rise slightly. This prediction stems from the reduced stigma attached to divorce and the expectation that the gains from marriage, for women, will continue to decline. Higher divorce rates coupled with lower marriage rates and older ages at first marriage will result in an even smaller proportion of this generation's life being spent married. The vast majority will marry as generations have in the past, but the average duration of marriages will continue to fall.

Fertility rates also are expected to decline slightly for this generation. This decline will not be dramatic and will be primarily due to a small increase in the proportion of all married couples who remain childless. We expect there to be little or no decline in the average family size of those couples who have children. As contraceptive technology improves, a higher proportion of children will be planned and timed in a fashion that minimizes the conflict between the duties of child-rearing and the other goals and aspirations of the parents.

We have speculated that women's participation in the labor force will continue to increase without any significant decrease in the value they place on marriage and rearing children. Assuming that the numbers of women desiring to combine employment, marriage, and parenthood will stabilize at their current levels, we conclude that one of the major issues confronting families, employers, social-policy makers, and individual women is the resolution of problems associated with their efforts to "have it all."

For both sexes, marriage and family, including children, remain essential elements of the "good life." The key to understanding the transition that has taken place is that women are no longer willing to choose between family life and a career: they want and expect both, just as men always have.

But in order to accommodate both a career and a family, women are making adjustments to their life course that have enormous demographic consequences. But even these adjustments in the life course have not eliminated all tension between the workplace and the family, for individual flexibility is severely limited in its ability to resolve conflicts that stem from the inherent nature or current organization of these institutions without sacrificing commitment to one or the other. For example, delaying marriage beyond the mid-thirties severely limits a woman's chances of ever marrying; delaying childbearing to the forties reduces the likelihood of her being able to have children and has significant implications for her health; and delaying a career until after her family is established or dropping out of the work force during childbearing years limits her job opportunities and income growth as well as curtails access to many higher-level occupations. A woman's work role suffers as well when she takes time off because of sick children or problems with child care, or is unable to assume a new position that requires a geographic move.

If women are to play a central, productive role in the economy while retaining their commitment to family life, then the structural characteristics of the family and the workplace will have to be adjusted. To date most of the adjustment to conflicts arising out of women's multiple roles has been limited to individuals, primarily women (Rapoport 1971; Myrdal and Klein 1956; Rossi 1964). However, men are beginning to make some adjustments as well—for example, by increasing their involvement with their children. In addition, when household work and outside employment are both considered, recent data indicate a narrowing of the gap between employed wives and employed husbands in total workload. This change, however, is due primarily to women's spending less time on housework rather than to husbands' spending more time (Pleck 1985). To some extent this reflects the increasing use of service industries such as professional day care and restaurants. It may also signal less willingness on the part of employed women to carry most of the household workload. Both men and women today enter marriage with altered expectations for the division of domestic labor. Most young men as well as most young women agree that both husband and wife should share household work (Borus et al. 1980). Whether this equitable belief will be put into practice remains to be seen.

While today's women clearly plan to combine employment and family, and most men also expect this, the actual structure of employment has changed only slightly. Women's demand for changes in the workplace will continue to rise, as will men's. Men are also experiencing the difficulties of combining work and family life, both indirectly—through the impact on their wives—and often directly as they attempt to cope with their own conflicting commitments. Employers are similarly facing the problems raised by relocation of dual-career families, the growing demand for flexible work schedules, and the appeal for employer-provided day care.

Although some employers have responded in limited ways to their workers' needs, changes in work requirements (e.g., weekly hours, schedules, leaves) are often introduced only on an ad hoc basis to accommodate a highly valued individual employee. With the combination of higher education, longer job tenure, and delayed childbearing, we anticipate that many more women (and men) will be well-established, valued employees at the time they first assume parental responsibilities. Eventually, the pressures from this growing group may be sufficient to create broad policy changes in the workplace. However, absorption of the impact of workers' competing responsibilities is likely to continue to fall to the family for some time to come.

Appendixes

Female Labor Force Participation Rates by Age

Year	Total	16–19[1]	20–24	25–34	35–44	45–54	55–64	65+
					Age			
1890	18.2%	24.5%	30.2%	15.1%		12.1%		7.6%
1900	20.0	26.8	31.7	17.5		13.6		8.3
1920	22.7	28.4	37.5	21.7		16.5		7.3
1930	23.6	22.8	41.8	24.6		18.0		7.3
1940	25.8	18.9	45.6	30.5		20.2		6.1
1945	35.8	39.2	55.3	39.0		31.2		9.0
1950	33.9	41.0	46.0	34.0	39.1	37.9	27.0	9.7
1955	35.7	39.7	45.9	34.9	41.6	43.8	32.5	10.6
1960	37.7	39.3	46.1	36.0	43.4	49.8	37.2	10.8
1965	39.3	38.0	49.9	38.5	46.1	50.9	41.1	10.0
1970	43.3	44.0	57.7	45.0	51.1	54.4	43.0	9.7
1975	46.3	49.1	64.1	54.6	55.8	54.6	41.0	8.3
1980	51.5	52.9	68.9	65.5	65.5	59.9	41.3	8.1
1981	52.1	51.8	69.6	66.7	66.8	61.1	41.4	8.0
1982	52.6	51.4	69.8	68.0	68.0	61.6	41.8	7.9
1983	52.9	50.8	69.9	69.0	68.7	61.9	41.5	7.8

[1] 14–19 years for 1940 and 1945.

Sources: U.S. Bureau of the Census 1975 and 1984i; U.S. Department of Labor, Bureau of Labor Statistics, 1983.

National Longitudinal Surveys of Labor Market Experience

The original National Longitudinal Surveys of Labor Market Experience (NLS) samples were drawn in 1967 by the United States Bureau of the Census. Each cohort was a multistage probability sample within 235 sample areas representing 485 counties and every state, as well as the District of Columbia. Sampling weights were assigned to each case so that estimates of the entire population could be made. These weights have been adjusted each year to reflect sample attrition for reasons other than death. In order to meet the data set's original objective of examining racial differences in labor force participation, blacks were over-sampled. The older cohort began with a sample of 5,393 women and the younger cohort with 5,533 women. After reductions due to ineligible households, the actual samples were 5,083 and 5,159 for the older and younger cohorts, respectively.

These two cohorts were initially selected by the Department of Labor because they represented very different sets of employment problems. The younger group was useful for examining the process of choosing an occupation, finding the first job, and preparing for employment. The older group was selected because it provided an opportunity to study the process by which married women reentered the labor force as their children grew older and no longer required their presence in the home. Although this rationale seems dated today—given the high rates of women's participation in the labor force regardless of their children's ages—labor force participation was, for this older cohort, closely linked to the presence of dependent children.

Although attrition from the sample was a major concern, the actual loss of respondents was quite low. Ten years after the first survey, the completion rates were 78 percent for older women and 76 percent for the younger women. By 1982, fifteen years after the first interview, the completion rates were 71 percent for the younger women and 70 percent for the older women. These are remarkably high rates for a national survey that follows the same individuals for fifteen years, and they suggest that the results described in this report may be generalized to the population of American women in the selected age ranges.

The schedule and format of respondent contacts for the two female cohorts is illustrated in Appendix Table B-1.

APPENDIX TABLE B-1
Timing and Methods of Data Collection

Year	Women Aged 30–44 in 1967	Women Aged 14–24 in 1968
1967	Interview	—
1968	Mailed Questionnaire	Interview
1969	Interview	Interview
1970	—	Interview
1971	Interview	Interview
1972	Interview	Interview
1973	—	Interview
1974	Telephone Survey	—
1975	—	Telephone Survey
1976	Telephone Survey	—
1977	Interview	Telephone Survey
1978	—	Interview
1979	Telephone Survey	—
1980	—	Telephone Survey
1981	Telephone Survey	—
1982	Interview	Telephone Survey

In order to clarify these comparisons, Appendix Table B-2 shows the year of birth of each NLS cohort used in the analysis and the ages of each cohort at several interview years. The first type of comparison involves following one or more cohorts as the women age. This corresponds to an analysis of women from one or more of the rows of Appendix Table B-2. The second type of comparison involves studying women of different ages at a particular point in time. This corresponds to an analysis of one or more columns of Appendix Table B-2. Finally, comparisons of same-aged women can be made at different times. Women who were 30–34 years old in 1967 can be compared to women who were 30–34 years old in 1978. Each of these types of comparisons is used in our analysis.

APPENDIX TABLE B-2

Ages of Women by Interview Year and Year of Birth

	Interview Year			
Year of Birth	1967–68	1972–73	1977–78	1982
1928–1932[a]	(35–39)	(40–44)	(45–49)	(50–54)
1933–1937	(30–34)	(35–39)	(40–44)	(45–49)
1944–1948	(20–24)	(25–29)	(30–34)	(34–38)
1949–1953[a]	(15–19)	(20–24)	(25–29)	(29–34)

[a]Mothers of the baby boom
[b]The baby-boom cohort

The scheduling of the various NLS attitude items used in this report is illustrated in Appendix Table B-3.

APPENDIX TABLE B-3

Timing of Attitude Items for the Two Birth Cohorts

Attitude Variables	Women Aged 30–44 in 1967	Women Aged 14–24 in 1968
Locus of Control	1969, 1972, 1977	1970, 1973, 1978
Desired Occupations at Age 35	—	1968, 1973, 1978, 1982
Attitude Toward Mothers' Employment	1967, 1972, 1977, 1982	1968, 1972, 1978
Commitment to Employment	1967, 1972, 1976, 1982	1970, 1972, 1978

The Construction of Life-Course Stages from the National Longitudinal Surveys

For each respondent and for each year, the National Longitudinal Survey data contain information on marital status, employment, children, and student status. The "student" variable was useful only for two age groups: the group aged 15–19 and, to a lesser extent, the group aged 20–24. Consequently, we formed a classification scheme based on the "marital status," "children," and "employment" variables and then classified any remaining respondent who was enrolled in school full-time as a "student." The resulting life-course stages are defined below:

1. Student: all full-time students who are not married, not employed, and who have no children under 18 years old. This classification is used only for the two youngest age groups.

2. Jobholder: all never-married women who are currently in the labor force and who have no dependent children.

3. Wife: all currently married women who are not in the labor force and who have no dependent children.

4. Employed Wife: all currently married women who are in the labor force and who have no dependent children.

5. Mother: all currently married women who are not in the labor force and who live with at least one child under 18 years old.

6. Employed Mother: all currently married women who are in the labor force and who live with at least one child under 18 years old.

7. Divorced Employed Mother: all ever-married women not currently married who are in the labor force and who live with at least one child under 18 years old.

8. Divorced Mother: all ever-married women who are not currently married, who are not in the labor force, and who live with at least one child under 18 years old.

9. Other: the residual category containing all combinations not classified above.

When these categories are applied to the NLS data, three different types of comparisons can be made. First, it is possible to compare the distribution of women of different ages within the same year(s). This reveals differences in life course within the same year among women born in different years. Second, it is possible to compare the distribution of the same group of women as they aged between 1967 and 1982. This demonstrates the effect of aging on life-course stage. The third comparison is among women of the same age in different years. This describes changes in life course among women of the same age at different points in time.

Appendix Table C-1 presents the results of applying the life-course stages to all four cohorts in each of the four years used in this report. The table reports unweighted sample counts on which the population estimates reported in the text are based.

APPENDIX TABLE C-1

Unweighted Sample Size for Each Cohort, Period, and Life-Course Stage

Women Born 1949–1953	1968 Age=15–19		1973 Age=20–24		1978 Age=25–29		1982 Age=29–33	
	N	%	N	%	N	%	N	%
Student	1,037	37.7%	205	9.1%				
Jobholder	324	11.8%	485	21.5%	267	13.4%	167	9.0%
Wife	92	3.3%	107	4.7%	43	2.2%	23	1.2%
Employed Wife	93	3.4%	356	15.8%	268	13.4%	151	8.1%
Mother	193	7.0%	355	15.7%	449	22.5%	370	19.9%
Employed Mother	65	2.4%	362	16.0%	526	26.4%	665	35.8%
Divorced Employed Mother	10	0.4%	83	3.7%	151	7.6%	212	11.4%
Divorced Mother	15	0.5%	56	2.5%	65	3.3%	54	2.9%
Other	925	33.6%	247	10.9%	225	11.3%	213	11.5%
Total	2,754	100.0%	2,256	100.0%	1,994	100.0%	1,855	100.0%

Women Born 1944–1948	1968 Age=20–24		1973 Age=25–29		1978 Age=30–34		1982 Age=34–38	
	N	%	N	%	N	%	N	%
Jobholder	514	23.5%	156	8.6%	97	6.1%	78	5.2%
Wife	125	5.7%	49	2.7%	25	1.6%	15	1.0%
Employed Wife	300	13.7%	182	10.0%	80	5.0%	46	3.1%
Mother	550	25.1%	600	33.1%	495	31.0%	320	21.5%
Employed Mother	330	15.1%	513	28.3%	582	36.5%	657	44.1%
Divorced Employed Mother	45	2.1%	114	6.3%	149	9.3%	207	13.9%
Divorced Mother	34	1.6%	66	3.6%	62	3.9%	51	3.4%
Other	289	13.2%	132	7.3%	106	6.6%	115	7.7%
Total	2,187	100.0%	1,812	100.0%	1,596	100.0%	1,489	100.0%

Women Born 1949–1953	1967 Age = 30–34		1972 Age = 35–39		1977 Age = 40–44		1982 Age = 45–49	
	N	%	N	%	N	%	N	%
Jobholder	73	4.5%	46	3.2%	33	2.6%	31	2.7%
Wife	21	1.3%	21	1.5%	42	3.3%	68	5.9%
Employed Wife	59	3.7%	44	3.1%	70	5.5%	144	12.4%
Mother	720	44.7%	512	36.1%	337	26.3%	226	19.5%
Employed Mother	488	30.3%	518	36.5%	499	38.9%	382	32.9%
Divorced Employed Mother	116	7.2%	140	9.9%	153	11.9%	137	11.8%
Divorced Mother	55	3.4%	69	4.9%	53	4.1%	56	4.8%
Other	80	5.0%	69	4.9%	95	7.4%	117	10.1%
Total	1,612	100.0%	1,419	100.0%	1,282	100.0%	1,161	100.0%

Women Born 1928–1932	1967 Age = 35–39		1972 Age = 40–44		1977 Age = 45–49		1982 Age = 50–54	
	N	%	N	%	N	%	N	%
Jobholder	53	3.3%	41	2.9%	34	2.7%	27	2.4%
Wife	30	1.8%	41	2.9%	87	6.8%	154	13.5%
Employed Wife	64	3.9%	74	5.1%	124	9.7%	193	16.9%
Mother	652	40.1%	464	32.3%	310	24.4%	193	16.9%
Employed Mother	576	35.4%	541	37.6%	441	34.6%	269	23.6%
Divorced Employed Mother	135	8.3%	134	9.3%	133	10.4%	115	10.1%
Divorced Mother	58	3.6%	71	4.9%	58	4.6%	64	5.6%
Other	59	3.6%	72	5.0%	86	6.8%	127	11.1%
Total	1,627	100.0%	1,438	100.0%	1,273	100.0%	1,142	100.0%

APPENDIX D

Supporting Tables for National Longitudinal Surveys

APPENDIX TABLE D-1

Life-Course Stage Distribution for the Mothers of the Baby Boom and the Baby-Boom Cohort: 1967–1982

Mothers of the Baby Boom

	1967 Age = 35–39		1972 Age = 40–44		1977 Age = 45–49		1982 Age = 50–54	
Life-Course Stage	N	%	N	%	N	%	N	%
Jobholder	242,490	4.1%	196,100	3.4%	178,380	3.1%	143,084	2.5%
Wife	102,570	1.7%	177,180	3.0%	419,890	7.4%	842,162	15.0%
Employed Wife	216,680	3.7%	279,980	4.8%	588,470	10.4%	1,041,836	18.6%
Mother	2,628,540	44.8%	2,057,500	35.4%	1,477,130	26.0%	1,017,810	18.1%
Employed Mother	2,055,410	35.0%	2,230,420	38.4%	2,044,800	36.0%	1,345,621	24.0%
Divorced Employed Mother	332,230	5.7%	448,970	7.7%	510,300	9.0%	453,266	8.1%
Divorced Mother	144,070	2.5%	196,840	3.4%	148,590	2.6%	229,018	4.1%
Other	151,060	2.6%	222,390	3.8%	316,930	5.6%	538,606	9.6%
Total	5,873,230	100.0%	5,809,380	100.0%	5,684,490	100.0%	5,611,403	100.0%

Baby-Boom Cohort

Life-Course Stage	1968 Age = 15–19		1973 Age = 20–24		1978 Age = 25–29		1982 Age = 30–33	
	N	%	N	%	N	%	N	%
Student	6,171,880	68.0%	876,150	9.9%	1,201,890	13.6%	810,120	9.1%
Jobholder	1,152,380	12.7%	2,019,950	22.9%	225,730	2.6%	108,810	1.2%
Wife	267,570	2.9%	478,230	5.4%	1,389,750	15.8%	828,110	9.3%
Employed Wife	339,930	3.7%	1,614,580	18.3%	2,208,890	25.1%	2,001,590	22.6%
Mother	309,370	3.4%	1,465,150	16.6%	2,277,240	25.8%	3,303,880	37.3%
Employed Mother	183,310	2.0%	1,306,110	14.8%	545,120	6.2%	833,040	9.4%
Divorced Employed Mother	18,810*	0.2%	260,550	3.0%				
Divorced Mother	29,480*	0.3%	174,520	2.0%	192,300	2.2%	187,320	2.1%
Other	608,860	6.7%	628,520	7.1%	771,320	8.8%	794,760	9.0%
Total	9,081,590	100.0%	8,823,760	100.0%	8,812,240	100.0%	8,867,630	100.0%

*Cell is based on fewer than 25 unweighted cases.

APPENDIX TABLE D-2
Life-Course Stages of Women in Their Thirties: 1967 versus 1982

	Women in Their Thirties in 1967[a]		Women in Their Thirties in 1982[b]		Change: 1967–1982	
	N	%	N	%	N	%
Jobholder	497,720	4.5%	1,185,870	7.3%	688,150	138.3%
Wife	154,680	1.4%	188,130	1.2%	33,450	21.6%
Employed Wife	397,040	3.6%	1,047,520	6.5%	650,480	163.8%
Mother	5,448,760	49.6%	3,717,500	23.0%	−1,731,260	−31.8%
Employed Mother	3,272,120	29.8%	6,660,390	41.1%	3,388,270	103.6%
Divorced Employed Mother	644,520	5.9%	1,763,810	10.9%	1,119,290	173.7%
Divorced Mother	219,520	2.0%	383,780	2.4%	164,260	74.8%
Other	353,920	3.2%	1,249,300	7.7%	895,380	253.0%
Total	10,988,280	100.0%	16,196,300	100.0%	5,208,020	47.4%

[a]Actual age at 1967 interview was 30–39.
[b]Actual age at 1982 interview was 29–38.

APPENDIX TABLE D-3
Life-Course Stages by Age Group

Women Aged 30–34 in:

Life-Course Stage	1967 N	1967 %	1978 N	1978 %	1982[a] N	1982[a] %
Jobholder	248,860	4.5%	411,160	5.6%	810,120	9.1%
Wife	77,340	1.4%	117,510	1.6%	108,810	1.2%
Employed Wife	198,520	3.6%	398,360	5.5%	828,110	9.3%
Mother	2,724,380	49.6%	2,396,560	32.9%	2,001,590	22.6%
Employed Mother	1,636,060	29.8%	2,759,040	37.9%	3,303,880	37.3%
Divorced Employed Mother	322,260	59.0%	595,710	8.2%	833,040	9.4%
Divorced Mother	109,760	2.0%	220,170	3.0%	187,320	2.1%
Other	176,960	3.2%	385,620	5.3%	794,760	9.0%
Total	5,494,140	100.0%	7,284,130	100.0%	8,867,630	100.0%

(continued on next page)

Women Aged 35–39 in:

Life-Course Stage	1967		1972		1982[b]	
	N	%	N	%	N	%
Jobholder	242,490	4.1%	167,020	3.1%	375,750	5.1%
Wife	102,570	1.7%	88,130	1.6%	79,320	1.1%
Employed Wife	216,680	3.7%	154,910	2.9%	219,410	3.0%
Mother	2,628,540	44.8%	2,140,820	39.6%	1,715,910	23.4%
Employed Mother	2,055,410	35.0%	2,083,110	38.5%	3,356,510	45.8%
Divorced Employed Mother	332,410	5.7%	437,590	8.1%	930,770	12.7%
Divorced Mother	144,070	2.5%	161,800	3.0%	196,460	2.7%
Other	151,060	2.6%	175,820	3.3%	454,540	6.2%
Total	5,873,230	100.0%	5,409,200	100.0%	7,328,670	100.0%

[a]Actual age at 1982 interview was 29–33.
[b]Actual age at 1982 interview was 34–38.

APPENDIX TABLE D-4

Percent of Women Intending to Become a "Housewife" at Age 35, by Age and Year

Age	Year 1968	1973	1978	1982
15–19	64.6		25.3[a]	
20–24	57.6	40.7	26.1	
25–29		37.2	20.7	
30–34			22.1	21.0

[a]Data from Borus et al. 1980 for those aged 16–19 and 20–22 in 1979.

APPENDIX TABLE D-5
Attitude toward Mothers' Working if Husband Approves[a]

| | Mothers of the Baby Boom | | | | Baby-Boom Cohort | | |
| | 1967 | 1972 | 1977 | 1982 | 1968 | 1972 | 1978 |
Life-Course Stage	Age = 35–39	Age = 40–44	Age = 45–49	Age = 50–54	Age = 15–19	Age = 19–23	Age = 25–29
Jobholder	3.80	3.95	4.39	4.24	3.37	4.08	4.53
Wife	3.80	3.67	4.01	4.29	3.33	3.97	4.19
Employed Wife	3.64	4.30	4.28	4.42	3.49	4.10	4.49
Mother	3.62	3.86	3.99	4.13	3.63	4.20	4.27
Employed Mother	4.09	4.08	4.25	4.36	3.88	4.31	4.58
Divorced Employed Mother	3.81	4.23	4.27	4.55	2.54	4.43	4.46
Divorced Mother	3.73	3.82	4.08	4.27	3.95	4.49	4.67
Other	4.06	4.10	4.28	4.36	3.86	4.22	4.54
Average	3.82	4.00	4.17	4.33	3.54	4.15	4.49

[a]Measured on a scale from 1 to 5, with higher scores indicating more positive attitude. Cell is based on fewer than 25 unweighted cases.

Attitude toward Mothers' Working if Husband Disapproves[a]

| | Mothers of the Baby Boom | | | | Baby-Boom Cohort | | |
| | 1967 | 1972 | 1977 | 1982 | 1968 | 1972 | 1978 |
Life-Course Stage	Age=35–39	Age=40–44	Age=45–49	Age=50–54	Age=15–19	Age=19–23	Age=25–29
Jobholder	2.13	2.46	2.96	2.95	1.67	3.01	3.44
Wife	1.75	1.97	2.17	2.61	1.48	2.74	2.76
Employed Wife	2.10	2.34	2.74	3.02	1.59	3.03	3.40
Mother	1.61	1.88	2.22	2.65	1.64	2.76	2.74
Employed Mother	1.93	2.25	2.69	2.92	2.05	2.96	3.10
Divorced Employed Mother	1.94	2.04	2.48	2.92	1.60	2.99	3.06
Divorced Mother	1.63	2.16	2.31	2.46	1.52	2.84	2.75
Other	2.37	2.29	2.56	3.21	2.18	3.00	3.19
Average	1.80	2.11	2.51	2.85	1.78	2.95	3.09

[a]Measured on a scale from 1 to 5, with higher scores indicating more positive attitude. Cell is based on fewer than 25 unweighted cases.

APPENDIX TABLE D-7
Female Labor Force Participation Rates by Age

Year	Total	Age						
		16–19	20–24	25–34	35–44	45–54	55–64	65 +
1968	41.6%	41.9%	54.5%	42.6%	48.9%	52.3%	42.4%	9.6%
1969	42.7	43.2	56.7	43.7	49.9	53.8	43.1	9.9
1970	43.3	44.0	57.7	45.0	51.1	54.4	43.0	9.7
1971	43.3	43.4	57.7	45.5	51.6	54.3	42.9	9.5
1972	43.9	45.8	59.0	47.6	52.0	53.9	42.1	9.3
1973	44.7	47.8	61.1	50.1	53.3	53.7	41.1	8.9
1974	45.6	49.1	63.0	52.4	54.7	54.6	40.7	8.2
1975	46.3	49.1	64.1	54.6	55.8	54.6	41.0	8.3
1976	47.3	49.8	65.0	57.1	57.8	55.0	41.1	8.2
1977	48.4	51.2	66.5	59.5	59.6	55.8	41.0	8.1
1978	50.0	53.7	68.3	62.1	61.6	57.1	41.4	8.4
1979	51.0	54.2	69.1	63.8	63.6	58.4	41.9	8.3
1980	51.5	52.9	68.9	65.5	65.5	59.9	41.3	8.1
1981	52.1	51.8	69.6	66.7	66.8	61.1	41.4	8.0
1982	52.6	51.4	69.8	68.0	68.0	61.6	41.8	7.9

Sources: U.S. Bureau of the Census 1975 and 1984; U.S. Department of Labor, Bureau of Labor Statistics, 1983.

References

Akers, D. S. 1967. "On Measuring the Marriage Squeeze." *Demography* 4:907–24.

Alexander, K. L., and T. W. Reilly. 1981. "Estimating the Effects of Marriage Timing on Educational Attainment: Some Procedural Issues and Substantive Clarifications." *American Journal of Sociology* 87:143–56.

Althauser, R. P., and M. Wigler. 1972. "Standardization and Component Analysis." *Sociological Methods and Research* 1:97–135.

American Council on Education. 1967, 1969, 1970, 1974, 1977, 1982, 1984. *National Norms for Entering College Freshmen*. Washington, D.C.: American Council on Education.

Ariès, P. 1962. *Centuries of Childhood: A Social History of Family Life*. New York: Vintage Books.

Bachrach, C. A. 1980. "Childlessness and Social Isolation among the Elderly." *Journal of Marriage and the Family* 42:627–36.

———. 1984. "Contraceptive Practice among American Women, 1973–1982." *Family Planning Perspectives* 16:253–59.

Bachrach, C. A., and M. Horn. 1985. *Marriage and First Intercourse, Marital Dissolution, and Remarriage: U.S., 1982*. Advance Data National Center for Health Statistics, no. 107. Washington, D.C.: U.S. Department of Health and Human Services.

Baldwin, W. H., and C. W. Nord. 1984. "Delayed Childbearing in the U.S.: Facts and Fictions." *Population Bulletin* 39:3–42.

Bancroft, G. 1958. *The American Labor Force*. New York: Wiley.

Barrett, N. S. 1979. "Women in the Job Market: Unemployment and Work Schedules." In *The Subtle Revolution: Women at Work*, ed. R. E. Smith. Washington, D.C.: Urban Institute.

Becker, G. S. 1974. "A Theory of Marriage." In *Economics of the Family*, ed. T. W. Schultz, pp. 299–344. Chicago: University of Chicago Press.

———. 1981. *A Treatise on the Family*. Cambridge, Mass.: Harvard University Press.

———. 1985. "Human Capital, Effort, and the Sexual Division of Labor." *Journal of Labor Economics*, pt. 3:S33–58.

Becker, G. S., E. M. Landes, and R. T. Michael. 1977. "An Economic Analysis of Marital Stability." *Journal of Political Economy* 85:1141–89.

Beller, A. H. 1985. "Changes in the Sex Composition of U.S. Occupations, 1960–1981." *Journal of Human Resources* 20:236–50.

Beresford, J. C., and A. M. Rivlin. 1966. "Privacy, Poverty, and Old Age." *Demography* 3:247–58.

Bianchi, S. M., and N. F. Rytina. 1984. "Occupational Change, 1970–1980." Paper presented at the annual meeting of the Population Association of America, Minneapolis, Minn., 3–5 May 1984.

Bianchi, S. M., and D. Spain. 1986. *American Women in Transition*. New York: Russell Sage Foundation.

Billy, J. O. G., N. S. Landale, and S. D. McLaughlin. 1985. "The Effect of Marital Status at First Birth on Marital Dissolution among Adolescent Mothers." *Demography* 23:329–49.

Billy, J. O. G., D. M. Zimmerle, W. R. Grady, and S. D. McLaughlin. 1987. "Racial Differences and Changes over Time in the Adolescent Illegitimacy Rate." Paper presented at the annual meeting of the American Sociological Association, Chicago, Ill., 17–21 August 1987.

Blake, J. 1965. "Demographic Science and the Redirection of Population Policy." *Journal of Chronic Diseases* 18:1181–1200.

———. 1979. "Is Zero Preferred? American Attitudes toward Childlessness in the 1970s." *Journal of Marriage and the Family* 41:245–57.

———. 1981. "The Only Child in America: Prejudice versus Performance." *Population and Development Review* 7(1):43–54.

Bloom, D. E. 1982. "What's Happening to the Age at First Birth in the United States? A Study of Recent Cohorts." *Demography* 19:351–70.

Bloom, D. E., and N. G. Bennett. 1985. *Marriage Patterns in the U.S.* Discussion Paper Series. Cambridge, Mass.: Harvard Institute of Economic Research.

Bloom, D. E., and J. Trussell. 1984. "What Are the Determinants of Delayed Childbearing and Permanent Childlessness in the United States?" *Demography* 21:591–612.

Booth, A., and J. Edwards. 1985. "Age at Marriage and Marital Instability." *Journal of Marriage and the Family* 47:67–75.

Booth, A., D. R. Johnson, L. White, and J. N. Edwards. 1984. "Women, Outside Employment, and Marital Instability." *American Journal of Sociology* 90:567–83.

Borus, M. E., J. E. Crowley, R. W. Rumberger, R. Santos, and D. Shapiro. 1980. *Pathways to the Future: A Longitudinal Study of Young Americans*. Columbus: Ohio State University Press.

Bowen, W. G., and T. A. Finegan. 1969. *The Economics of Labor Force Participation*. Princeton, N.J.: Princeton University Press.

Bumpass, L. L. 1973. "Is Low Fertility Here to Stay?" *Family Planning Perspectives* 5:67–69.

Bumpass, L. L., R. R. Rindfuss, and R. B. Janosik. 1978. "Age and Marital Status at First Birth and the Pace of Subsequent Fertility." *Demography* 15:75–86.

Bumpass, L. L., and C. F. Westoff. 1970. *The Later Years of Childbearing*. Princeton, N.J.: Princeton University Press.

Burch, T. K., K. Thomas, P. Loring, M. McQuillan, and F. McGillvary. 1983.

"Changing Household Headship in the United States, 1900 to 1970: A Preliminary Test of the Income Threshold Hypothesis." Paper presented at the annual meeting of the Population Association of America, Pittsburgh, Pa., 14–16 April 1983.

Burnham, D. 1983. "Induced Terminations of Pregnancy: Reporting States, 1980." *Monthly Vital Statistics Report* 32(8).

Caldwell, J. C. 1982. *Theory of Fertility Decline*. New York: Academic.

Call, V. R. A., and L. B. Otto. 1979. "On 'The Effect of Early Marriage on the Educational Attainment of Young Men.'" *Journal of Marriage and the Family* 41:217–23.

Caplow, T. 1954. *The Sociology of Work*. New York: McGraw-Hill.

Card, J. J. 1977. "Consequences of Adolescent Childbearing for the Young Parent's Future Personal and Professional Life." Final Report to National Institute of Child Health and Human Development, Contract # HD-62831. Palo Alto, Calif.: American Institutes for Research.

Carliner, G. 1975. "Determinants of Household Headship." *Journal of Marriage and the Family* 37:28–38.

Carnoy, M., and D. Marenbach. 1975. "The Return to Schooling in the United States, 1939–1969." *Journal of Human Resources* 10:312–31.

Carter, H., and P. C. Glick. 1976. *Divorce: A Social and Economic Study*. Rev. ed. Cambridge, Mass.: Harvard University Press.

Chafe, W. H. 1972. *The American Woman: Her Changing Social, Economic, and Political Roles, 1920–1970*. New York: Oxford University Press.

Cherlin, A. J. 1977. "The Effect of Children on Marital Dissolution." *Demography* 14:265–96.

————. 1980. "Postponing Marriage: The Influence of Young Women's Work Expectations." *Journal of Marriage and the Family* 42:355–65.

————. 1981. *Marriage, Divorce, Remarriage*. Cambridge, Mass.: Harvard University Press.

Clark, R., and G. Martire. 1979. "Americans, Still in a Family Way." *Public Opinion* 2:16–19.

Cochrane, S. H. 1979. "Fertility and Education: What Do We Really Know?" *World Bank Staff Occasional Papers*, no. 26. Baltimore: Johns Hopkins University Press.

Coleman, J. S., R. H. Bremmer, B. R. Clark, J. B. Davis, D. H. Eichorn, Z. Griliches, J. F. Kett, N. B. Ryder, Z. B. Doering, and J. M. Mays. 1974. *Youth: Transition to Adulthood*. Chicago: University of Chicago Press.

Collver, O. A., and E. Langlois. 1962. "The Female Labor Force in Metropolitan Areas: An International Comparison." *Economic Development and Cultural Change* 10:367–85.

Corcoran, M., G. J. Duncan, and M. S. Hill. 1984. "The Economic Fortunes of Women and Children: Lessons from the Panel Study of Income Dynamics." *Signs* 10(2):232–48.

Coser, R. L., and G. Rokoff. 1971. "Women in the Occupational World: Social Disruption and Conflict." *Social Problems* 19:535–54.

Cramer, J. C. 1980. "Fertility and Female Employment: Problems of Causal

Direction." *American Sociological Review* 45:167–90.

Darling, C. A., D. J. Kallen, and J. E. VanDusen. 1984. "Sex in Transition, 1900–1980." *Journal of Youth and Adolescence* 13(5):385–99.

Das Gupta, P. 1978. "A General Method of Decomposing a Difference between Two Rates into Several Components." *Demography* 15:99–112.

Davis, J. A. 1982. "Achievement Variables and Class Cultures: Family, Schooling, Job, and Forty-Nine Dependent Variables in the Cumulative GSS." *American Sociological Review* 47:569–86.

Davis, K. 1984. "Wives and Work: The Sex Role Revolution and Its Consequences." *Population and Development Review* 10:397–417.

Davis, K., and J. Blake. 1956. "Economic Development and Cultural Change." In *Theory of Fertility Decline*, ed. John C. Caldwell. New York: Academic.

Davis, M. J., and L. L. Bumpass. 1976. "The Continuation of Education after Marriage among Women in the United States: 1970s." *Demography* 13:161–74.

Dawson, D. A., D. J. Meny, and J. C. Ridley. 1980. "Fertility Control in the United States Before the Contraceptive Revolution." *Family Planning Perspectives* 12:76–86.

Degler, C. 1980. *At Odds: Women and the Family in America from the Revolution to the Present*. New York: Oxford University Press.

Demos, J. 1972. "Demography and Psychology in the Historical Study of Family Life: A Personal Report." In *Household and Family in Past Time*, ed. P. Laslett and R. Wall. London: Cambridge University Press.

Dubnoff, S. 1978. "Long Term Trends in the Adequacy of Individual Incomes in the United States, 1860–1974." Paper presented at the Social Science History Association, in Columbus, Ohio, on 3–5 November 1978.

Duncan, B., and O. D. Duncan, eds. 1978. *Sex Typing and Social Roles*. New York: Academic.

Duncan, G. J. 1983. "Prepared Statement on Broken Families." In Hearings before the Subcommittee on Family and Human Services of the Committee on Labor and Human Resources, U.S. Senate, March 22 and 24, 1983. Washington, D.C.: U.S. Government Printing Office, pp. 223–38.

Duncan, O. D. 1969. "Inheritance of Poverty or Inheritance of Race?" In *On Understanding Poverty*, ed. D. P. Moynihan, pp. 85–110. New York: Basic Books.

Duncan, O. D., D. L. Featherman, and B. Duncan. 1972. *Socioeconomic Background and Achievement*. New York: Seminar.

Easterlin, R. A. 1962. *The American Baby Boom in Historical Perspective*. National Bureau of Economic Research, Occasional Paper 79. New York.

———. 1966. "On the Relation of Economic Factors to Recent and Projected Fertility Changes." *Demography* 3:131–53.

———. 1973. "Relative Economic Status and the American Fertility Swing." In *Family Economic Behavior*, ed. E. B. Sheldon, pp. 170–223. Philadelphia: J. B. Lippincott.

———. 1978. "What Will 1984 Be Like? Socioeconomic Implications of Recent Twists in Age Structure." *Demography* 15:397–432.

———. 1980. *Birth and Fortune: The Impact of Numbers on Personal Welfare.* New York: Basic Books.

Elder, G. H., Jr. 1972. "Role Orientations, Marital Age, and Life Patterns in Adulthood." *Merrill-Palmer Quarterly* 18:3–14.

———. 1974. *Children of the Great Depression.* Chicago: University of Chicago Press.

———. 1978. "Approaches to Social Changes and the Family." *American Journal of Sociology* 84:S1–38.

———, ed. 1985. *Life Course Dynamics: Trajectories and Transitions, 1968–1980.* Ithaca, N.Y.: Cornell University Press.

Elder, G. H., Jr., and R. C. Rockwell. 1976. "Marital Timing in Women's Life Patterns." *Journal of Family History* 1:34–53.

England, P. 1981. "Assessing Trends in Occupational Sex Segregation, 1900–1976." *Sociological Perspectives on Labor Markets*, ed. Ivar Berg. New York: Academic.

Espenshade, T. J. 1983a. "Black-White Differences in Marriage, Separation, Divorce, and Remarriage." Paper presented at the annual meeting of the Population Association of America, Minneapolis, Minn., 14–16 April 1983.

———. 1983b. "Marriage, Divorce, and Remarriage from Retrospective Data: A Multiregional Approach." *Environment and Planning* 15A:1633–52.

———. 1985. "Marriage Trends in America: Estimates, Implications and Underlying Causes." *Population and Development Review* 11:193–245.

Farkas, G. 1976. "Education, Wage Rates, and the Division of Labor between Husband and Wife." *Journal of Marriage and the Family* 38:473–83.

Feldberg, R. L. 1984. "Comparable Worth: Toward Theory and Practice in the United States." *Signs* 10(2):311–28.

Fogarty, M. P., R. Rapoport, and R. Rapoport. 1971. *Sex, Career, and Family.* Beverly Hills: Sage Publications.

Forisha, B. L., and B. H. Goldman. 1981. *Outsiders on the Inside: Women and Organizations.* Englewood Cliffs, N.J.: Prentice-Hall.

Forrest, J. D., E. Sullivan, and C. Tietze. 1979. "Abortion in the United States, 1977–1978." *Family Planning Perspectives* 11:329–41.

Freedman, R. C. 1961–62. "The Sociology of Human Fertility: A Trend Report and Bibliography." *Current Sociology* 10/11(2):35–121.

Freedman, R. C., P. L. Whelpton, and A. A. Campbell. 1959. *Family Planning, Sterility, and Population Growth.* New York: McGraw-Hill.

Freeman, R. B. 1980. "The Facts about the Declining Economic Value of College." *Journal of Human Resources* 15:124–42.

Fuchs, V. R. 1974. "Women's Earnings: Recent Trends and Long-run Prospects." *Monthly Labor Review* 97:23–26.

Furstenberg, F. F., Jr. 1976. *Unplanned Parenthood: The Social Consequences of Teenage Childbearing.* New York: Free Press.

Gallup. 1985. "Majority Now Considers Premarital Sex Acceptable" (16 May) Princeton, N.J.: Gallup Poll.

Gendell, M. 1965. "The Influence of Family-Building Activities on Women's Rate of Economic Activity." World Population Conference, Belgrade, Yugoslavia, 30 August–10 September 1965.

Giele, J. Z. 1984. "Cohort Shifts in Women's Life Patterns, 1934–1979." Paper presented at the annual meeting of the American Sociological Association, San Antonio, Texas, 27–31 August 1984.

Glenn, N. D. 1980. "Values, Attitudes, and Beliefs." In *Constancy and Change in Human Development*, ed. O. Brim, Jr., and J. Kagan. Cambridge, Mass.: Harvard University Press.

Glick, P. C. 1984. "Marriage, Divorce, and Living Arrangements: Prospective Changes." *Journal of Family Issues* 5:7–26.

Glick, P. C., and A. J. Norton. 1977. "Marrying, Divorcing and Living Together in the U.S. Today." *Population Bulletin* 32(5):3–39.

Glick, P. C., and G. B. Spanier. 1980. "Married and Unmarried Cohabitation in the U.S." *Journal of Marriage and the Family* 42:19–30.

Goldin, C. 1979. "Household and Market Production of Families in a Late Nineteenth-Century American City." *Explorations in Economic History* 16:111–31.

Goldman, N., C. F. Westoff, and C. Hammerslough. 1984. "Demography of the Marriage Market in the U.S." *Population Index* 50(1):5–25.

Goldscheider, C. 1971. *Population, Modernization, and Social Structure.* Boston: Little, Brown and Company.

Goode, W. J. 1963. *World Revolution and Family Patterns.* New York: Free Press.

Goodman, J. D. 1979. "The Economic Returns of Education." *Social Science Quarterly* 60:269–83.

Goodman, L. A. 1976. "The Relationship between the Modified and More Usual Multiple Regression Approach to the Analysis of Dichotomous Variables." In *Sociological Methodology*, ed. D. R. Heise, pp. 83–110. San Francisco: Jossey-Bass.

Grady, W. R. 1980. *Remarriages of Women 15–44 Years of Age Whose First Marriage Ended in Divorce: United States, 1976.* Advance Data, National Center for Health Statistics, no. 58. Washington, D.C.: U.S. Department of Health and Human Services.

Granberg, D., and B. W. Grandberg. 1980. "Abortion Attitudes, 1965–1980: Trends and Determinants." *Family Planning Perspectives* 12:250–61.

Grant, W. V., and L. J. Eiden. 1980. *Digest of Education Statistics, 1980.* Washington, D.C.: National Center for Education Statistics.

———. 1981. *Digest of Education Statistics, 1981.* Washington, D.C.: National Center for Education Statistics.

Greven, P. 1966. "Family Structure in Seventeenth-Century Andover." *William and Mary Quarterly* 23:234–56.

———. 1970. *Four Generations: Population, Land, and Family in Colonial Andover, Massachusetts.* Ithaca, N.Y.: Cornell University Press.

_____. 1972. "The Average Size of Families and Households in the Province of Massachusetts in 1764 and in the United States in 1970: An Overview." In *Household and Family in Past Time*, ed. P. Laslett and R. Wall. London: Cambridge University Press.

Griffith, J. D., H. P. Koo, and C. M. Suchindran. 1984. "Childlessness and Marital Stability in Remarriages." *Journal of Marriage and the Family* 46:577–85.

_____. 1985. "Childbearing and Family in Remarriage." *Demography* 22:73–88.

Gross, E. 1986. "Plus Ça Change . . . ? The Sexual Structure of Occupations over Time." *Social Problems* 16:198–208.

Grossman, A. S. 1978. "Children of Working Mothers, March, 1977." *Monthly Labor Review* 101:30–33.

_____. 1983. *Children of Working Mothers*. Washington, D.C.: Bureau of Labor Statistics, U.S. Department of Labor.

Guttentag, M., and P. Secord. 1983. *Too Many Women: Demography, Sex, and Family*. New York: Basic Books.

Gwartney, J., and R. Stroup. 1973. "Measurement of Employment Discrimination According to Sex." *Southern Economic Journal* 39:575–87.

Haines, M. R. 1981. "Poverty, Economic Stress, and the Family in a Late Nineteenth-Century American City: Whites in Philadelphia, 1880." In *Philadelphia: Work, Space, Family, and Group Experience in the Nineteenth Century*, ed. T. Hershberg. New York: Oxford University Press.

Hannan, M. T., N. B. Tuma, and L. P. Groeneveld. 1978. "Income and Independence Effects of Marital Dissolution: Results from the Seattle and Denver Income-Maintenance Experiments." *American Journal of Sociology* 84:611–33.

Hareven, T. K. 1978. "The Dynamics of Kin in an Industrial Community." *American Journal of Sociology* 84:S151–82.

Hastings, D., and J. Robinson. 1974. "Incidence of Childlessness for United States Women, Cohorts Born 1891–1945." *Social Biology* 21:178–84.

Hawthorn, G. P. 1970. *The Sociology of Fertility*. London: Collier-Macmillan.

Hayghe, H. 1984. "Working Mothers Reach Record Numbers in 1984." *Monthly Labor Review* 107:31–34.

Heckman, J. J. 1974. "Shadow Prices, Market Wages, and Labor Supply." *Econometrica* 42:679–94.

Heer, D. M., and A. Grossbard-Shechtman. 1981. "The Impact of the Female Marriage Squeeze and the Contraceptive Revolution on Sex Roles and the Women's Liberation Movement in the United States, 1960–1975." *Journal of Marriage and the Family* 43:49–65.

Henderson, A. M., and T. Parsons. 1947. *Introduction to Max Weber, the Theory of Social and Economic Organization*. New York: Free Press.

Henshaw, S. K., N. J. Binkin, E. Blaine, and J. C. Smith. 1985. "A Portrait of American Women Who Obtain Abortions." *Family Planning Perspectives* 17:90–96.

Henshaw, S. K., and K. O'Reilly. 1983. "Characteristics of Abortion Patients in the United States, 1979 and 1980." *Family Planning Perspectives* 15:5–16.

Herrenkohl, E. C., and R. C. Herrenkohl. 1979. "A Comparison of Abused Children and Their Nonabused Siblings." *Journal of the American Academy of Child Psychiatry* 18:260–69.

Heyns, B., and J. A. Bird. 1982. "Recent Trends in the Higher Education of Women." In *The Undergraduate Woman*, ed. P. J. Perun, pp. 43–69. Lexington, Mass.: Lexington Books.

Hofferth, S. L., and K. A. Moore. 1979. "Early Childbearing and Later Economic Well-Being." *American Sociological Review* 44:784–815.

Hoffman, L. W. 1975. "The Employment of Women, Education, and Fertility." In *Women and Achievement: Social and Motivational Analyses*, ed. M. T. Mednick, S. S. Tangri, and L. W. Hoffman. Washington, D.C.: Hemisphere Publishing.

Hoffman, S. 1977. "Marital Instability and the Economic Status of Women." *Demography* 14:67–76.

Holsinger, D. B., and J. D. Kasarda. 1976. "Education and Human Fertility: Sociological Perspectives." *Population and Development*, ed. R. G. Ridker. Baltimore: Johns Hopkins University Press.

Houseknecht, S. K., S. Vaughan, and A. S. Macke. 1984. "Marital Disruption among Professional Women: The Timing of Career and Family Events." *Social Problems* 31(3):273–84.

Huber, J., and G. Spitze. 1980. "Considering Divorce: An Expansion of Becker's Theory of Marital Instability." *American Journal of Sociology* 86:75–89.

Hymowitz, C., and M. Weissman. 1978. *A History of Women in America*. New York: Bantam Books.

Iams, H., and A. Thornton. 1975. "Decomposition of Differences: A Cautionary Note." *Sociological Methods and Research* 3:341–52.

Johnson, T. R., and J. H. Pencavel. 1984. "Dynamic Hours of Work Functions for Husbands, Wives, and Single Females." *Econometrica* 52:363–89.

Jones, E. F. 1981. "The Impact of Women's Employment on Marital Fertility in the U.S., 1970–1975." *Population Studies* 35:161–73.

Kaestle, C. F., and M. A. Vinovskis. 1978. "From Apron Strings to ABCs: Parents, Children, and Schooling in Nineteenth-Century Massachusetts." *American Journal of Sociology* 84:S39–80.

Kanter, R. M. 1978. "Families, Family Processes, and Economic Life: Toward Systematic Analysis of Social Historical Research." *American Journal of Sociology* 84:S316–39.

Kaplan, D. L., and C. M. Casey. 1958. *Occupational Trends in the United States, 1900 to 1950*. U.S. Bureau of the Census, Working Paper No. 5. Washington, D.C.: U.S. Government Printing Office.

Kasarda, J. D., J. O. G. Billy, and K. B. West. 1986. *Status Enhancement and Fertility: Reproductive Responses to Social Mobility and Educational Opportunity*. New York: Academic.

Katz, M. B., and I. E. Davey. 1978. "Youth and Industrialization in a Canadian City." *American Journal of Sociology* 84:S80–119.

Kerckhoff, A. C., and A. A. Parrow. 1979. "The Effect of Early Marriage on the Educational Attainment of Young Men." *Journal of Marriage and the Family* 41:97–107.

Kinsey, A. C., W. B. Pomeroy, and C. E. Martin. 1948. *Sexual Behavior in the Human Male*. Philadelphia: W. B. Saunders.

Kinsey, A. C., W. B. Pomeroy, C. E. Martin, and P. H. Gebhard. 1953. *Sexual Behavior in the Human Female*. Philadelphia: W. B. Saunders.

Kitagawa, E. M. 1955. "Components of a Difference between Two Rates." *Journal of the American Statistical Association* 50:1168–94.

Knoke, D. 1975. "Comparison of Log-Linear and Regression Models for Systems of Dichotomous Variables." *Sociological Methods and Research* 3:416–34.

Kobrin, F. E. 1973. "Household Headship and Its Changes in the United States, 1940–1960, 1970." *Journal of the American Statistical Association* 68:793–800.

————. 1976a. "The Fall in Household Size and the Rise of the Primary Individual in the United States." *Demography* 13:127–38.

————. 1976b. "The Primary Individual and the Family: Changes in Living Arrangements in the United States Since 1940." *Journal of Marriage and the Family* 38:233–39.

————. 1978. "The Fall in Household Size and the Rise of the Primary Individual in the United States." In *The American Family in Social-Historical Perspective*, second edition, ed. M. Gordon. New York: St. Martin's Press.

Kohn, M. L., and C. Schooler. 1983. *Work and Personality: An Inquiry into Social Stratification*. Norwood, N.J.: Ablex.

Koo, H. P., C. M. Suchindran, and J. D. Griffith. 1984. "The Effects of Children on Divorce and Remarriage: A Multivariate Analysis of Life Table Probabilities." *Population Studies* 38:451–71.

Kreps, J., ed. 1976. *Women and the American Economy: A Look to the 1980s*. Englewood Cliffs, N.J.: Prentice-Hall.

Kupinsky, S. 1971. "Non-Familial Activity and Socio-Economic Differentials in Fertility." *Demography* 8:353–67.

————. 1977. *The Fertility of Working Women. A Synthesis of International Research*. Praeger Special Studies. New York: Praeger.

Langer, J. 1985. "The New Mature Mothers." *American Demographics* 7:29–50.

Laslett, B. 1973. "The Family as a Public and Private Institution: An Historical Perspective." *Journal of Marriage and the Family* 35:480–92.

Laslett, P., ed. 1972. *Household and Family in Past Time*. London: Cambridge University Press.

Lazear, E. P., and R. T. Michael. 1980. "Family Size and Distribution of Real Per Capita Income." *American Economic Review* 70:91–107.

Leon, C., and R. W. Bednarzik. 1978. "A Profile of Women on Part-time Schedules." *Monthly Labor Review* 101:3–12.

Lesthaeghe, R. 1983. "A Century of Demographic and Cultural Change in Western Europe: An Exploration of Underlying Dimensions." *Population and Development Review* 9:411–35.

Long, C. D. 1958. *The Labor Force under Changing Income and Employment.* Princeton, N.J.: Princeton University Press.

Lopata, H. Z., and K. F. Norr. 1980. "Changing Commitments of American Women to Work and Family Roles." *Social Security Bulletin* 43:3–14.

McCarthy, J. 1978. "A Comparison of the Probability of the Dissolution of First and Second Marriages." *Demography* 15:345–60.

McCarthy, J., and J. Menken. 1979. "Marriage, Remarriage, Marital Disruption, and Age at First Birth." *Family Planning Perspectives* 11:21–30.

McGuigan, D. G., ed. 1980. *Women's Lives: New Theory, Research, and Policy.* Ann Arbor: University of Michigan Center for Continuing Education of Women.

McLanahan, S., and J. Adams. 1985. *Explaining the Decline in Parents' Psychological Well-Being.* Center for Demography and Ecology Working Paper 85-25. Madison: University of Wisconsin.

McLaughlin, S. D. 1977. *Consequences of Adolescent Childbearing for the Mother's Occupational Attainment.* Final Report to National Institute for Child Health and Human Development, Contract #NO1-HD-62832. Minneapolis: University of Minnesota.

――――. 1982. "Differential Patterns of Female Labor-Force Participation Surrounding the First Birth." *Journal of Marriage and the Family* 44:407–20.

McLaughlin, S. D., J. O. G. Billy, T. R. Johnson, B. D. Melber, L. D. Winges, and D. M. Zimmerle. 1985. *The Cosmopolitan Report: The Changing Life Course of American Women.* Vol. 1. New York: Hearst Publications.

McLaughlin, S. D., W. R. Grady, J. O. G. Billy, and L. D. Winges. 1985. *The Effects of the Decision to Marry on the Consequences of Adolescent Pregnancy.* Final Report to the Office of Adolescent Pregnancy Programs, Department of Health and Human Services. Seattle: Battelle Human Affairs Research Centers.

McLaughlin, S. D., W. R. Grady, and N. Landale. 1985. *Changes in the Propensity to Live Alone.* Final Report to National Institute of Child Health and Human Development. Seattle: Battelle Human Affairs Research Centers.

McLaughlin, S. D., and B. D. Melber. 1986. *The Cosmopolitan Report: The Changing Life Course of American Women.* Vol. 2. New York: Hearst Publications.

McLaughlin, S. D., and M. Micklin. 1983. "The Timing of the First Birth and Changes in Personal Efficacy." *Journal of Marriage and the Family* 45:47–55.

McLaughlin, S. D., and D. Zimmerle. 1987. *The Cosmopolitan Report: The Changing Life Course of American Women.* Vol. 3. New York: Hearst Publications.

Magarell, J. 1981. "The Enrollment Boom among Older Americans: 1 in 3 College Students Is Now Over 25 Years Old." *Chronicle of Higher Education.* 4 May 1981, p. 3.

Margolis, M. L. 1984. *Mothers and Such: Views of American Women and Why They Changed*. Berkeley: University of California Press.

Marini, M. M. 1978a. "The Transition to Adulthood: Sex Differences in Educational Attainment and Age at Marriage." *American Sociological Review* 43:483–507.

———. 1978b. "Sex Differences in the Determination of Adolescent Aspirations: A Review of Research." *Sex Roles* 4:723–53.

———. 1984a. "Women's Educational Attainment and the Timing of Entry into Parenthood." *American Sociological Review* 49:491–511.

———. 1984b. "The Order of Events in the Transition to Adulthood." *Sociology of Education* 57:63–84.

Marini, M. M., and P. J. Hodsdon. 1981. "Effects of the Timing of Marriage and First Birth on the Spacing of Subsequent Births." *Demography* 18:529–48.

Masnick, G., and M. J. Bane. 1980. *The Nation's Families: 1960–1990*. Cambridge, Mass.: Joint Center for Urban Studies of MIT and Harvard University.

Mattessich, P. W. 1979. "Childlessness and its Correlates in Historical Perspective: A Research Note." *Journal of Family History* 4:299–307.

Mednick, M. T., S. S. Tangri, and L. W. Hoffman. 1975. *Women and Achievement: Social and Motivational Analyses*. Washington, D.C.: Hemisphere Publishing.

Melber, B. 1981. "Efforts to Equalize Educational Opportunity for Women in the United States." In *Bildungschancen für Mädchen und Frauen im internationalen Vergleich* (An International Comparison of Equal Opportunity for Girls and Women), ed. I. Schmid-Jorg, S. Hubner, C. Krebsbach-Gnath, B. D. Melber, and F. Escher. Munich, West Germany: Oldenbourg.

Mellor, E. F. 1984. "Investigating the Differences in Weekly Earnings of Women and Men." *Monthly Labor Review* 107:17–28.

Menken, J. 1980. "The Health and Demographic Consequences of Adolescent Pregnancy and Childbearing." In *Adolescent Pregnancy and Childbearing: Findings from Research*, ed. C. S. Chilman, pp. 157–200. National Institutes of Health Publication No. 81-2077. Washington, D.C.: U.S. Government Printing Office.

Merton, R. K. 1968. *Social Theory and Social Structure*. New York: Free Press.

Michael, R. T. 1978. "The Rise in Divorce Rates, 1960–1974: Age-Specific Components." *Demography* 15:177–82.

———. 1985. "Consequences of the Rise in Female Labor Force Participation Rates: Questions and Probes." *Journal of Labor Economics* 3(1), pt. 2:S117–46.

Michael, R. T., V. R. Fuchs, and S. R. Scott. 1980. "Changes in the Propensity to Live Alone—1950–1976." *Demography* 17:39–56.

Millman, S. R., and G. E. Hendershot. 1980. "Early Fertility and Lifetime Fertility." *Family Planning Perspectives* 12:139–49.

Mincer, J. 1962. "Labor Force Participation of Married Women: A Study of Labor Supply." In *National Bureau of Economic Research, Aspects of Labor Economics*. Princeton, N.J.: Princeton University Press.

Modell, J., F. Furstenberg, Jr., and T. Hershberg. 1976. "Social Change and Transitions to Adulthood in Historical Perspective." *Journal of Family History* 1:7–32.

Modell, J., F. Furstenberg, Jr., and D. Strong. 1978. "The Timing of Marriage in the Transition to Adulthood: Continuity and Change, 1860–1975." *American Journal of Sociology* 84:S120–50.

Modell, J., and T. K. Hareven. 1973. "Urbanization and the Malleable Household: An Examination of Boarding and Lodging in American Families." *Journal of Marriage and the Family* 35:467–79.

Moen, P. 1985. "Continuities and Discontinuities in Women's Labor Force Activity." In *Life Course Dynamics: Trajectories and Transitions, 1968–1980*, ed. Glen H. Elder, Jr. Ithaca, N.Y.: Cornell University Press.

Moore, K. A. 1978. "Teenage Childbirth and Welfare Dependency." *Family Planning Perspectives* 10:233–37.

Moore, K. A., and L. J. Waite. 1977. "Early Childbearing and Educational Attainment." *Family Planning Perspectives* 9:22–25.

Morgan, J. M., I. Sirageldin, and N. Baerwaldt. 1966. *Productive Americans*. Ann Arbor: University of Michigan.

Morgan, S. P. 1982. "Parity Specific Fertility Intentions and Uncertainty: The United States, 1970–1976." *Demography* 19:315–34.

Morgan, S. P., and R. R. Rindfuss. 1982. "Delayed Childbearing in the United States: 'Depression'-Style Childbearing in the 1970s and 1980s." Paper presented at the annual meeting of the American Sociological Association, San Francisco, Calif., 6–10 September 1982.

Morison, S. E. 1965. *The Oxford History of the American People: 1869 to the Death of John F. Kennedy, 1963*. New York: Oxford University Press.

Mosher, W. D., and C. A. Bachrach. 1982. "Childlessness in the United States: Estimates from the National Survey of Family Growth." *Journal of Family Issues* 3:517–43.

Mott, F. L. 1982. "Women: The Employment Revolution." In *The Employment Revolution*, ed. F. L. Mott. Cambridge, Mass.: MIT Press.

Mott, F. L., and S. F. Moore. 1979. "The Causes of Marital Disruption among Young American Women: An Interdisciplinary Perspective." *Journal of Marriage and the Family* 41:355–65.

Mott, F. L., and S. H. Mott. 1985. "Attitude Consistency Among American Youth." Washington, D.C.: U.S. Department of Labor.

Mott, F. L., and D. Shapiro. 1983. "Complementarity of Work and Fertility among Young American Mothers." *Population Studies* 37:239–52.

Myrdal, A., and V. Klein. 1956. *Women's Two Roles: Home and Work*. London: Routledge and Kegan Paul.

Namboodiri, N. K. 1964. "The Wife's Work Experience and Child Spacing." *Milbank Memorial Fund Quarterly* 42:65–77.

National Center for Education Statistics. 1984. *Digest of Education Statistics, 1983–1984.* Washington, D.C.: U.S. Government Printing Office.

National Longitudinal Survey. 1985. *The National Longitudinal Surveys Handbook, 1983–1984.* Columbus: Ohio State University.

Nye, F. I., and L. W. Hoffman. 1963. *The Employed Mother in America.* Chicago: Rand McNally.

O'Connor, J. F. 1977. "A Logarithmic Technique for Decomposing Change." *Sociological Methods and Research* 6:91–192.

O'Neill, J. 1985. "The Trend in the Male-Female Wage Gap in the United States." *Journal of Labor Economics* 3(1):S91–116.

Oppenheimer, V. K. 1968. "The Sex Labeling of Jobs." *Industrial Relations* 7:219–34.

———. 1970. *The Female Labor Force in the United States.* Population Monograph Series, no. 5. Berkeley: University of California Press.

———. 1973. "Demographic Influence on Female Employment and the Status of Women." *American Journal of Sociology* 78:946–61.

———. 1982. *Work and the Family: A Study in Social Demography.* New York: Academic.

Oppong, C. 1983. "Women's Roles, Opportunity Costs, and Fertility." In *The Determinants of Fertility in Developing Countries,* ed. R. A. Bulatao and R. D. Lee with P. E. Hollerbach and J. Bongaarts, 1:547–89. New York: Academic.

Pampel, F. C. 1981. *Social Change and the Aged: Recent Trends in the U.S.* Lexington, Mass.: Lexington Books.

———. 1983. "Changes in the Propensity to Live Alone: Evidence from Consecutive Cross-sectional Surveys, 1960–1976." *Demography* 20:433–48.

Parelius, A. P. 1975. "Change and Stability in College Women's Orientations Toward Education, Family, and Work." *Social Problems* 22:420–32.

Parsons, T. 1949. "The Structure of Social Action." In *The Family: Its Function and Destiny,* ed. R. N. Anshen. New York: Harper.

Parsons, T., and R. F. Bales. 1955. *Family, Socialization and Interaction Process.* Glencoe, Ill.: Free Press.

Phelps, O. W. 1967. *Introduction to Labor Economics.* New York: McGraw-Hill.

Philliber, W. W., and D. V. Hiller. 1983. "Relative Occupational Attainments of Spouses and Later Changes in Marriage and Wife's Work Experience." *Journal of Marriage and the Family* 45:161–70.

Plateris. A. 1978. "Divorces and Divorce Rates." National Center for Health Statistics, DHHS (PHS) 79-1907, ser. 21, no. 29.

———. 1979. "Divorces by Marriage Cohort." National Center for Health Statistics, DHHS (PHS) 79-1912, ser. 21, no. 34.

Pleck, J. 1981. "The Work-Family Problem: Overloading the System." In *Outsiders on the Inside: Women and Organizations,* ed. B. L. Forisha and G. H. Goldman. Englewood Cliffs, N.J.: Prentice-Hall.

———. 1985. *Working Wives, Working Husbands.* Beverly Hills: Sage Publications.

Pleck, J., and M. Rustad. 1980. *Husbands' and Wives' Time in Family Work and Paid Work in the 1975–76 Study of Time Use*. Working Paper No. 63. Wellesley, Mass: Center for Research on Women, Wellesley College.

Poston, D. L., and E. Gotard. 1977. "Trends in Childlessness in the United States, 1910–1975." *Social Biology* 24:212–24.

Pratt, L., and P. K. Whelpton. 1958. "Extra-Familial Participation of Wives in Relation to Interest in and Liking for Children, Fertility Planning, and Actual and Desired Family Size." In *Social and Psychological Factors Affecting Fertility*, ed. P. K. Whelpton and C. V. Kiser, 5:1211–44. New York: Milbank Memorial Fund.

Pratt, W. F., W. D. Mosher, C. A. Bachrach, and M. C. Horn. 1984. "Understanding U.S. Fertility: Findings from the National Survey of Family Growth, Cycle III." *Population Bulletin* 39:1–42. Washington, D.C.: Population Reference Bureau.

Preston, S. H. 1975. "Estimating the Proportion of American Marriages That End in Divorce." *Sociological Methods and Research* 3:435–60.

Preston, S. H., and J. McDonald. 1979. "The Incidence of Divorce within Cohorts of American Marriages Contracted since the Civil War." *Demography* 16:1–25.

Preston, S. H., and A. T. Richards. 1975. "The Influence of Women's Work Opportunities on Marriage Rates." *Demography* 12:209–22.

Pryor, E. T., Jr. 1972. "Rhode Island Family Structure: 1875 and 1960." In *Household and Family in Past Time*, ed. P. Laslett and R. Wall. London: Cambridge University Press.

Pullum, T. W. 1980. "Separating Age, Period, and Cohort Effects in White U.S. Fertility, 1920–1970." *Social Science Research* 9:225–44.

Randour, M. L., G. L. Strasburg, and J. Lipman-Blumen. 1982. "Women in Higher Education: Trends in Enrollments and Degrees Earned." *Harvard Educational Review* 52(2):189–202.

Rapoport, R. 1971. *Dual-Career Families*. Middlesex, England: Penguin.

Regan, M. C., and M. E. Roland. 1982. "University Students: A Change in Expectations and Aspirations Over the Decade." *Sociology of Education* 55:233–28.

Reiss, I. L. 1967. *The Social Context of Premarital Sexual Permissiveness*. New York: Holt, Rinehart and Winston.

Reskin, B. F., and H. I. Hartmann. 1986. *Women's Work, Men's Work: Sex Segregation on the Job*. Washington, D.C.: National Academy Press.

Reynolds, L. C. 1974. *Labor Economics and Labor Relations*. Englewood Cliffs, N.J.: Prentice-Hall.

Ridley, J. C. 1959. "Number of Children Expected in Relation to Non-Familial Activities of Wife." *Milbank Memorial Fund Quarterly* 37:277–96.

———. 1969. "The Changing Position of American Women in Education, Labor Force Participation, and Fertility." In *The Family in Transition*. Fogarty International Proceedings, No. 3. Washington, D.C.: U.S. Government Printing Office.

Rindfuss, R. R., and L. L. Bumpass. 1977. "Fertility during Marital Disruption." *Journal of Marriage and the Family* 39:517–30.

Rindfuss, R. R., L. L. Bumpass, and C. St. John. 1980. "Education and Fertility Roles in Women's Occupations." *American Sociological Review* 45: 431–48.

———. 1983. "Social Determinants of Age at First Birth." *Journal of Marriage and the Family* 45:553–65.

Rindfuss, R. R., S. P. Morgan, and C. G. Swicegood. 1984. "The Transition to Motherhood." *American Sociological Review* 49:359–72.

Robinson, J. P. 1977. *How Americans Use Time: A Socio-Psychological Analysis.* New York: Praeger.

Robinson, J. P., and E. Rogers-Millar. 1979. "Housework, Technology, and Quality of Life: Implications from Longitudinal Time-Use Surveys." In *Household Work*, ed. Sarah F. Berk. Beverly Hills: Sage Publications.

Robinson, J. P., J. Yerby, M. Fieweger, and N. Somerick. 1977. "Sex-Role Differences in Time Use." *Sex Roles* 3:443–58.

Rodgers, W. L., and A. Thornton. 1985. "Changing Patterns of First Marriage in the U.S." *Demography* 22:265–79.

Roper, Inc. 1986. *The 1985 Virginia Slims American Women's Opinion Poll.* New York: Roper Organization.

Rosen, H. 1976. "Taxes in a Labor Supply Model with Joint Wage-Hours Determination." *Econometrica* 44:485–508.

Rosenfeld, R. A. 1980. "Race and Sex Differences in Career Dynamics." *American Sociological Review* 45:583–609.

Rossi, A. 1964. "Equality between the Sexes: An Immodest Proposal." *Daedalus* 93:607–52.

Rupp, L. J. 1978. *Mobilizing Women for War.* Princeton, N.J.: Princeton University Press.

Ryan, M. P. 1983. *Womanhood in America: From Colonial Times to the Present.* New York: Franklin Watts.

Ryder, N. B. 1973. "Recent Trends and Group Differences in Fertility." In *Toward the End of Growth: Population in America*, ed. C. F. Westoff, pp. 57–68. Englewood Cliffs, N.J.: Prentice-Hall.

Ryder, N. B., and C. F. Westoff. 1971a. "Fertility Planning Status: United States, 1965." *Demography* 4:435–44.

———. 1971b. *Reproduction in the United States, 1965.* Princeton, N.J.: Princeton University Press.

Safilios-Rothschild, C. 1972. "The Relationship between Work Commitment and Fertility." *International Journal of Sociology of the Family* 2:64–71.

Schoen, R. 1983. "Measuring the Tightness of a Marriage Squeeze." *Demography* 20:61–78.

Schoen, R., W. Urton, K. Woodrow, and J. Baj. 1985. "Marriage and Divorce in Twentieth Century American Cohorts." *Demography* 22:101–14.

Schoen, R., and K. Woodrow. 1980. "Labor Force Status Life Tables for the United States, 1972." *Demography* 17:297–322.

Schultz, T. W., ed. 1973. *Economics of the Family: Marriage, Children, and Human Capital.* Chicago: University of Chicago Press.

Sennett, R. 1970. *Families Against the City: Middle Class Homes of Industrial Chicago, 1872–1890.* Cambridge, Mass.: Harvard University Press.

Sewell, W. H., and R. M. Hauser. 1975. *Education, Opportunity and Earnings: Achievement in the Early Career.* New York: Academic.

Shapiro, D., and J. E. Crowley. 1983. "Hopes and Plans: Education, Work Activity, and Fertility." In *Tomorrow's Workers*, ed. M. E. Borus. Lexington, Mass.: Lexington Books.

Shaw, L. B. 1983. *Unplanned Careers: The Working Lives of Middle-Aged Women.* Lexington, Mass.: Lexington Books.

———. 1985. "Determinants of the Increasing Work Attachment of Married Women." *Work and Occupations* 12(1):41–57.

Shorter, Edward. 1977. *The Making of the Modern Family.* New York: Basic Books.

Sieling, M. S. 1984. "Staffing Patterns Prominent in Female-Male Earnings Gap." *Monthly Labor Review* 107:19–33.

Simkins, L., and M. G. Eberhage. 1984. "Attitudes Toward AIDS, Herpes II, and Toxic Shock Syndrome." *Psychological Reports* 55:779–86.

Smelser, N. J., and S. Halpern. 1978. "The Historical Triangulation of Family, Economy, and Education." *American Journal of Sociology* 84:S288–315.

Smith, J. P. 1984. "The Paradox of Women's Poverty: Wage-earning Women and Economic Transformation." *Signs* 10(2):291–310.

Smith, J. P., and M. P. Ward. 1984. *Women's Wages and Work in the Twentieth Century.* Report prepared for the National Institute of Child Health and Human Development, Grant nos. 1 RO1 HD-17357-01 and 1 RO1 HD-15811-01A1. Rand Publication Series.

———. 1985. "Time-series Growth in the Female Labor Force." *Journal of Labor Economics* 3(1), pt. 2:S59–90.

Smith, R. E., ed. 1979a. *The Subtle Revolution: Women at Work.* Washington, D.C.: Urban Institute.

———. 1979b. *Women in the Labor Force in 1990.* Washington, D.C.: Urban Institute.

Smith, S. J. 1980. "Tables of Working Life for the United States, 1977: Substantive and Methodological Implications." Paper presented at the annual meeting of the Population Association of America, Denver, Colo., 10–12 April 1980.

———. 1983. "Estimating Annual Hours of Labor Force Activity." *Monthly Labor Review* 106:13–22.

Smith, S. J., and F. W. Horvath. 1984. "New Developments in Multistate Working Life Tables." Paper presented at the annual meeting of the Population Association of America, Minneapolis, Minn., 3–5 May 1984.

Smith-Lovin, L., and A. R. Tickamyer. 1978. "Non-Recursive Models of Labor Force Participation, Fertility, Behavior, and Sex Role Attitudes." *American Sociological Review* 43:541–57.

Spanier, G. B. 1983. "Married and Unmarried Cohabitation in the U.S.: 1980." *Journal of Marriage and the Family* 45:277–88.

Spanier, G. B., and P. Glick. 1980. "The Life Cycle of American Females: An Expanded Analysis." *Journal of Family History* 5:97–111.

Spitze, G., and J. Huber. 1980. "Changing Attitudes toward Women's Nonfamily Roles: 1938–1978." *Sociology of Work and Occupations* 7:317–35.

SRI International. 1983. *Final Report of the Seattle/Denver Income Maintenance Experiment*. Vol. 1. Washington, D.C.: U.S. Government Printing Office.

Stafford, F. P. 1980. "Women's Use of Time Converging with Men's." *Monthly Labor Review* 103:57–59.

Steinberg, L. D., and E. Greenberger. 1980. "The Part-Time Employment of High School Students—A Research Agenda." *Child Youth* 2:159–83.

Stevenson, M. 1973. "Women's Wages and Job Segregation." *Politics and Society* 4:83–95.

Stolzenberg, R. M., and L. J. Waite. 1977. "Age, Fertility Expectations, and Plans for Employment." *American Sociological Review* 42:769–82.

Sweet, J. A. 1973. *Women in the Labor Force*. New York: Seminar.

———. 1977. "Demography and the Family." *Annual Review of Sociology* 3:363–405.

———. 1984. "Components of Change in the Number of Households: 1970–1980." *Demography* 21:129–41.

Sweet, J. A., and R. Teixeira. 1984. *Breaking Tradition: Schooling, Marriage, Work, and Childbearing in the Lives of Young Women, 1960–1980*. Center for Demography and Ecology Working Paper, 84-13. Madison: University of Wisconsin.

Taeuber, K. E., and J. A. Sweet. 1976. "Family and Work: The Social Life Cycle of Women." In *Women and the American Economy: A Look to the 1980s*, ed. J. M. Kreps, pp. 31–60. New York: Columbia University Press.

Tan, H. W., and M. P. Ward. 1985. *Forecasting the Wages of Young Men: The Effects of Cohort Size*. Rand Corporation Report no. R-3115-Army, prepared for the Department of the Army. Santa Monica, Calif.: Rand Corporation.

Taylor, L. 1968. *Occupational Sociology*. New York: Oxford University Press.

Tella, A. 1964. "The Relation of Labor Force to Employment." *Industrial and Labor Relations Review* 17:454–69.

Thadani, V. N. 1978. "The Logic of Sentiment: The Family and Social Change." *Population and Development Review* 4:457–99.

Thornton, A. 1977. "Children and Marital Stability." *Journal of Marriage and the Family* 39:531–40.

———. 1985. "Changing Attitudes Toward Separation and Divorce: Causes and Consequences." *American Journal of Sociology* 90:856–72.

Thornton, A., and D. Freedman. 1982. "Changing Attitudes Toward Marriage and Single Life." *Family Planning Perspectives* 14:297–303.

———. 1983. "The Changing American Family." *Population Bulletin* 38:1–43.

Tien, H. Y. 1965. *Social Mobility and Controlled Fertility: Family Origins and Structure of the Australian Academic Elite*. New Haven, Conn.: College and University Press.

―――. 1967. "Mobility, Non-familial Activity, and Fertility." *Demography* 4:218–27.

Treiman, D. J., and H. I. Hartmann, eds. 1981. *Women, Work, and Wages: Equal Pay for Jobs of Equal Value*. Washington, D.C.: National Academy Press.

Trussell, J., and D. E. Bloom. 1983. "Estimating the Covariates of Age at Marriage and Age at First Birth." *Population Studies* 37:403–16.

Tsuchigane, R., and N. Dodge. 1974. *Economic Discrimination against Women in the United States: Measures and Changes*. Lexington, Mass.: Lexington Books.

Tsui, A. O. 1984. "Zero, One or Two Births: 1975 and 1980." Paper presented at the annual meeting of the Population Association of America, Minneapolis, Minn., 3–5 May 1984.

Udry, J. R. 1977. "A Biosocial Model of Adolescent Sexual Behavior." National Institute of Child Health and Human Development Grant Application.

Udry, J. R., K. E. Bauman, and N. M. Morris. 1975. "Changes in Premarital Coital Experience of Recent Decade-of-Birth Cohorts of Urban American Women." *Journal of Marriage and the Family* 37:783–87.

Uhlenberg, P. 1974. "Cohort Variations in Family Life Cycle Experience of U.S. Females." *Journal of Marriage and the Family* 5:284–92.

U.S. Bureau of the Census. 1949. *Historical Statistics of the United States, 1789–1945*. Washington, D.C.: U.S. Government Printing Office.

―――. 1969. "Marriage, Fertility, and Childspacing: June 1965." *Current Population Reports*, ser. P-20, no. 186.

―――. 1973. *United States Census of Population: 1970. Age at First Marriage*. Report PC(2)-4D. Washington, D.C.: U.S. Government Printing Office.

―――. 1975. *Historical Statistics of the United States, Colonial Times to 1970*, pt. 1. Washington, D.C.: U.S. Government Printing Office.

―――. 1976a. "Number, Timing, and Duration of Marriage and Divorces in the U.S.: June, 1975." *Current Population Reports*, ser. P-20, no. 297.

―――. 1976b. "A Statistical Portrait of Women in the U.S." *Current Population Reports*, ser. P-23, no. 58.

―――. 1977. "Characteristics of the Population below the Poverty Level: 1975." *Current Population Reports*, ser. P-60, no. 106.

―――. 1978a. "Perspectives on American Fertility." *Current Population Reports, Special Studies*, ser. P-23, no. 70.

―――. 1978b. *The Current Population Survey: Design and Methodology*. Technical Paper 40. Washington, D.C.: U.S. Government Printing Office.

―――. 1980a. "Households and Families by Type: March 1980 (Advance Report)." *Current Population Reports*, ser. P-20, no. 57.

―――. 1980b. "Families Maintained by Female Householders: 1970–1979." *Current Population Reports*, ser. P-23, no. 107.

―――. 1981. "School Enrollment—Social and Economic Characteristics of Students: October 1979." *Current Population Reports*, ser. P-20, no. 360.

———. 1982. "Characteristics of the Population below the Poverty Level: 1980." *Current Population Reports*, ser. P-60, no. 133.

———. 1983. "Marital Status and Living Arrangements: March 1982." *Current Population Reports*, ser. P-20, no. 380.

———. 1984a. "Childspacing among Birth Cohorts of American Women: 1905 to 1959." *Current Population Reports*, ser. P-20, no. 385.

———. 1984b. "Fertility Of American Women: June 1982." *Current Population Reports*, ser. P-20, no. 387.

———. 1984c. "Educational Attainment in the United States: March 1981 and 1980." *Current Population Reports*, ser. P-20, no. 390.

———. 1984d. "Understanding U.S. Fertility: Findings from the National Survey of Family Growth, Cycle III." *Population Bulletin* 39:1–42.

———. 1984e. "Marital Status and Living Arrangements: March, 1983." *Current Population Reports*, ser. P-20, no. 389.

———. 1984f. "Household and Family Characteristics: March 1983." *Current Population Reports*, ser. P-20, no. 388.

———. 1984g. "School Enrollment—Social and Economic Characteristics of Students: October, 1982." *Current Population Reports*, ser. P-20, no. 392.

———. 1984h. "School Enrollment—Social and Economic Characteristics of Students: October, 1983." *Current Population Reports*, ser. P-20, no. 394.

———. 1984i. *Statistical Abstracts of the United States, 1985.* Washington, D.C.: U.S. Government Printing Office.

———. 1986. *Statistical Abstracts of the United States, 1987.* Washington, D.C.: U.S. Government Printing Office.

U.S. Department of Labor, Bureau of Labor Statistics. 1980. *Employment in Perspective: Working Women.* BLS Report 643. Washington, D.C.: U.S. Government Printing Office.

———. 1981. *Employment and Earnings*, vol. 27, January. Washington, D.C.: U.S. Government Printing Office.

———. 1982. *Tables of Working Life: The Increment-Decrement Model.* BLS Bulletin 2135. Washington, D.C.: U.S. Government Printing Office.

———. 1983. *Handbook of Labor Statistics.* BLS Bulletin 2175. Washington, D.C.: U.S. Government Printing Office.

———. 1985. *Employment and Earnings*, vol. 31, July. Washington, D.C.: U.S. Government Printing Office.

U.S. National Center for Health Statistics. 1980. "Advance Report of Final Natality Statistics." *Monthly Vital Statistics Report* 31 (8), 30 November 1982.

———. 1982. "Advance Report of Final Natality Statistics." *Monthly Vital Statistics Report* 33 (6), 28 September 1984.

———. 1983a. "Advance Report of Final Divorce Statistics, 1980." *Monthly Vital Statistics Report* 32 (3), 27 June 1983.

———. 1983b. "Advance Report of Final Marriage Statistics, 1980." *Monthly Vital Statistics Report* 32 (5), 18 August 1983.

———. 1984a. "Advance Report of Final Marriage Statistics, 1981." *Monthly*

Vital Statistics Report 32 (11), 17 January 1984.

————. 1984b. "Births, Marriages, Divorces and Deaths, United States, 1983." *Monthly Vital Statistics Report* 32 (12), 26 March 1984.

————. 1985a. "Advance Report of Final Marriage Statistics, 1982." *Monthly Vital Statistics Report* 34 (3), 28 June 1985.

————. 1985b. "Advance Report of Final Divorce Statistics, 1982." *Monthly Vital Statistics Report* 33 (11), 28 February 1985.

Ventura, S. J. 1980. "Trends and Differentials in Births to Unmarried Women: United States, 1970–1976." *Vital and Health Statistics*, DHHS Pub. no. (PHS)80-1914, ser. 21, no. 36.

Vickery, C. 1979. "Women's Economic Contribution to the Family." In *The Subtle Revolution: Women at Work*, ed. R. E. Smith. Washington, D.C.: Urban Institute.

Voss, P. R. 1977. "Social Determinants of Age at First Marriage in the United States." Paper presented at the annual meeting of the Population Association of America, St. Louis, Mo., 21–23 April 1977.

Waite, L. J. 1975. "Working Wives and the Life Cycle." Ph.D. dissertation, University of Michigan.

————. 1981. "U.S. Women at Work." *Population Bulletin* 36:1–43.

Waite, L. J., and K. A. Moore. 1978. "The Impact of an Early First Birth on Young Women's Educational Attainment." *Social Forces* 56:845–65.

Waite, L. J., and R. M. Stolzenberg. 1976. "Intended Childbearing and Labor Force Participation of Young Women: Insights from Nonrecursive Models." *American Sociological Review* 41:235–51.

Walker, K., and M. Woods. 1976. *Time Use: A Measure of Household Production of Goods and Services*. Washington, D.C.: American Home Economics Association.

Ware, H. 1976. "Fertility and Work-Force Participation: The Experience of Melbourne Wives." *Population Studies* 30:413–27.

Watkins, S., J. Menken, and B. Vaughan. 1981. "The Fertility of the Formerly Married." Paper presented at the annual meeting of the Population Association of America, Washington, D.C., 26–28 March 1981.

Weed, J. A. 1980. "National Estimates of Marriage, Dissolution, and Survivorship." National Center for Health Statistics, DHHS pub. no. (PHS) 581-1403, ser. 3.

Weinstock, E., C. Tietze, F. S. Jaffe, and J. G. Dryfoos. 1975. "Legal Abortions in the United States since the 1973 Supreme Court Decision." *Family Planning Perspectives* 7:23–31.

Weller, R. H. 1968. "The Employment of Wives, Role Incompatibility, and Fertility: A Study among Lower- and Middle-Class Residents of San Juan, Puerto Rico." *Milbank Memorial Fund Quarterly* 16:507–27.

Westervelt, E. M. 1975. *Barriers to Women's Participation in Postsecondary Education*. Washington, D.C.: National Center for Education Statistics, U.S. Department of Health, Education, and Welfare.

Westoff, C. F. 1976. "Trends in Contraceptive Practice: 1965–1973." *Family Planning Perspectives* 8:54–57.

Westoff, L. A., and C. F. Westoff. 1971. *From Now to Zero: Fertility, Contraception and Abortion in America.* Boston: Little, Brown and Company.

Williams, G. 1979. "The Changing U.S. Labor Force and Occupational Differentiation by Sex." *Demography* 16:73–88.

Wolf, D. A. 1983. "Kin Availability and the Living Arrangements of Older Women." Paper presented at the annual meeting of the Population Association of America, Pittsburgh, Pa., 14–16 April 1983.

Zelnik, M., and J. F. Kantner. 1980. "Sexual Activity, Contraceptive Use, and Pregnancy among Metropolitan Area Teenagers: 1971–1979." *Family Planning Perspectives* 12:230–37.

Index